Agile User Experience Design

Agile User Experience Design

A Practitioner's Guide to Making It Work

Diana DeMarco Brown

AMSTERDAM • BOSTON • HEIDELBERG • LONDON • NEW YORK • OXFORD
PARIS • SAN DIEGO • SAN FRANCISCO • SINGAPORE • SYDNEY • TOKYO

Morgan Kaufmann is an imprint of Elsevier

Acquisitions Editor: Meg Dunkerley
Development Editor: Heather Scherer
Project Manager: Mohanambal Natarajan
Copyeditor: Gnomi Schrift Gouldin

Morgan Kaufmann is an imprint of Elsevier
225 Wyman Street, Waltham, MA 02451, USA

First edition 2013

Library of Congress Cataloging-in-Publication Data
Application submitted

British Library Cataloguing in Publication Data
A catalogue record for this book is available from the British Library

For information on all Morgan Kaufmann publications
visit our website at www.mkp.com

ISBN: 978-0-12-415953-2

To my daughter, my best creation

Contents

INTRODUCTION xi
  Acknowledgment xii
ABOUT THE AUTHOR xiii

CHAPTER 1 Introduction to Agile 1
  Introduction 2
  Agile Values + UX 4
  Agile Principles + UX 9
  Common Methods 20
  Common Terms 28
  Case Study—Jeff Gothelf, TheLadders.com 36
  Summary 38

CHAPTER 2 Agile Methods + UX = Agile UX 39
  Introduction 39
  Fitting a UX Peg Into an Agile-Shaped Hole 42
  The UX Work 48
  Case Study—Catherine Robson, Seachange
  International 66
  Summary 68

CHAPTER 3 Case Studies 71
  Introduction 72
  Suzanne O'Kelly, AppNexus 72
  Thyra Rauch, IBM 77
  Archie Miller, Snagajob.com 79
  Carol Smith, Perficient 83
  Kayla Block, PAR Springer Miller 87
  Anonymous 1, at an Enterprise Software Company ... 92
  Christina York, ITHAKA 94
  Anonymous 2, a Large Desktop Software Company ... 99

Austin Govella, Avanande 104
Josh O'Connor, National Council for the Blind, Ireland 109
Adrian Howard, Quietstars..110
Elisa Miller, Senior User Experience Engineer
GE Healthcare 112
Summary 118

CHAPTER 4 Common Success Factors 121
Introduction 121
Project Over Process...124
Team Dynamics...127
Communication 129
Define the Big Picture 133
Training...134
Adapt and Evolve 139
Case Study—Sarah Kahn, Adzerk..140
Case Study—Anonymous 3, a Company Specializing
in Direct Marketing Products 143
Summary 146

CHAPTER 5 Frequently Asked Questions 147
Introduction 147
Should we Even be Agile?..148
How Long Should Sprints Be?..150
What Deliverables Should UX Produce? 151
How Should the UX Team Fit in With the
Development Sprints? 153
How do you Get Developers to Talk About the
Design of One Thing While They are Busy
Implementing Another? 155
What if UX Team Members Have to Support More
Than One Project? 155
How do we Fit User Research Into the Sprint Cycle? 156
What if the Team Claims to be Agile, but Agile
Values are Nowhere to be Seen? 157
What if the Team is not Colocated? 158
What do i do When Someone Uses "That's not Agile"
As a Reason not to do Something?...158
How Does the UX Team Plan and Research for the
Next Release? 159

How do you Manage Internal Stakeholders? 160

Summary 160

CHAPTER 6 Using Agile Concepts for UX Teams 163

Introduction 163

Creating a User Experience Backlog...164

Recurring User Testing 165

Breaking the Work in to Smaller Pieces 165

Constant Feedback and Iteration...166

Recurring Events and Rituals.....................................166

No Design Divas or Heroes...167

Focusing on Communication Over Documentation 168

Thinking and Communicating in Terms of User Stories..........169

Defining Acceptance Criteria 169

Using Less Up-Front Design..170

Summary 170

INDEX.. 173

Introduction

When I found out that I was going to be supporting a project using Scrum, I was immediately wary. I did not really know much about Scrum or Agile but had the sense that these things moved at a fast pace and did not really take UX into consideration. However, I had no choice about which development process my team chose, so I set my trepidations aside and got ready to support my team.

I was fortunate that some internal experts who were advocates of the UX team were working in parallel sprints, or working a sprint ahead, to the development team. Their model seemed very logical and comfortable, and I was happy to apply the technique. Once I got started though, I noticed that a lot of factors in my situation did not match their experience and I was not entirely sure how to modify the technique to fit. My team was not colocated (although not extremely so), the team was larger than recommended, and the project had a significant infrastructure piece in addition to the user interface. None of the issues was a deal breaker, but I needed to adjust my process and I was always very uncertain about whether I was being Agile enough.

After finishing the project, I shared my experience at a local usability professionals' conference, and it was eye-opening. People were so hungry for insight and guidance and had many of the same questions. However, since there was a wide variety in situations, the answer to those questions might be different for everyone. I was blown away by the different implementations of Agile UX and felt like I was not seeing enough of that diversity reflected in the dialog happening around Agile and UX. I felt that had I known there were so many ways to do Agile UX and what they were, this would have given me more confidence about my approach. I thought, "Someone should write a book." Then, a few years later, I did.

The goal of this book is to show that there are many ways for a UX team to succeed, and fail, at being Agile and to illustrate that using the same set of tactics could lead to either outcome, depending on the situation. The case studies show that there are many ways to be Agile and more than a few ways for a UX team to do well in an Agile environment. I examine what contributes to a team's success and what factors to consider to determine the best path for your team to take to achieve a positive outcome. After reading this book, you will have the tools you need to determine what Agile UX means for you in your situation.

ACKNOWLEDGMENT

Doug DeMarco of DeMarco Interactive created the fantastic illustrations in this book.

About the Author

Diana Brown has been designing interactions and software interfaces for over a decade. She spent a good portion of that time talking to end users and finding ways to encourage them to talk to her. Much of the rest of her time has been spent talking to her development teams and finding ways to encourage them to talk to her. She continues to be amazed by all the cool things that software can do.

CHAPTER 1

Introduction to Agile

CONTENTS

Introduction 2

Agile Values + UX 4
Individuals and interactions over processes and tools 5
Working software over comprehensive documentation 6
Customer collaboration over contract negotiation 7
Responding to change over following a plan 8

Agile Principles + UX 9
Principle 1 10
Principle 2 11
Principle 3 11
Principle 4 12
Principle 5 13
Principle 6 14
Principle 7 15
Principle 8 16
Principle 9 17
Principle 10 18
Principle 11 19
Principle 12 19

Common Methods 20
Crystal 20
Extreme Programming (XP) 20
Scrum 21
Hybrid agile, or custom agile 23
Kanban 25
Scrumban 26
Lean UX 27

Common Terms 28
Chickens and pigs 28
Product owner 28
Scrum master 29
Sprint 30
Product backlog 30
User stories 31

Agile User Experience Design. http://dx.doi.org/10.1016/B978-0-12-415953-2.00001-7

1

Epic.. 32
Planning poker 32
Story-point estimation 32
Acceptance criteria... 34
Burn-down chart 34
Spike 35
AgileFall.. 35
Jeff Patton.. 36

Summary 38

References 38

INTRODUCTION

To understand what it means to practice an Agile form of user-centered design, it is important to have a sense of what exactly *Agile* means and where the term came from. Since the Agile methodology has a deep, rich history and is continually evolving, it has become the subject of many books, blogs, white papers, conference presentations, and websites, all of which have their own take on the value system and its methods. This chapter touches on only the most common terms and concepts and those that might be most relevant to a user experience practitioner. I encourage everyone to spend some time exploring the many resources that are available to get a deeper understanding of the philosophy and the various methods for applying it that have grown up along the way. It is also important to recognize that there is no one single right way to implement Agile design. At its core, "Agile" is a set of values to use as compass to guide a team through the production of software. Whatever process or tools are used and how they are applied are secondary to the overall goals of empowering a highly functional team as it builds great software to the delight of its end users.

Agile is a term that grew out of efforts in the 1990s to find a better development method for producing software. Traditional methods, such as the waterfall method, were starting to be recognized as a bit unwieldy. Consumers were expecting more of their software in terms of quality and functionality, and production cycles needed to change in order to create a product that would satisfy end users. Additionally, production cycles needed to be able to adapt and accommodate the reality of shifting requirements. Waterfall development makes it especially challenging for teams to respond to issues, mostly because it is inherently unable to discover serious problems with the design, architecture, or the code itself early in the cycle and can really identify them only when it is too late for a correction. Not knowing what problems might exist until the end of the release cycle results in a lower-quality product or longer release cycle. Traditional methods are also prone to creating silos, where product managers throw requirements "over the wall" to designers, who then throw their design specifications over the wall to development teams, who throw their code over to a quality team, that eventually authorizes the release of a product. Due to the limited interaction and communication among these teams during the production of each deliverable, each team is playing a game of telephone and putting its own interpretation on the requirements or the specifications. As in the telephone game, the end result very rarely matches the original intention.

Development teams began experimenting with new techniques like Extreme Programming, Adaptive Programming, Scrum, and other methods to find a better way to produce high-quality software and meet demands without requiring developers to write code 24 hours a day. In 2001, practitioners of a variety of these philosophies got together in Utah and created the Agile Manifesto. The manifesto, and its accompanying 12 principles, captures the spirit of what all these methods were trying to achieve and is an important starting point for an organization that is consider adopting Agile practices. Reading the values expressed in the Agile Manifesto is always a good way to check on whether or not you are on track with your own Agile implementation. While the methods, techniques, and terminology have evolved since 2001, the core values of Agile have not. The manifesto eloquently states:

> "We are uncovering better ways of developing
> software by doing it and helping others do it.
> Through this work we have come to value:
> **Individuals and interactions** over processes and tools
> **Working software** over comprehensive documentation
> **Customer collaboration** over contract negotiation
> **Responding to change** over following a plan
> That is, while there is value in the items on
> the right, we value the items on the left more"
> **The Manifesto for Agile Software Development, agilemanifesto.org**

FIGURE 1.1
The agile process.

AGILE VALUES + UX

The manifesto provides the best guidance for and is the most succinct expression of the values that should drive an Agile organization. A description of the principles behind the Agile Manifesto is provided on the website, and it gives additional insight into the manifesto, but the heart of the matter is very well expressed in the manifesto itself. While referencing something that was written so long ago might feel old fashioned, I find that these values are just as relevant now as when they were first created. In software years, 2001 was a very long time ago; and while it was not quite the Dark Ages, it might well be analogous to the Atomic Age. After all, 2001 was the year that many overvalued dotcoms went under, the first-generation iPods were introduced, Microsoft released XP, and several years ahead of the introduction of the ubiquitous Facebook. UX (user experience) practitioners are working today who have no memory of that time. With all the focus on Agile in recent years and the birth of so many variations on the theme, it is fair to assume that the movement has evolved beyond its original manifesto. After all, how many software concepts still hold water over a decade later? That assumption is false. All the children of the original Agile movement still share the core values expressed in the Agile Manifesto and really just use different tactics to create an environment that embodies the spirit of the original statement. All these years later, software production teams still struggle with processes that often focus on the milestone deliverables instead of keeping their eyes on the shipping product. Rarely is a release cycle not subject to changing needs from stakeholders, but rarer still is the process that can support responding to such a change—unless you are working in an Agile environment. The intention of the Agile Manifesto is to define a value system that allows for the creation of a culture that can respond to these situations, while recognizing the value of the individual team member, and produce good software. While the Agile Manifesto lays out the core values of an Agile environment, many techniques can build a process and a framework to support those values. Examining these values through a UX lens can show that there is a natural relationship between the two.

Unfortunately, at no time have UX professionals gotten together and hashed out a manifesto of UX values and principles that came to be the standard to which we all hold ourselves. In fact, despite definitions of the process for user-centered design, there is no formal expression of its value system, beyond the idea that we want to keep the user's needs central to the design process. Things start to get even more vague regarding UX principles. It is not that no UX principles are written down, but that different UX principles are written down by many people. Quite a few people have their own spin on UX design principles, including Microsoft, which has defined the UX principles for Windows and shared these principles on its website (see http://msdn.microsoft.com/en-us/library/windows/desktop/dd834141.aspx). Most of the definitions of UX principles tend to mention the mission of keeping the user involved in the process, then identify additional guidelines for best supporting the user. Rather than picking a favorite to use for a comparison to the Agile principles, since I have yet to see a set that did not offer some interesting food for thought, or creating yet another set of UX principles, we will review the Agile principles and values and explore the way they fit with and support the type of activities in which UX practitioners tend to engage.

Individuals and interactions over processes and tools

Despite being the first value expressed in the Agile manifesto, it can often be the first one that is forgotten as teams explore the different tools used to manage tasks, user stories, and generate burn-down charts. Excitement over various ceremonies, like daily scrums, backlog grooming, planning poker, and retrospectives, and a desire to properly execute those meetings can often distract the teams from focusing on the people and the communication these things are intended to support and inform. Add to that the fun of exploring and using new software tools to support the process, and the team's attention can be easily aimed in the wrong direction. If a daily standup meeting needs to run for 20 minutes while the team becomes accustomed to the brevity of the status reports, that can be okay as long as the teams are learning how to give brief status reports and they are improving their ability to share only the relevant information. The point of 15 minute meetings is less about that specific amount of time, although it is a very good target, and more about providing the least amount and most relevant information in a meeting short enough to not create a burden for the team to attend. If the team is consistently allowing such meetings to run for 30 or 45 minutes, then it has a problem that needs to be resolved. Similarly, if planning poker is taking too long, does not feel productive, or is causing team members to become disengaged, then it is time to look at whether planning poker is the best technique for the team to use, or if there might be a better way to estimate effort. While it is fun to play with a set of cards, the event is just one way to get the team to participate in effort estimations, and it is not the only way to do that. If the team is several sprints into the cycle and members put more time and energy into the task management tools than they get out of them, the team needs to talk about a different way to handle and track tasks. Even if it would be too disruptive to switch process managment tools during the release, a healthy discussion about the tool will identify problems and potential solutions and help determine if something different needs to be used in the future. It is a critical part of the Agile method to refine the process throughout rather that pick an approach and stick to it no matter what. All these techniques are meant to be the means to an end; and if they are not moving the team toward increased and improved communication, then it is time to revisit the Agile Manifesto and think about how to actually be more Agile.

From a user experience perspective, the idea of treating the process with the same iterative design techniques used on the product should feel very comfortable. We ask customers for their feedback on the product and refine it accordingly; the product team is the consumer of the process and should be able to provide input into its design. Additionally, designers and usability specialists are used to thinking about the individual end user rather than a set of features; this lends itself well to a process built around the idea of user stories. Improving the interaction between the end user and the system is always foremost in our thoughts. After all, some of us have even had "interaction designer" as part of our job title. Going Agile means taking the same perspective that we have on our users and applying it to our teammates and our work. Some UX folks do this naturally and focus on relationship as a matter of course. Since UX teams are rarely able to realize their designs and implement them for the shipping product on our own, we rely on the development team to do so; and it is always in our best interest to build healthy relationships with the team and other functional groups with which we work. However, it also happens that there are team who perhaps have fallen into a more "us vs. them" mentality with their colleagues from other functional areas. Practicing Agile is a great opportunity to let go of any divisive mentalities and focus on team building. The good news is that this particular Agile value gives everyone on the team permission or instruction to focus on communication and the individual team members rather than on the process. Recognizing that each team member brings a unique set of skills to the team is also a change from traditional processes, where the developers often are seen as interchangeable code producers. Valuing individual skills provides an opportunity to recognize what the user experience team members bring to the table. It also allows the process to be tailored to the individuals that constitute the team.

Working software over comprehensive documentation

Obviously, the highest priority in any production cycle should be the thing that is created, sold, and generates revenue. However, if a functional area is rated and rewarded more for the artifacts it produces than for the shipping software, this priority can easily get lost. People want to do the right thing, but they also want to be recognized for their work; and if such recognition is given to only a very specific piece work or deliverable, then that is where their energy and attention will go. Unfortunately, many traditional methods also require so much documentation that they end up creating environments where it is more important to generate the items that support the process than to produce the software itself. Obviously, the well-intentioned thought is that the whole of the software is made better by the increased quality of its parts, but the myopic focus on the production of the bits and pieces can create silos that inhibit the communication that might bring this hope to fruition. The idea of putting the attention on the development of the software over generation of the supporting documentation can represent an interesting challenge for UX practitioners who want to take this value to heart. While we certainly contribute to the product, in most cases we usually are not responsible for building it, but we can and do create plenty of supporting artifacts.

In many ways, this principle is asking us to let go of our most visible and tangible contribution to the release. But, if we can make peace with that idea and recognize that the product is more important than the detailed internal deliverables, we can also see that this could positively affect our relationship the other functional areas, as it can reduce barriers to communication and put our efforts toward attending to what gets implemented rather than being satisfied with achieving a good design. Designers, despite our best efforts to remain open to all solutions, often get focused or attached to a particular design solution and wrapped up in the process of creating and documenting that design. However, if little or none of that elegant solution makes it in to the product, was it a good investment for the company or the designer and did it do anything to improve the end user's experience? This does not mean that a UX person should live in a constant state of compromise and cave in on important issues just to get some of the design elements implemented. But, it does mean reminding ourselves that the design unto itself is not the end goal; instead, the design of the shipping product should be the focus of all efforts.

This more holistic approach requires that we to take a closer look at the way we work with our colleagues to see if we are doing everything we can to educate all the functional areas about the value of a good user experience and exactly why a given design solution is important to the customer. If our teammates truly understand the value of a particular design element and why it is of benefit to the end user, they will not be as quick to make trade-offs that compromise its value and may make more effort to work with the designer to find an equitable solution when any kind of trade-offs need to be made. It would also support this core value to emphasize relationship building with other functional areas to improve the dialog about design and user experience as well as generally working toward creating a more collaborative environment.

Customer collaboration over contract negotiation

This may be the easiest value to fit in to a user-centered design mentality. Since our work tends to be so user-centric, our focus is naturally on the customer.

There has also been a lot more motion in recent years around using the customer as a design partner or collaborator and there are many techniques to facilitate this. Personas are certainly a step in that direction, using a representation of the end user based on user research to inform design and influence decisions. Personas can be leveraged quite effectively within an organization to get agreement about target users and share the information in a digestible format that makes them easy to communicate broadly and even easier for the product teams to remember. Once the personas have become part of the collective consciousness, they become part of the conversation and ultimately influence the design. Indi Young's (2008) *Mental Models* describes techniques for modeling and visualizing customer behaviors, so that the user behaviors, and not just their wants and needs, can be communicated to a broader team with a goal of designing to these activities. The information to create the visualizations can come from observing or interviewing customers and can result in a very solid understanding of the user actions most important for the software to address. Collaboration can even be taken a step further by engaging the customers directly in design creation, using codesign activities or testing methods such as Rapid Iterative Testing and Evaluation (RITE; Medlock et al., n.d.). As user-centered designers, we are always customer centric, but there are always new ways to bring the end user into the design process; and this value gives us encouragement to work with our customers and to create an understanding among the team members that there is value in doing so.

Responding to change over following a plan

Many things can change during the course of a release cycle—technologies, market demands, user needs, and organizational structures. Things always come up that have the potential to cause the schedule to slip or feature work to be dropped. Even if there are no changes, work can often be more complicated or take longer to implement than originally planned. The longer the release cycle, the more potential there is for some kind of a disruption, especially within a product's competitive landscape. Sticking blindly to a schedule or roadmap in the face of evidence that the company should do otherwise is not a path to success. But it often happens, because a late cycle change in direction can be very expensive or result in an even later delivery of functionality. Of course, not all changes are dramatic enough to force or necessitate a major reshuffling of effort and resources. In fact, the most common adjustments teams are asked to accommodate are much smaller but can derail a release in a "death by a thousand paper cuts" fashion—the dreaded and, it seems, ubiquitous changes in scope or requirements. The need to make a change can occur for any number of reasons—time estimates were off and features need to drop to make the release date, new information came in from a key customer requiring additional features to be added, or maybe a product manager simply needed to shift the priorities. Since these events occur more often than not, any good process should anticipate their occurrence, and Agile does that. This makes the process more adaptive and generally more able to achieve a successful outcome.

For the UX team, building in this kind of responsiveness to change can present an opportunity to incorporate more user feedback into the product. Ideally, some user research would have been done in the planning stages to help define the requirements, so that the starting point for the design and development work is on target. However, validation and refinement of the design necessarily occur during the development cycle, just as it does in more traditional development environments. A natural outcome of these activities is a list of changes to the design; although if the requirements and the user stories are well informed, the required alterations should be relatively small in scope. The difference when this value is in play is that the development team is more willing and able to respond to revisions in the design, because it is more ready and able to respond to change. It also helps that the team expects the possibility that it might need to respond to a new direction, not simply because history has taught this but because the process indicates that it will happen. In an Agile method, the frustration around dealing with change is mitigated, because activities are in place to support the introduction of new tasks or user stories that come from usability testing and events that allow these items to be given priority and potentially incorporated in to the release. It is easier to respond to change when the process provides a way to do so without disrupting the release. The process is also geared toward discovering these things as early as possible, so that their overall impact on the release schedule is much smaller.

AGILE PRINCIPLES + UX

"We follow these principles:
Our highest priority is to satisfy the customer through early and continuous delivery of valuable software.
Welcome changing requirements, even late in development. Agile processes harness change for the customer's competitive advantage.
Deliver working software frequently, from a couple of weeks to a couple of months, with a preference to the shorter timescale.
Business people and developers must work together daily throughout the project.
Build projects around motivated individuals. Give them the environment and support they need,
and trust them to get the job done.

The most efficient and effective method of conveying information to and within a development team is face-to-face conversation.

Working software is the primary measure of progress.

Agile processes promote sustainable development. The sponsors, developers, and users should be able to maintain a constant pace indefinitely.

Continuous attention to technical excellence and good design enhances agility.

Simplicity—the art of maximizing the amount of work not done—is essential.

The best architectures, requirements, and designs emerge from self-organizing teams.

At regular intervals, the team reflects on how to become more effective, then tunes and adjusts its behavior accordingly. "

From "Principles behind the Agile Manifesto," AgileManifesto.org

Principle 1 - Our highest priority is to satisfy the customer through early and continuous delivery of valuable software

This principle could not be more relevant, given that many products are constantly releasing updates and new versions of their sites or their apps to meet ever-changing customer needs and keep up with the constant improvements from competitors. For most teams, the days of 18-month or two-year release cycles are long gone or were never an option for their markets. Shorter cycles and increased responsiveness to customer needs do not always translate in to an increased focus on a great user experience. In the rush to delivery, features and functionality can still take priority over design. However, customers are much more demanding about the quality of the design and much less patient with features that are put together haphazardly. Expectations have changed to the point where users have little patience for software that is difficult to use, no matter how complex the application is. Not a designer among us has not been asked by an internal or external stakeholder to "Make it like a video game," or "It should be easy to use like TurboTax," or the newest favorite comparison, "Make it work like my iPhone." Whether or not these analogies are appropriate for a particular software project, and generally they are not, is less relevant than that the experiences people are having on a daily basis change the way we all think about software. So much good design is everywhere now and users have come to recognize it as important to their experience and expect a certain amount of usability from all their experiences. Along with this increased sophistication and awareness about ease of use comes the reality that the market responds to good design. This translates into an easier sell for the UX team to be a part of a process committed to generating products that satisfy customer needs and have frequent releases to meet market demands.

Principle 2 - Welcome changing requirements, even late in development. Agile processes harness change for the customer's competitive advantage

Changing requirements have been a reality as long as requirements have been written. Teams that recognize this and are encouraged to embrace these changes and view them as an opportunity are more likely to produce something that actually meets or exceeds customer needs. This Agile principle accepts that changes occur and acknowledges that they will come, as they often do, late in the release cycle. What is most exciting about this principle, however, is that it changes the mentality about this fact of life from resigned acceptance (or dread and fear) and positions it as positive and something that can be used to the benefit of the customer. This is so valuable for the UX team, that often findss itself in the position of delivering customer feedback late in the cycle and is often treated as the bearer of bad news. Instead of presenting change requests and knowing that only the smallest items, if even those, have a chance to make it in to the release or that everything will be deferred to an unspecified future release that never seems to come, with an Agile method in place, the changes are seen as the helpful information that it is. The change in attitude comes not just from accepting Agile values and principles but because Agile methods support this principle, by building in to the process a mechanism for dealing with late changes and ensuring that this information is solicited early and often. In traditional methods, feedback is deferred, because there is often no way to accommodate it without compromising the quality or the schedule of the release. Very often the entire team can see the value of the changes, but traditional methods created a momentum around the planned functionality that leaves the team a bit helpless to do anything differently. Not only does Agile support a different mindset with respect to course correction, Agile processes have mechanisms for accommodating these changes.

Principle 3 - Deliver working software frequently, from a couple of weeks to a couple of months, with a preference to the shorter timescale

The frequent delivery of working software is of great benefit to the UX team. In more traditional environments, UX people generally have to work with rough prototypes or no working code at all, which may or may not be sufficient for expressing the complexity of an application. Even if a prototype was done by the UX team, it may not match the actual implementation unless someone on the UX team is directly responsible for building the front end of the UI (user interface). In a traditional environment, a functioning development prototype is rarely available for review or testing until late in the release cycle. Generally, by the time working code is available, it is too late for usability testing results to influence shipping the release. Frequent deliveries of working code not only lends itself to more opportunities to do user research on the actual software, but shorter and more frequent shipping cycles mean that, when design changes are relegated to a future release, that day might actually come, since the next "release" might be only a few weeks away. When the software delivery happens more often, there is less pressure to squeeze every last item into the current release, since the customers will not have to wait years for the next version. This opens the door to allowing the focus of the product team to expand its focus beyond being exclusively centered on features and to consider the user experience as part of the release.

Principle 4 - Business people and developers must work together daily throughout the project

Of course, this principle would be even better if it referenced the designers, but if you read *developers* as "all functional areas supporting the production of the software," then it makes the statement even more powerful. Organizationally, the people who are connected to the business needs are often fairly far removed from the production team. Even if there is no distance between the business and production teams, there is often tension between the two areas. It is very rare for these two groups to work closely together, mainly because they have separate paths and few intersection points. Regardless of whether the issue is tension or distance, the dynamic contributes to a decreased awareness of and sensitivity to the business drivers on the part of the development team. Often, simply a lack of exposure and communication gaps create this lack of insight.

In one of my roles, I reported directly into product management and was amazed at what a difference it made to be a part of the conversations about business initiatives and product strategy on a daily basis. With that information in my consciousness, decisions based on strategic business goals seemed more obvious and product-specific trade-offs were easier to make. But, with their focus intentionally on the production of the software, development teams can find it hard to lift their heads up from the work of building the release to get involved in other interests, even though the purpose of producing the software is to meet the business needs. Often, it is difficult for them to access this information, even if they wanted to.

Usually, only the development managers attend high-level meetings where information is shared about business priorities. Contrast that with this principle, which has a simplicity and a genius to it, as it encourages a partnership with daily involvement between the production and business teams. It reduces the amount of communication necessary to keep each other in the loop by increasing the frequency, it builds relationships, and it increases knowledge about the business for both sides. The two teams truly are partners, and not only recognizing this but fostering it is the healthiest thing for the product and, ultimately, the customers. The UX team benefits from this as much as the rest of the teams, since having an awareness of the business needs makes it easier to be more strategic about where we put our resources and attention. Left to our own devices, designers want to redesign everything that needs the help, and the list of potential candidates for design attention is usually infinitely long. It can be hard to admit that not every fix is worth making, but the more in touch the UX team is with the business needs, the easier it is to be aware of those needs. A product might contain some embarrassingly bad screens, but if only 2 percent of the users see those and they are able to perform their tasks despite the flaws on the screens, it probably is not worth spending design cycles fixing them. Just as the production team needs to be conscious of the user personas, it also needs to be aware of the revenue numbers and product strategy related to those personas.

Principle 5 - Build projects around motivated individuals. Give them the environment and support they need, and trust them to get the job done

One thing that is common, especially within the management teams of large development organizations, is to treat all staff as interchangeable resources instead of human beings with different strengths and skill sets. When looking at spreadsheet after spreadsheet of projects, level of effort estimates, and full-time-equivalent numbers, it is tempting to pretend that all resources are equal. It is often the case that availability is the most relevant factor in getting assigned to a project rather than interest or ability. This means that a developer who is much more comfortable and capable of tackling complex infrastructure issues may end up being responsible for creating a user interface for which he has no interest and possibly limited ability to write code. Finding the work to fit the skillsets of the team rather than trying to fit the team into the project at hand can be more difficult but can yield significantly better results and produce higher morale. Putting team members where they are best able and willing to contribute guarantees that more positive energy and enthusiasm is brought to bear on a project. This can be a boon for the UX team, as it is more likely to work with team members who are genuinely interested in and capable of producing a great UX.

The focus on creating an environment and providing the team with the support to accomplish its work clearly benefits everyone. This principle takes this concept a step further by positing the idea that trusting people to get the work done not only eliminates the micromanagement inherent in most traditional environments but also empowers the team to make the necessary decisions that affect the final output and make it better. After all, because a specification has the four to six required electronic signatures on it does not necessarily make it any better or more relevant than something that the team sketched out on a whiteboard. The fact that design document was sent up the reporting chain, often to managers or executives who are quite distant from the project does not actually make that design any more effective at meeting user needs than trusting the team to make the right decisions. This principle assumes that, as part of their enthusiasm for the project and knowing that they will be allowed to take on the responsibility of decision making, the team has ramped up and done all the relevant user research, business requirements, market analysis, and technical constraints that affect the product. The team knows its project the best and is the most qualified to understand what should be done to make it successful. When team members are trusted to do that and feel that there is faith in their ability to execute on the work, the team will be motivated to work harder and prove this principle to be true.

Principle 6 - The most efficient and effective method of conveying information to and within a development team is face-to-face conversation

In an age of instant message tools, video chats, wiki pages, emails, and remote employees, there is often no need to interact in person with your coworkers anymore. Many companies take advantage of these technologies and a more global economy to have employees and team members scattered across the globe. However, nothing is more challenging to express over the phone than a design concept that is still in the early stages, and it is nearly impossible to collaboratively whiteboard a design via conference call. Not only will my colleagues miss out on seeing my excessive hand gestures, which admittedly convey enthusiasm more than any information about the design intent, they will be unable to grab a pencil or marker and join me at the whiteboard to hash out a concept and come up with a shared understanding of the design problem or solution. And rarely will an email thread, even one with embedded sketches, result in a common understanding and agreement to a design. Of course, more and more teams are distributed and travel budgets are growing smaller, so efforts need to be made to use technology to replicate the types of meetings from which a colocated team can participate and benefit. Certainly, if colleagues are remote, then digital sketching tools like Balsamiq combined with a screen sharing application like WebEx or GoToMeeting can absolutely replicate a sketching session in a conference room. However, if your colleagues are within walking distance of your cube, the more face-to-face contact you have with them, the better. Not only does this increase the efficacy of information sharing, it increases the sense of a team. It can be easy to ignore the blinking instant message icon in the corner, if you are busy. It is a little harder to completely ignore the blinking human standing in your cube. Also, much more information can be gained by an in-person discussion. Facial expression and body language can color an interaction and transmit so much information that would be lost otherwise. Remote situations can be managed and work quite well, with a little creativity, but if you are not having frequent in-person conversations with the team members near you and opt to rely on technology, then you are building walls instead of relationships.

Principle 7 - Working software is the primary measure of progress

The siren call of metrics can be hard to resist. It can be so comforting to have all these numbers and graphs, providing you with tons of information about all the different things that need to be tracked as part of the release. The numbers can be followed, evaluated, plotted, managed, and discussed. Despite the best intentions behind most metrics, however, once any measure is put in place, people work to the number and not necessarily the spirit of what it is trying to achieve. But, at the end of the day, only one metric really matters and it is the progress of the production team—the existence of working software. Hitting the release date is also important, but the ability and likelihood of hitting that target becomes much easier to track when working code is available to asses and evaluate. The same is true for quality metrics, which are also very important but are much easier to accurately gauge when working software can be tested. In the end, you know you made the release date only when you have working software available on a given date, until then it remains at a level of uncertainty, no matter what metrics are in place.

For the UX team, this means that the measure progress can be evaluated by the incorporation of the research finding or design work into that working software. Someone once said that his UX team would be judged only by the designs produced and the designs that were implemented. At the time, I thought working on a team with this philosophy would be really freeing, because it would mean not being penalized for working with a difficult team that did not care about design and would be rewarded for having created wonderful designs even if they never made it into the product. Then, it dawned on me that such a philosophy also meant that a designer would not be penalized for being a difficult designer to work with or for coming up with designs that might be beautiful or represent a fantastic user experience but were impossible to implement. While I am very supportive of the idea of creating aspirational designs, when time and resources are tight, most efforts need to be spent on creating work that might actually make it into the hands of the customer. If working software is the primary measure of progress for the team, it makes sense that, for the UX team, the design and usability of that working software be the primary measure of their progress. This not only incentivizes the UX team to create a good experience for the customer given the technology available, but emphasizes the responsibility in working with team members to bring that design to life.

Principle 8 - Agile processes promote sustainable development. The sponsors, developers, and users should be able to maintain a constant pace indefinitely

For some, it may be a surprise to see that the Agile principles include the idea of working at a sustainable pace, since Agile development cycles are have a reputation for feeling like a marathon run at a sprint pace (no pun intended). However, one of the original motivations behind the Agile Manifesto and its principles was to create a more hospitable work environment that did not routinely include 80-hour workweeks. The reality is that 80-hour workweeks are not sustainable and if that is what it takes to release a product, something is going wrong somewhere. Either the project is understaffed, has taken on too much work, or is grossly mismanaged; the bottom line for this type of project is that some issue that needs to be resolved. Ultimately, such an extreme pace leads to burn out and low morale, and neither condition is fertile ground for producing good software. While the rhythm of an Agile cycle is different than that of traditional methods and may take getting used to, if the pace is feels so intense that it seems unmanageable, then it is a sign that something in the process is broken and needs to be reworked.

It may be especially challenging for the UX teams get used to properly estimating the effort for small increments of work, but that is a skill that develops over time and with more experience in Agile. Until this happens, the UX team needs to engage in frequent communication with the rest of the project team and to discuss the issue in retrospective until the kinks are worked out. The goal is for the skill of estimating effort to be developed, and the UX team needs to understand how to load balance and size their work to fit into the new schedule. No one on the team, including the UX members, is supposed to work at a pace that he or she cannot sustain. This is not because Agile is a warm and fuzzy process; it is really a practical issue. If you are working around the clock to keep up, it means that you are overcommitting and you and the team do not have a good sense of what can be done in a given period of time. It is an indication that there is a risk for failing to meet deliverable dates looming in the team's future. While you may be able to push through and get the work done, the quality of the work may suffer as a result, or at some point you will burn out and be unable to continue taking on that much work. There are times when the workload spikes, for whatever reason, and if the team has been stretched beyond its means all along, it may not be able to accommodate an unexpected surge. It is better for the team to know what is reasonable and plan accordingly than to realize later that the expectations were completely unrealistic and were known to be so, but the team was not given the opportunity to adjust.

Principle 9 - Continuous attention to technical excellence and good design enhances agility

If we think of *agility* as meaning the production of high-quality code that meets or exceeds the customer's needs, then it is clear that using the best technology in the most elegant way and creating a great user experience design moves a team further down the path toward agility. What makes this statement so Agile, is the use of the word *continuous*. Not only does it mean not just settling on a platform, technology, or a design then never revisiting the topic, but it means continually and constantly considering and refining these decisions throughout the cycle. This does not mean that a heavyweight desktop app should change course halfway through a release cycle and try to ship as an iPad application instead, just because it is a cooler technology. (However, it is worth mentioning that this kind of change in direction is not outside the realm of possibility. Such a major adjustment would only be likely to be done if a key customer or entire group of users switched platforms and the product would fail if it did not release on the right platform.) It does mean that opportunities to evolve the underlying technology or improve the architecture should be at the forefront of the development team's consciousness. It does not require that the team consider only what is being done for the current release but have an eye toward the future and consider whether the current version will support future possibilities. Similarly, the UX team should be looking around to see if new technologies or design paradigms might allow it to improve the design for the customer. And, as the team moves through the release, the UX staff should be looking for opportunities to improve the design. These improvements can be inspired by customer feedback, conversations with developers and internal stakeholders, or witnessing an innovative and relevant implementation. Unlike more traditional methods, the design is not done when the specification is completed and put on a shelf, with no real way to revisit it until the next release. The UX team needs to look at the design as a living thing that can and should be revised when information is available to improve it and provide a better experience for the customer.

Having a principle that speaks to the importance of continuous attention to good design makes the job of a UX person that much easier. After all, if I had a magic wand to wave at work, this might be one of the things I would wish for. It might be true that the original intention of the use of the word *design* could have been to speak to the architecture of the code, but we can certainly broaden the context of the statement to encompass all the work that goes on to produce the front end. As with the focus on technical excellence, it is the element of "continuous" that makes this principle so interesting and so powerful. In more traditional methods, design can often be talked about at the kickoff of the project, at a certain milestone, like the delivery of the specification, or as a last minute addition once the code is written. This is less likely to be true with using the Agile method, since the work is constant and ongoing. However, saying that the attention to good design should occur throughout the process recognizes the need for it to be a deeply embedded part of the work and not something smacked on when the team thinks about it. To achieve a truly great design, the effort needs to be an integral part of everything that the team does.

Principle 10 - Simplicity—the art of maximizing the amount of work not done—is essential

Simplicity is the most valuable concept in design, and it seems appropriate to apply it to the work process. For the UX designers, this might not represent a great challenge in terms of changing our mindset, because we so often shrink to fit into the time we have available and often do it by focusing on doing only what is most necessary. The best thing about this principle is that it is a call to action in terms of being very conscious about where those on the UX team spend time, what they produce, and if there are places where we could spend less time or do things differently and achieve the same or a better outcome. This does not mean just doing less; it really means spending time and resources where they are the most effective and being as strategic as possible in choosing the activities in which we engage. By all means, if having that second brainstorming session did not yield much, then the next time you should consider whether a single brainstorming meeting might be sufficient. If you and your team to discuss what is and is not working and actively examine how you spend your time, the extraneous tasks are often easy to identify. Generally, your teammates will not hesitate to let you know when you have had one too many brainstorming sessions. Some areas of waste are not quite as obvious, because the only time being wasted is yours, and your teammates might not be as quick to flag it as a problem. It is important to be very conscious of the impact your work has when looking for opportunities for efficiency. If you spent time coming up with a design solution with a developer and he is already well on his way to implementing it as agreed and you then spend your time producing sketches or wireframes to reflect that agreement, you may want to ask yourself, Why? Is it out of habit or the feeling that, if you did not write it down, then it did not really get designed? If so, then it may not be time well spent and you should consider saving your effort. If the answer is that you did it so you could communicate the design to a QE (Quality Engineering) team in another country, then it might be the right thing to do, but make sure that you are producing only what you need to in order to provide that team with an understanding of the UI. It is important to look at everything you do and ensure that you are being as simple as possible in your efforts.

Principle 11 - The best architectures, requirements, and designs emerge from self-organizing teams

Much like the idea of building teams around motivated individuals and trusting them to do the work, this principle is geared toward allowing the teams the freedom to make the necessary decisions to achieve great software. The team should be allowed to control the timing and flow of its work because, as the people closest to the project, the members best understand the right course of action. Additionally, the team is in the best position to know which person is the best choice to execute a given task. For the UX practitioner, this can also mean being more open to working collaboratively with other team members on design and allowing the design work to be supported by those whose are able to execute it. This certainly does not mean treating design tasks in a random or haphazard way but recognizing that, if a developer has a good eye for design or creative implementation solution, then it might make sense for that person to handle those decisions for a particular piece of the project. Perhaps, you can seed the effort with some discussion, then let the person take it from there. The UX person always is responsible for the outcome, so this is less about dumping your design work on a willing victim and more about allowing people with the interest and skill to contribute to the design in a more meaningful way. This can give the team a greater sense of ownership with respect to the design, and it can help maximize what is most likely a limited design resource.

Principle 12 - At regular intervals, the team reflects on how to become more effective, then tunes and adjusts its behavior accordingly

It may be the last principle, but I see it as the most critical. Without this, there can be no successful Agile implementation. These moments of reflection, done as a group or individually, allow the team to work more efficiently. This evaluation is especially important for teams beginning their Agile journey, as it is necessary for them to identify and learn as a group what is or is not working, the need for this does not go away when teams get more experienced. The only difference is that the necessary course corrections or process tweaks might be smaller. It is not realistic to think that a team can be completely efficient and Agile as soon as the project kicks off, with no need to examine how the members work as their way through the release cycle.

In looking at effective teams, it seems that the ability to do this well is the best predictor of a positive outcome. The first retrospective session that a team has may certainly be awkward, but if the team is engaged and the conversation generally heads in the right direction, the odds are pretty good that it will not take long for the individuals to master this skill and ultimately find success with an Agile process. However, if in the first retrospective, team members' conversations are shut down or they feel like their feedback is not being heard, it can be tough to recover from that first experience. The team will have a much harder time refining its effort, because the members have no a forum in which they can express their concerns and work through solutions. If that dynamic continues in the retrospectives, not only will the team miss out on their best chance to improve its process but this could be a red flag that other communication issues are going on and need attention. The scrum master is responsible for making sure that this meeting is productive, but depending on his or her background, this person may not have to skills to get the discussion moving in a healthy direction if it is not doing so naturally. As experienced facilitators and moderators, it is the responsibility of the UX team members to help make the exchange as fruitful as possible. In an official scrum retrospective, the scrum master runs the meeting, but that is not to say that the UX person cannot help guide the conversation in a positive direction. If a discussion is about how the process is going is being done in a more informal way, then it may be easier for the UX person to jump in and manage the tone of the discussion.

COMMON METHODS

Crystal

Crystal refers to a family of methodologies developed by Alistair Cockburn that are color-coded based on the size of the team. It is one of the first entrants into the pool of Agile methods, since it was created even before Extreme Programming and given a formal name prior to the creation of the Agile Manifesto. In terms of method and process, this is probably the most light-weight and flexible of them all. Rather than create a series of ceremonies or events, it focuses on addressing risk on teams and using a process that allows the development team to achieve certain characteristics by using a set of methods, some of which are identified as optional. It is a framework that offers some specific tactics and techniques and is more specific than the principles of the Agile Manifesto but less prescriptive than most other Agile methods. The best source for more information about how to apply this framework to small teams would be *Crystal Clear* by Alistair Cockburn (2005).

Extreme Programming (XP)

Extreme Programming is one of the earlier Agile methods, and it remains very much a part of the current discussion of Agile. It is worth mentioning not only for its historical significance but also because, for many developers, this method is often their earliest and defining experience with Agile. They may have moved on it using other Agile methods, but this is the technique that sets the tone for their understanding of how Agile processes work. One of the most interesting elements of this method is the "Customer Bill of Rights" and the

"Developer Bill of Rights," which introduced the concept that the process of producing software needs to take in to consideration its obligations to both its customers and the people who are writing the code. It is a fairly detailed development process, the main purpose of which is to empower the team to take real ownership of the project, encourage frequent communication among team members, participate in honest planning, incorporate customer engagement into the process, and acknowledge that iteration is a desired part of the process. The emphasis on refactoring seen in all Agile methods was born from this practice.

This is a very well-defined methodology with a very heavy focus on code production to the exclusion of considering the roles of other functional areas. This is not a flaw in the method; it simply is meant to address the faster, higher-quality production of code and speaks to that part of the production process. A UX team should be prepared to be highly communicative and integrated with a development team that will move rapidly to find solutions and implement them. There is a high likelihood that there will be access to working prototypes to use for testing very early on, when working with this method. Additionally, if the developers have really embraced the values of this approach, there will be an openness to rework and refine the design, as refactoring is highly valued in this technique.

Scrum

This is one of the more popular of the Agile methods right now. The two key features in this process are the roles of the team members (the product owner, the development team, and the scrum master) and the product backlog. Each project team has a scrum master, who is responsible for moving the process forward and removing obstacles that might prevent it from doing so, and a product owner, who is responsible for setting the priorities of the work items. The team itself also plays an important role, as the members' consensus on and commitment to a given scope of work is an integral part of the process. The team commits to contents of a sprint, after discussing each element and estimating its required effort. Should a need arise to change that scope or timing, only the team can agree to make that adjustment during the course of the sprint. Of course, the request to change scope or direction in mid-sprint can come from within or external to the team, but since the team has made a commitment to do a specific amount of work within a specific amount of time, only the team members can decide to alter that commitment. In practice, the issue around changing direction during the course of the sprint does not often come up, but there is value in knowing that the team controls its own destiny, at least for a set period of time. In an environments where the scope of the development work can change on the whimsy of executives, creating a safe place, where the work cannot be disrupted, allows teams to focus in a way that they might not have been able to do in more traditional environments. The product backlog is the repository for the user stories, the tasks needed to satisfy them, bugs, and nonfunctional requirements. Anyone on the team can contribute to the backlog, although a larger team needs to determine the priority and timing of the work. The product owner represents the voice of the customer, owns the priorities of the work items, and works with the team to define user stories.

Scrum also has many events geared to facilitating productive and frequent communication between team members. There is a daily scrum meeting, also called *daily standup*, which is a recurring 15-minute meeting. While anyone can attend, only the contributors can speak, and they are meant to share only what they did yesterday, what they intend to do today, and what obstacles they face that might inhibit their work. Some organizations may also have a daily scrum of scrum meeting, where representatives from multiple scrum teams meet to discuss work that overlaps or affects the different teams. Both events provide predictable, daily opportunities for team members to engage in conversation and facilitate communication in an efficient way. Also, events occur for every sprint cycle as part of the maintenance and planning for each sprint. There is generally a backlog grooming session, in which the team estimates the effort for a given story, refines and negotiates the acceptance criteria for a story, and breaks down large stories, or epics, in to smaller chunks. This meeting is supposed to be only an hour long, but more than one of these may be necessary for a given sprint, especially at the beginning of the release cycle, when more decisions are made about what work needs to happen and when it should occur. Sprint planning should also take place at the beginning of each sprint, the first day of the sprint, so that the team can scope out the work and commit to a specific set of deliverables for that sprint. This is the longest event in scrum, time boxed at a maximum of eight hours. Smaller or more focused teams may find that they do not need that much time for planning; larger project teams may have to work harder to stay within that time frame. At the end of each sprint, there should also be a sprint review and a sprint retrospective. The sprint review is where the team discusses what work was or was not completed, according to its ability to meet the acceptance criteria and definition of *done*, and demonstrate the results of the sprint to the team and stakeholders. The sprint retrospective is where the team acknowledges what went well in that sprint and discusses what did not go well and how to do better going forward. Fostering a candid and open forum in this meeting is critical to making scrum a process that works well for a project and for the team. This is the event that requires the most open, honest communication; and if that type of discourse is not facilitated or the feedback is not acted upon, it can inhibit the ability of the team to work well together.

This approach is not very prescriptive where design and usability testing are concerned, so it provides a great opportunity for the UX team to be proactive about defining its role in the process. Depending on the scope of the project, the dynamics of the team, the length of the sprints, and when the designer gets on board, you can decide if it makes the most sense to work within the sprint to produce the deliverables. It is not uncommon for designers to work ahead of the development teams to define the interfaces and gather feedback while still maintaining constant communication with the rest of the team. Working in this fashion is also referred to as *working in parallel* to the development team. When the design team works independently of the development team by working on a design problem in a separate sprint from its implementation, this can give the design and research teams a little more room to breathe. They can determine their own velocity and have the entire length of the sprint or sometimes multiple sprints to work on their design solution or to complete their testing and analyze the results before the implementation begins. If the UX person is working within a sprint, along with the rest of the team, he or she generally has less time to work on a given item before it needs to be coded. This can be fine if the designer is partnered very closely with a developer or is working on a very small piece of work. For user research or when addressing larger design issues, to do so in a different sprint than the implementation tasks can often be advantageous. While some UX teams work exclusively in parallel to or within a sprint, it is certainly possible to mix both techniques over the course of a release. When thinking about how to include user research in the cycle, it helps to decide at the beginning of the release if doing weekly user testing is possible or if dedicating a sprint or two to usability sessions is more realistic. Larger pieces of research ideally are done ahead of the cycle, if possible, or in an early sprint or sprints, if there is no time to research ahead. What is really critical is to thoughtfully consider what the UX role should be in the framework of a specific team's implementation of Scrum and with the team dynamics in mind. If it is your first time participating in Scrum, just take your best guess at what has the best chance of success based on the culture, the team dynamics, and the project and be prepared to iterate on that approach.

Hybrid agile, or custom agile

Hybrid Agile, or *Custom Agile* is used to describe what happens when a company takes the elements of any Agile methodologies that are appealing to it and uses them in a way that makes sense for the organization. The company may do this because only a part of an organization is using Agile methods and the efforts need to conform to a broader project management framework. Or, perhaps, combining Agile methods with traditional methods is just a good fit for the company and the culture. This requires a project team to be conscious about how its adoption of Agile methods fits the broader framework and what striking this balance means for the team. Certainly, more effort is required in doing this, because a team cannot use a prepackaged process and will (ideally) invest time

FIGURE 1.2
Custom agile.

in making the best trade-offs. If this investment is made, then creating a custom process can potentially increase the odds of a successful and less painful transition in adopting Agile. There is a potential for trouble, however, if an organization is not being conscientious in defining this process—it can wind up with something that is called *Agile* but is more or less the same traditional process always used. This outcome is especially likely if an organization is hybridizing its Agile approach because it is simply reluctant to make a broad organizational change. This type of approach tends to have a high rate of failure, because it can often reflect a lack of genuine commitment to Agile rather than fully embracing the concept, instead just trying to squeeze it into the existing culture.

If the organization is genuinely committed to customization, then this type of implementation can be the most open to allowing the UX team to define its own role and be a very active voice in the process. If there is dedication to defining a homegrown method, the process definition should include all the functional areas involved and account for their needs in a way that fits best for the organization If your organization has taken this tack for adopting Agile, the odds are pretty good that stakeholders from all areas will be involved and the result will be something that works well for all the teams. The good news is that a culture that embraces this approach will likely get it right or be open to course correction if it did not. On the other hand, if an organization is choosing this approach because it is hesitant to give up processes that are old, comfortable, and well established or there is a sporadic application of Agile throughout the organization, this method can be the most challenging approach of all. In is unlikely that much training will be available to people when that kind of dynamic is at play. The company might train a few key people but not see the value in providing training for something it feels will be defined in-house. This can be problematic, because it is very hard to know where to make changes if you lack a good understanding of that from which you are deviating.

Another potential issue is that this might mean that a UX person can find himself or herself supporting both Agile and non-Agile projects, which can be a scheduling and logistical nightmare. The design team can also find itself working with all of the urgency and speed of Agile but still producing heavy-handed specifications and experiencing the worst of both worlds. Another problem that often arises under these circumstances is that each team has a different understanding of Agile; and if the UX person is supporting multiple projects, it can be a challenge to know how a given team is working. It is hard to generalize knowledge of an hybrid method if no single method is in use.

Kanban

The Kanban technique is not as widely adopted as Scrum but has definitely gained traction recently and seems to be part of the next wave of Agile methods. The term is derived from the Japanese for "visual card" and is a relative of Toyota's Lean production processes. The central element of this method is a formalized version of the type of board often used by Agile teams. On a Kanban board, there is a "Goals" column on the far left that describes the team's goals, to provide a reminder of the overall purpose of the project. A "Stories" column contains all of the stories that will be worked on, and a story remains in this column until it moves through the process toward completion. Each subsequent column represents the work steps necessary to get to the final state. These columns are defined by the team and could include "UI design," "Development," "Validation." The top part of each column is for stories in progress for that step, the bottom is for stories that are complete for that step but have not yet moved to the next step. The final column holds the stories that are complete and of shipping quality. For this method, a little less structure is given to the time it takes to complete a task; the task moves from one column to the next as it is ready. This can allow for a more a natural cadence for the team, as the work can flow as it needs to, in contrast with Scrum's sprint cycles and formal commitments.

It is very important that UX activities are included in the column to create visibility around the importance of those tasks and the necessity of completing them for a task to be "done" or move forward. Design work always warrants having a column; and it can be very powerful to have the visual reminder that design work should precede implementation. It can also be educational for the team to see how long a given card spends in the design column. For that reason alone, there is value in having design as its own column. If other UX activities, such as usability testing, are only going to happen for a few features or will be done infrequently, then they might not require their own column on the board. Another challenge for teams working in a Kanban environment is that often

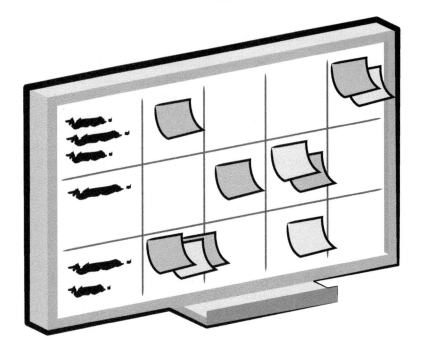

FIGURE 1.3

Kanban.

seeing the "big picture" across projects is difficult, since the Kanban boards are for a single project and very local. Of course, when this happens, it is not just a problem for the designers, but it can make their lives especially challenging if they support multiple project teams and do not feel that they have an adequate sense of how all of those projects fit together.

Since this process is, in fact, very light on process, it works best in environments where the team and the culture already support a high level of communication and collaboration. One of the reasons that methods like Scrum exist is to provide a framework that facilitates the creation of a highly communicative culture and to provide events that create the opportunities for the team to realize Agile values. Choosing to use Kanban should be done when your team does not need these cultural training wheels and is ready and able to simply execute the work using a lightweight process to give the work some structure.

Scrumban

As its name might imply, this is a hybrid of Scrum and Kanban, the term coined by Corey Ladas (2008) to describe the method that his team developed. It is essentially a leaner form of Scrum but does away with some of the events typically associated with Scrum and uses the Kanban board to visualize the project; however, it adds a value to the cards to show their relative weight within the project. To learn more, read Corey's paper online at http://leansoftwareengineering.com/ksse/scrum-ban/. The idea of adding weight seems interesting, as it can help to expose and highlight some of the complexity that might not be as obvious on a Kanban board, where all the tasks look the same. At the same time, it can also provide a little more structure for a team that is either transitioning from Scrum to Kanban or for those teams where this type of approach simply fits their needs.

Lean UX

This is another of the next generation Agile methods and the first one to consider UX explicitly. While not exactly in its infancy, Lean UX is still very much in its youth and is gathering an increasing amount of momentum and attention. The term was born as a result of Eric Ries's (2011) *The Lean Startup* book and movement, which encourages rapid prototyping and user validation and the continuous deployment of production code in response to a fast-moving market. The idea of integrating design into this process led to the creation of the idea of Lean UX. While there are several definitions and many strong opinions about what Lean UX is or is not (and more than a few books being written on the topic), all of the current definitions seem to have a few commonalities. As its name implies, there is no waste in this process. For some adopters, this means no deliverables at all, for others it simply means no unnecessary deliverables and few products from the UX team. This process moves fast, so it needs to be very streamlined, and the focus of the UX team needs to be on influencing the design and processing customer feedback to guide the next round (or current cycle, if possible) of designs. In some ways, the emphasis in the name on UX is almost misleading, because a Lean UX team must be seamlessly integrated into the production team to be as efficient and effective as possible. While UX is a prominent consideration, it is most certainly the method that is the least likely to have any silos.

The other element that everyone agrees on as being a part of Lean UX is frequent and continuous feedback from customers. These types of UX teams are the most likely to have found a way to incorporate weekly customer testing sessions into their cycles, despite also generally having the fastest-moving and shortest production cycles. They have recurring usability testing sessions, which often occur in person. In addition, these sessions are often complemented by remote or automated web testing tools that gather feedback. Teams that lack access to local users rely on the remote techniques, as these still yield valuable results, even if they do not offer the same kind of face-to-face contact. The team plans the recurring sessions with customers, and the topics can range from getting feedback on concepts or wireframes to full-fledged user testing. The concept of "test what you have" is very common among Lean UX teams. While I

FIGURE 1.4
Lean UX.

have not heard anyone explicitly include this in their official Lean UX definitions, I notice that these teams are also the most likely to have very organic, highly adaptive ways of working with the other functional areas. This makes sense, really, since these teams need to function at such a high level of efficiency. It can almost be challenging to talk about "process" with Lean UX practitioners, because so many of them have managed to fall into a very natural and almost transparent rhythm of working, to the point where the artifice of process just falls away.

COMMON TERMS

Chickens and pigs

Every project has people in the role of chickens or pigs. The chickens are the team members involved in the project, but not necessarily directly, and need to be informed of its progress. The pigs are the team members committed to doing the work and are directly responsible for the outcome of the project. The terminology comes from a description of a bacon and egg breakfast, in which chickens are involved, but pigs are committed. The UX team usually falls in to the pig category since it directly contributes to the outcome of the release and is "committed."

Product owner

The product owner is the owner of the product backlog and the deciding authority on priorities and user story definitions. Which functional area fills this role is dependent on the organization, but typically it is a product manager or other type of business owner. It is not unusual for a development manager to be in this role, if the organization has no product managers, the product managers are in another location, or the product managers are not usually involved in the release in a hands-on way. It is uncommon, but not unheard of, for someone from the UX team to be in this role. Regardless of the functional area from which they come, the UX staff members should expect to work as closely as possible with whomever does fill that role. One reason that it is critical to establish a good working relationship with the product owner is because that individual is ultimately responsible for the shipping product. The UX person is responsible for the creation of the design, but the product owner actually "owns' the product, which includes the design. Since the product owner oversees the assignment of priorities to the user stories and the work in general, it is important that he or she understand the value of user-centered design so that those efforts are not constantly put at the bottom of the priority list. In general, the product owner works well with UX, as that individual appreciates the research produced by the UX team and is happy to know that someone is looking after the design.

Scrum master

This is the person responsible for keeping the Scrum process on track. As the person responsible for facilitating the removal of impediments raised in the daily scrum meetings, he or she keeps the meetings on track and on time and generally is responsible for enforcing the agreed-upon Agile process. The non-Agile analogy would be a project manager, and the role tends to be most effective when it is filled by a neutral third party who is not directly involved in the production of the releasing deliverable. Scrum masters act as time cops for the scrum events that are time boxed; they facilitate the retrospectives and generally make sure that the team follows the process it has chosen to follow. Ideally, however, scrum masters do not act as the "scrum police," which is not an actual Scrum term but my own description for scrum masters so enamored of the Scrum process that they cannot see the forest for the trees. It is not their role to be rigid about following Scrum to the letter and in the way they saw presented during the scrum master training. At first, the scrum master might well insist the team does follow the process exactly, so that team members can properly identify where they need to make change. This initial adherence to the formal process is entirely appropriate and of benefit to the team. However, if the team agrees that something about the process does not suit it and identifies an alternative approach, the scrum master should be open to supporting the team in that change and keeping them on track with it. He or she should not declare the change to be "not Agile" and try to talk the team out of doing it. This role is really that of a facilitator who has a good working understanding of Agile processes and helps the team get the most that it can out of working in an Agile way.

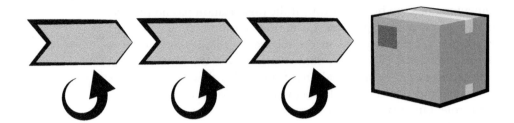

FIGURE 1.5
Sprints.

Sprint

Essentially, a sprint is single development iteration in a given release. Each sprint has a scope to which the team commits and its goal is to have demonstrable software at the end. A single release cycle is made up of a series of sprints. A sprint's length is typically between one and four weeks, with a three weeks being a nice balance between meeting time and work time. Most teams use a consistent sprint length throughout the release, unless some need arises for adjustment as the team moves through the development process. Teams using Kanban or a less formal Agile method may not use a specific sprint length and allow the work to follow its own pace. The estimation of the level of effort, using the abstract of story points, are tracked to determine the team's overall velocity. The velocity helps determine how much work the team tends to complete in a given sprint, so that it can plan the appropriate scope to take on in future releases. The UX members can be tracked as part of the team's overall velocity, which may or may not be helpful to the process. Each team should determine the value of this work and if it is helpful to the greater team. It may be interesting to the UX person that the team are 10 hours into a 20-hour design task, but if that person is straddling multiple projects that 20 hours could be evenly spread across the sprint or occur all at once at the beginning or the end. This might not help the team or the UX person know if the team is on track for the sprint, especially if all of his or her work occurs in the last few days. Regardless, the issue of tracking UX velocity should be discussed by the team and agreed upon ahead of time, although it can be revisited in a retrospective if necessary.

Product backlog

At a high level, the product backlog is a prioritized list of things related to a product, typically for the current release. Because the team reviews the product backlog often, it may be a distraction for the backlog to contain items that are out of scope for the release at hand. Some teams manage this by coding these items with an exceptionally low priority and a specific numerical value, so that they can remain available for consideration in the event of a schedule slip or other dramatic change in circumstances. If the items never make it in to the release, the team may roll them into the backlog for the next release. Other teams create release-specific backlogs and move out-of-scope items into the backlog for the next release or review in the future.

Items in the backlog can include epics, user stories, tasks, or bugs. When the team does its planning, it pulls from the backlog to inform the scope of the release. When the team engages in backlog grooming, it reprioritizes items, fleshing out acceptance criteria and refining the estimates. While the product owner is the ultimate owner of the backlog, it can be very helpful if the UX person is part of the process of creating the backlog. If any high-level design has been done, the UX person can make sure that this perspective is supported by the user stories and tasks in the backlog.

User stories

Instead of functional requirements, which can inspire a myopic focus on features and functionality, Agile methods rely on user stories, in an effort to keep the attention and awareness on the needs of the user. User stories have a consistent format that phrases everything in terms of the users and their needs—"As a …, I want to … ." Additionally, "in order to…" can be added to the end of user story to provide more insight into the motivation behind the story, but the shorter format is the more typical of the two. While its helpful for the team members to be involved in the creation of the user stories, UX people tend to be more accustomed to thinking of the user perspective when considering functionality. Strong UX participation during the population of the product backlog is also the earliest opportunity to influence the process and incorporate user-centered values into the work well ahead of executing any design tasks.

A good example of a user story is "As a mom of an active preschool girl, I want to see all the skorts available in a size 5T so that I can buy as many as possible." This describes who the customer is—a person shopping for someone else. What that person is doing—looking at a list of available skorts (skirts with built-in shorts) in a specific size. And, if your team takes the extra step, the story ,explain why the user is doing the task—to purchase multiple items. While not every team uses the "so that I …" part of the sentence, it is clear that having this extra phrase can be very helpful, especially for designers. A person who wants the list to compare prices against another site, identify the fabric content, or get a sense of how much variety is available on the site is really performing a different task than a person who wants to identify all available items and buy multiples of them. It could mean the difference between having a list of thumbnails with prices and a way to select multiple items to go into the shopping bag or having a broader list that also includes product details. If the various solutions for different motivations have commonalities, as they do in this case, it might make sense to provide a broad solution that will address several different "whys." Having the discussion with the product owner around this part of the user story could be very valuable, especially for the UX team. Knowing the "why" might lead the team to a different design solution than if it has to fill in the blank itself. Having it explicitly defined also ensures that everyone has the same motivation in mind, which can produce a more consistent outcome.

Epic

When a user story is so large that it cannot be completed in a single cycle or is defined in such a way that it needs to be broken down further, it is considered an epic. An epic needs to be broken down into more digestible pieces, which can potentially fit within a sprint cycle. It might seem like the best thing to do is to simply decompose the epic in to its smaller pieces and get rid of the high-level item once it has been identified as being too large to fit. However, preserving the larger story allows for relationships to be established between the smaller items and provides a more obvious picture of how things fit together. It also provides clarity about when this particular requirement is really met, if only four of the five smaller pieces have been implemented, then the epic has not been satisfied.

Planning poker

One technique that can be used to estimate effort for a user story is to give each team member a set of planning poker cards. In this way, team members can put up a card giving their estimate of effort, people who have a higher or lower estimate can explain their estimates, and the team can decide if an adjustment needs to be made. The outcome of the subsequent discussion is an estimate for relative size of the story. It is important for the team to be clear on what it is estimating, whether the overall team effort or just the effort for that functional area. Otherwise, a team can waste time doing a Delphi on the estimates, such as if a UX person is asked to estimate development effort or vice versa. Part of this clarity requires a decision around how the UX work will be handled in general. A user story should be applicable to all the functional areas, as it is really just a specifically formatted customer requirement. A task should be specific to the functional area, and if dependencies require a UX task related to a given story to be done prior to the implementation task for that story, these dependencies can be captured at the task level.

Story-point estimation

When estimating effort, most methods recommend using story points rather than hours or days to determine the relative effort of the work. It can be a challenge for teams to think so abstractly about effort, and if numbers are used (rather than small, medium, etc.), the natural tendency is to try to map a story-point number to hours of work. It is best if the team can fight that urge and instead determine the baseline of the story points against a specific task with which everyone is familiar to establish that a task like x is small, a task like y is medium. Once a baseline is established, the team can use these as a reference when trying to gauge the amount of work required to complete a particular user story. It can be quite difficult for team members who are more comfortable with precision to become accustomed to estimating effort in such abstract terms. However, the point of using a concept such as story points is to keep team members from getting caught up in a false precision during estimation. While it is certainly easier to conceive of what 10, 20, or 40 hours of project work looks like, that does not make an estimated effort of 10 hours any more accurate than a story-point estimate of small. If you think about the last estimation effort in which you tooka part, a certain level of abstraction was probably applied to the numbers; and you can see that what was perceived as a small task would always be estimated at 10 hours.

Estimation of story points is something that needs to be considered when defining the role of the UX team in the process. If the UX team is going to be on separate sprints, it may or may not be important to estimate its effort and track its velocity. Since UX teams are always expanding or shrinking to fit the time they are given, putting too much effort into estimating the effort of UX tasks might not be a great use of the team's time. However, if the UX team uses parallel sprints for its work, it might be interesting o track velocity to help it with its own planning. In most cases, the UX team can do its estimates solo and let the product team review them if interested. This is especially true if a UX person supports multiple projects. In which case, that individual's velocity is determined more by the time is available to be spent on a given project rather than how long it takes to do a particular task or tasks. Additionally, when it comes to estimation and tracking the velocity of user research, there might be nothing interesting or insightful to track. Six hours of testing takes six hours; and while some scheduling or posttest analysis might occur, these are pretty discrete events and estimating them may offer no value to the team. These tasks have no significant amount of potential for variability that represents a risk that requires management. It is probably sufficient to account for the time and know that a day or two days of testing activities occur at a certain point in the sprint. However, if the UX team needs to track effort to load balance or manage staffing resources or the product team wants keep track of UX efforts for some other reason, it may be useful to estimate user stories in a way that accounts for the UX team's time. As with the other elements of the process, it is important to work with the team to define the approach to this up front and revisit it as necessary throughout.

Acceptance criteria

These criteria determine what needs to be included in the working code for a given user story for it to be considered ready to ship. It defines the scope of that user story in terms of functionality and behavior for both the user and the system. For the user story "As a doctor, I want to see an overview of my critical activities, so that I can take action on them," the acceptance criteria might include "the total number of critical actions is displayed," "an overview of critical actions is displayed," and "the overview links to each critical action so they can be resolved." This way, the product owner can communicate the details about the user story, the designer can add his or her perspective, and the developer can have a better understanding of what the user story intends to achieve. It also allows the team to agree on what the implementation will contain to be considered shippable, so it represents a tacit agreement as to scope. Defining this ahead of doing the work also avoids difficult discussions later in the cycle. Often, it is not until the code has been written and submitted that team members realize that it does not quite do what they had in mind. Even in a responsive Agile environment, waiting to have that conversation during the team demonstration or just prior to the end of the sprint puts everyone in an awkward position. Either the work is not considered complete, which causes the team to miss its deliverable, date or the rework is pushed to the next sprint. Doing the rework later is fine, but it could have been avoided with a little more discussion at the beginning and a more explicit expression of expectations.

Burn-down chart

This chart is used in daily meetings to visualize the overall progress of the team and is a plot of the effort against the remaining hours. Ideally, this is a nice straight line down, as the amount of work left to do decreases throughout the sprint. In reality, the actual burn-down chart often has many spikes and valleys, which ideally have an overall downward trend. To track effort, the tasks must have estimates associated with them, and the team must track the completion of and time spent on each task. These charts tend to be most valuable for the development team, whose work occurs consistently throughout the sprint and the release cycle. It tends to be less insightful when used for tracking QE or UX efforts, as those may happen ahead or behind certain tasks and take place predominantly at the beginning or end of the sprint. It may give the team a picture that indicates less progress than is actually true, if the burn-down chart routinely includes tasks that typically happen at the end of the sprint, such as some QE testing tasks. Similarly, if the UX team is working in a sprint and its design tasks take place in the first few days, the burn-down chart may look a little more positive than it necessarily is, as the designers mark their work as complete. If the charts are reviewed by only the project team, this is not much of an issue, as it can take these things into consideration when reviewing the chart. However, if people outside the team are looking at these plots, they may not understand this and get the wrong message. When considering how to use these charts and generally approaching how to track velocity, the team should consider its audience.

Spike

Some teams use spikes to manage stories that cannot be estimated without some amount of investigation. Given the short time frames of sprints and the Scrum emphasis on committing to a specific amount of work, it makes no sense to simply sign up to do work of an indeterminate duration. Under any circumstances, tracking the progress of an effort that lacks an expected duration is hard, so a technique was created to address this problem. To deal with a spike, the team is given a set amount of time to do the necessary research, and the outcome of the spike is an estimate for the user story. Spikes can be used to accommodate UX design work or to account for user research, but the method is really intended to handle uncertainty around implementation solutions. Design and research should be predictable events that are a part of the normal planning. Spikes should be used to manage exceptions, such as a design task that requires research into available technology before it can be estimated or unexpected issues that come up and need user research to be properly defined.

AgileFall

While this may not be an official term yet, its use in conversation seems to be gaining popularity. The term refers to the situations in which Agile methods are fit into a waterfall organization or when a sort of mini-waterfall process starts to occur within an Agile environment. Sometimes, a team may be practicing Agile and the rest of the company is not or cannot, and the team strikes a balance between the Agile teamwork and satisfying higher-level requirements to meet more traditional milestones, checkpoints, or requirements. Depending on how rigid or extensive the requirements are, this can either be quite detrimental to the adoption of Agile or dovetail neatly, without too much effort or distraction.

If the team is engaging in a mini-waterfall process, that might be more of a red flag. This typically happens if the functional areas work separately and do not engage in a high level of communication. There might be a lack of transparency and insight into what each is doing, and handoffs of deliverables might still be a bit formal. The team might not be letting go of old habits and needs more support in adopting new ones. One contributing factor to this might be the UX team, if it is working in parallel sprints, although not every UX team that works in parallel contributes to a mini-waterfall dynamic. If your team is engaging in parallel sprint work and things start looking and feeling awfully like a waterfall, then it might be worth revisiting how the work is going and if attention needs to be paid to any communication issues.

Jeff Patton

While this is not exactly an Agile term, he is certainly an Agile institution. Many of the UX practitioners whose case studies are in this book received training and coaching from him directly or via webinars. He is a prominent thought leader on Agile and one of the most vocal in speaking about the design process (and the design team) as part of that process. His work and his blog can be found online at www.agileproductdesign.com/. Since most discussion about Agile UX began with him, his work would be the best place to start if you are beginning to explore Agile and UX design.

CASE STUDY—JEFF GOTHELF, THELADDERS.COM

One of the best ways to learn about a process is to hear how other people are doing it. UX teams have been adopting and adapting Agile practices for years and many teams achieved quite a bit of success in working this way. We examine a variety of real teams to see how they managed to implement an Agile process and what lessons they have to offer. Jeff Gothelf's story is interesting for many reasons. It gives a glimpse into an expert realization of Lean UX, which is one of the most recent innovations in Agile and UX. It also paints a picture of the challenges that teams face when making the transition away from traditional methods. We see how getting it wrong once or twice is just a step on the path to getting it right.

At the time of our interview, Jeff was the director of user experience at TheLadders.com, an online subscription job listing service targeted at filling senior-level positions. The organization decided to switch from a waterfall environment to an Agile process and deferred to the UX team to sort out what that would mean for it. Jeff did a lot of work figuring out how to help his team adapt to a wholesale change, and the transition had a rocky start. However, the team members were able to refactor their approach and hit their stride as a team.

Jeff did some research online to see how various UX teams tackle Agile. Since it was a bit early on in the days of Agile UX, few case studies of successful UX teams and an equal amount of horror stories were available online. Jeff started reaching out to people who experienced the transition to get their perspective on working within an Agile environment. Some of his early advisors included Andrew Sandler and Catherine Courage, the Agile UX pioneers at Salesforce.com. He also met Jeff Patton and listened to his take on Agile. The team also had Alistair Cockburn, one of the original authors of the Agile Manifesto, discuss the integration process with them. Essentially, Jeff was able to pick the brains of some of the MVPs of Agile and Agile UX. After getting a sense of the landscape, Jeff put together an idea of the process his team would follow, knowing that, in true Agile fashion, he would revisit the process along the way.

The team started with two-week sprints, working ahead of development and replacing functional specifications with story cards and wireframes. These wireframes started to get quite heavy as annotations were added to document the interaction rules. The team also created a vision document to keep track of the overall plan. Expressing an overall vision can be incredibly helpful for the entire team, not just the UX staff. A common complaint among Agile teams is that they lose track of the big picture, generally because so much of the focus is on the current sprint or immediate piece of work. Having a vision document of some kind, especially one that can be easily remembered, provides a reference point for everyone working on the project. This can go a long way to keeping the day-to-day decisions on the right track, since it is clear to all where they are going.

The first effort at becoming Agile resulted in Jeff being greeted one morning by a diagram created by his team illustrating that everything to do with Agile created a negative environment and low team morale. Jeff describes this as the "pinnacle of unhappiness" for the team in their integration effort. His assessment of what happened was that the UX team did not really know what to expect and did not know what it really meant to be Agile. Additionally, the development team was considered the expert on the process within the organization, but the members had no real idea of where UX should fit in. This situation is actually fairly typical for most UX teams. The UX team is entering new territory, and few, if any, team members have prior experience working with Agile. Regardless of how much training or research the team does, it can be hard to really know what to expect from working in such a new way. Since so much depends on the culture and personalities of the team members involved, every Agile situation is a bit different. Additionally, the interest in and decision to move to an Agile process generally originates from the development organization. If the development team invests in training, it quickly develops expertise, as the members are studying a process that is geared toward their work. Even if the UX team begins its research at the same time, the members have to do the additional homework of trying to figure out the best way to incorporate their work into a predefined process. In the best of situations, the UX team lags behind its development colleagues. This does not need to be a problem, but it can contribute to making the UX team feel like it ts not in control of its own fate.

Since the first approach was less than successful, the UX team members refactored. For their second attempt, they followed the advice of Andrew Sandler, of Salesforce.com, and created a style guide to alleviate some of the design burden and work more efficiently. Using techniques like style guides, style sheets, and pattern libraries can offer predefined solutions. This allows the team to focus on the communication and design of the higher-level elements of the design, rather than spend time and energy explaining how a widget should look or behave. Jeff's team also began prototyping its designs, so that members could communicate their design intentions without having to produce heavyweight documents. This allowed the team to engage in the more complex interaction design problems, rather than trying to do it all in two weeks. All of this put the team more in control of its deliverables with less effort and gave it the ability to more

fully engage in the rhythm of Agile. The members also communicated within the UX team about issues as they arose. If a cross-functional issue needed to be dealt with, the directors handled that.

Once the team members were able to execute their work, they started incorporating user testing. They began testing whatever was ready, every other week, mid-sprint. Additionally, two design reviews were added to each of the iterations to get feedback from stakeholders as well as customers. The process continues to evolve, and when I spoke with Jeff, some experienced team members are only sketching ahead then working in parallel with development. Less experienced teams still work ahead but only by a week or so.

In reflecting on the experience, Jeff noted that it is really important for UX team members to be comfortable with opening up their work to critique and collaboration and welcome the interactions with other disciplines. Jeff points out that Lean UX is not the place to try to be a rock star or a hero, and a UX person who is uncomfortable with a team-based culture will not be happy in an Agile environment. This can make the transition even more challenging for some team members. To read more about Jeff's experience getting started with Agile, in his own words, his story can be found at JohnnyHolland.org in the article "Beyond Staggered Sprints: How TheLadders.com Integrated UX into Agile" (Gothelf, n.d.).

What I found most powerful about Jeff's story is that he points out that things did not go well at first. But this does not make the attempt a failure; it is just an effort that needs revisiting and refining. The fact that his team was willing to let him know just how unhappy they were is actually a sign of success that the team culture is such that the members feel that if a problem is raised it will get addressed.

Key Points

- If at first you do not succeed, try again—and again—and again. An Agile process can put a spotlight on pre-existing communication issues and create stress on a UX team, because it introduces a completely new rhythm and way of working. These things take time and effort to overcome, but with time and effort, they can be overcome. The sign of success is not that it is easy but that everyone is communicating and working out problems and wanting to try new solutions.
- Talk to your peers. Many UX teams have gone before you and have lessons to share. The community is quite

generous and Agile veterans are generally very willing to help out anyone who wants it. In addition to the people mentioned in the case study, Jeff also spoke with Jeff Patton and found it valuable to learn from him. Before even speaking with peers, Jeff researched the state of UX and Agile online, so that he could get a sense of challenges. This tactic is a great place to start if you do not even know what questions to ask or who out there might have a good experience to share.

SUMMARY

There are many different ways to apply something called *Agile* to a development process. Regardless of which particular technique is used, it is always important to look to the Agile Manifesto to remember that the spirit of the method is not about adhering blindly to a process or producing copious amounts of documentation. *Being Agile* means working collaboratively as a team and with the customer to produce great software while adapting to change as the need arises. The values and the principles expressed in the Agile Manifesto are at the heart of all the methods, and appreciating them is the first step in being successful with Agile.

References

Cockburn, A., 2005. Crystal Clear: A Human-Powered Methodology for Small Teams. Addison-Wesley, Boston.

Gothelf, J., n.d. Beyond staggered sprints: How TheLadders.com integrated UX into Agile. In: Holland, J., Johnny Holland: It's All About Interaction. Retrieved April 2, 2012, from http://johnnyholland.org/2010/10/beyond-staggered-sprints-how-theladders-com-integrated-ux-into-agile/.

Ladas, C., n.d. Scrum-ban: Lean software engineering. Retrieved April 2, 2012, from http://leansoftwareengineering.com/ksse/scrum-ban/.

Manifesto for Agile Software Development. n.d. Manifesto for Agile Software Development. Retrieved April 2, 2012, from http://www.AgileManifesto.org.

Medlock, M.C., Wixon, D., Terrano, M., Romero, R., Fulton, B., n.d. Using the RITE method to improve products: A definition and a case study (Playtest Research). Retrieved April 2, 2012, from www.microsoft.com/en-us/download/details.aspx?id=20940Twelve.

Patton, J., n.d. Agile Product Design, Holistic Product Design and Agile Software Development. Retrieved April 2, 2012, from http://agileproductdesign.com.

Principles of Agile software. n.d. In: Manifesto for Agile Software Development. Retrieved April 2, 2012, from www.AgileManifesto.org.

Ries, E., 2011. The Lean Startup: How Today's Entrepreneurs Use Continuous Innovation to Create Radically Successful Businesses. Crown Business, New York.

Windows User Experience Design Principles. n.d. :n: MSDN—Explore Windows, Web, Cloud, and Windows Phone Software Development. Retrieved April 12, 2012, from http://msdn.microsoft.com/en-us/library/windows/desktop/dd834141.aspx.

Young, I., 2008. Mental Models: Aligning Design Strategy with Human Behavior. Rosenfeld Media, Brooklyn, NY.

CHAPTER 2

Agile Methods + UX = Agile UX

CONTENTS

Introduction 39

Fitting a UX Peg Into an Agile-Shaped Hole 42

The UX Work 48
Resourcing and staffing 48
Specifications 51
User research 55
Usability testing reports 61
Design activities 64

Summary 68

References 69

INTRODUCTION

Just as Agile is a really big term that can refer to the values, the manifesto, and all of the process that emerged from the movement, *user experience* is also a broad and sometimes controversial term. The formal definition that the Nielsen Norman Group uses ("User Experience: Our Definition," n.d.) is

> "'User experience' encompasses all aspects of the end-user's interaction with the company, its services, and its products. The first requirement for an exemplary user experience is to meet the exact needs of the customer, without fuss or bother. The next is the simplicity and elegance that produce products that are a joy to own, a joy to use. True user experience goes far beyond giving customers what they say they want, or providing checklist features. In order to achieve high-quality user experience in a company's offerings there must be a seamless merging of the services of multiple disciplines, including engineering, marketing, graphical and industrial design, and interface design."

Agile User Experience Design. http://dx.doi.org/10.1016/B978-0-12-415953-2.00002-9

(This definition can be found on the Nielsen Norman website at www. nngroup.com) Since Donald Norman is one of the earliest and most influential users of the term, the definition is the foundation of how many people understand the concept of user experience.

In my career, the words *usability, interaction design, product design*, and *user experience design* have appeared at different times in my title, even though my role in each of these positions was fundamentally the same. This is why, for some people, *user experience* feels like just another of the many buzz words used to describe user-centered design. For me, it means something specific or rather something that is very inclusive. I respectfully disagree slightly with the Nielsen Norman definition, which I think encompasses what many people now commonly refer to as *customer experience* (a term that evolved recently). I consider *user experience* to be slightly narrower than what the words describe, something that is more focused on the interactions and use of the product itself than speaking to the entire organization that produces, sells, and markets the software. Working with a sales representative to buy a license or a customer's ability to access helpful marketing materials seems to fall more appropriately under the broader term of *customer experience*, although it would be within the boundaries of *user experience* as defined by Norman. Part of this is because the customer and the user may not be the same person, especially in the case of enterprise software. When using these terms in this way, it is possible that the customer who negotiates the license or decides to upgrade to a new version may not be the same person as the user who actually touches the product. Of course, in many cases, they are the same, especially in the case of websites and consumer software.

I specifically see the idea and practice of user experience as an umbrella that describes only the end users' interaction with the product; including their environments, motivations, thoughts, and reactions to their interaction with the product. This means that UX considers not just the customers' ability to execute a task using an application but takes into account where they use it, why they use it, what other tasks and tools that they might need to use. It also speaks to their level of delight, frustration, comfort, and trust evoked as part of performing their tasks using that product. For example, if you design an application for use by business travelers and think of using audio and voice commands, you need to be aware that they will often use it at busy airports with lots of background noise, which might make it difficult to hear audio and challenging for the system to process voice commands. This could lead to a frustrating user experience, even if the user accomplishes the tasks after great effort and even though the product design might be very attractive. From a process perspective, UX also refers to the spectrum of activities that contribute to the resulting product—research, design and usability testing.

I refer to *UX practitioners* throughout this book for the sake of brevity. However, it is worth pointing out that t many people may not actually think of themselves as a UX practitioners even if it appears in their job title. People in many domains, collectively, could be considered as contributing to the user experience of a product—researchers, usability specialists, information architects, product/interaction/user experience/interface designers, and visual designers. So many job descriptions are used to classify those of us in roles that support the creation of a product's user experience, but in the end, all of us are focused on contributing to the creation of something that meets or exceeds the customer's wants and needs. A user researcher might study the target audience for a banking application and learn that trust is an important part of the user experience for a certain group and certain things influence that group's ability to trust in the application. A company may then have a product designer, an interaction designer, or a visual designer work on the design of the product to ensure that the elements establishing or influencing trust are incorporated in to the resulting application because of the information provided by the researcher. A usability specialist might facilitate usability tests to validate the design, and one of the many dimensions that he or she explores will be the issue of trust. The researcher then feeds the information back to the team, possibly with recommendations for improvements. In some companies, some or all of those roles might be filled by a single person. Because the theoretical "UX team" might be an actual team or teams or simply one person, I choose to use a single umbrella term to represent all of such efforts.

In describing the banking application, it is clear that there are many places for potential hand-offs, customer touch points, and activities just within the formation and refinement of the user experience. Looking at the list of tasks, it can be easy to imagine that these things require a lot of time to do thoroughly and properly. In good conscience, I have to acknowledge that, to do a truly thorough and proper research, design, and validation requires a certain amount of time, effort, and resources. Regardless of whether or not an organization is Agile, there are limits to how thorough a job one can do, due to normal constraints on time or resources. As a result, the various UX disciplines have not often had the luxury of time to conduct their efforts. Since it might be possible to spend an infinite amount of time creating a design or conducting research, often we make do with filling the time allocated to us. The crux of the challenge of fitting UX efforts into Agile methods is that we still need to do the same activities we have always done but do them even more quickly than before, because less time probably is allotted to the release in general. This is where we need to look at what we and how we are doing while thinking about what Agile values. It may not be a case of shrinking to fit as much as working differently and more efficiently to achieve and identify the tasks that contribute the most to creating a fantastic user experience.

FITTING A UX PEG INTO AN AGILE-SHAPED HOLE

In the previous chapter, we explored Agile values and principles and saw their connection to the goals and values of user-centered design. It is clear that many of the core values of Agile resonate quite well with those employed by your average user experience designer/researcher. It would be hard for a UX practitioner not to be excited about a process that emphasizes collaboration, communication, and consideration of the customer's needs and accommodates changes in requirements whenever they occur. That is exactly what most UX teams wish for. The core values that are the foundation of Agile methods can provide significant benefit to any organization that is genuinely committed to creating a culture that embodies those values. However, Agile methods are not a magic bullet and may not be an ideal fit for all projects or organizations. In fact, an organization that has existing challenges and simply trains one or two people in Scrum, then expects to "be Agile" will find that using an Agile process only shines a spotlight on those issues. The difficulty is because the obstacles that tend to undermine Agile processes are generally around communication or other cultural issues and typically the kind of problems with which organizations prefer not to deal. The reluctance to address these things is because they are tough to resolve and require a lot of soft skills that may not be available on the staff. The benefit of engaging fully in a detailed Agile process is that it can help to encourage better behavior on these fronts.

This especially affects the UX teams, because we are often in the role of supporting the work of development teams and tend to be directly affected by organizational issues and communication breakdowns. Just "going Agile" without laying the proper foundation does not result in an effortless transition to faster production of more user-centered products. Doing so really requires a team or organization to truly engage in fostering an environment of collaboration and communication. This means that if you are struggling to get usability feedback listened to by other functional areas or design specifications are considered to be more of a suggestion than an instruction with the development process currently in place, you are likely to find that is still the case if your company goes Agile. In fact, moving to an Agile methodology might serve only to make these issues more obvious to everyone on the team and bring things to a head quicker in the cycle. If there is a lack of communication between different team members or some functional areas are considered less important than others, these dysfunctions become more obvious when Agile methods are in place. However, if the move to Agile is thoughtful process and existing issues are acknowledged and dealt with properly, it certainly can be an effective change agent.

Instead of the organization trying, from the top down, to change the way that teams work, in an Agile environment, each team can contribute to a more grassroots level of fomenting change. In companies where only a few teams are Agile or all the teams are Agile but not necessarily embodying Agile values, the deck may seem stacked against you. However, ultimately, the team controls its own culture; and no matter how friendly or unfriendly the environment that the team is in, it is up to it to define its own values and set the tone for its behavior. Of course, this requires the teams to be very conscious of their adaptation of Agile, they need to be committed to the spirit of Agile and not focused exclusively on the details of the process. As part of the production team, the UX staff is in a position to influence the attitude of the team and model good behavior. Just as teams that model Agile values and have successful projects can persuade other teams to follow their example, UX team members can help set the tone of the production team by embodying Agile values themselves. The project team can be the agent of change within the organization and the UX person can be the agent of change, if necessary, within the team.

The best indicator of a project team's dedication to Agile values is the likelihood that it will be successful in Agile, the best opportunity to facilitate healthy communication and the most influential time to sway the culture is during the retrospectives. Regardless of which Agile method is practiced, there will be some form of re-evaluation and discussion. In Scrum, this activity is an explicit ceremony, which ensures that even teams not comfortable having this kind of discussion will at least make an attempt to do so. When these meetings allow for candid conversation and team member's feedback is taken seriously and acted on, there is a good chance of success for the project. Since this is the best time to raise issues and seek a resolution with the involvement of the entire team, it is critical that everyone feel comfortable doing so. If the team members feel like their suggestions will be dismissed, then this meeting will end up being a missed opportunity. The UX person will not likely be in the role of scrum master and so will not run the meeting or directly facilitate its tone. However, the UX person can help to set or change the dynamic of the meeting if he or she is willing to identify areas where the team could have done better during the sprint, is open to feedback on that topic, and acts on that feedback. Not only will the UX person benefit from the discussion but it allows the individual to be an active participant in driving the tone of the conversation and sets an example for the broader team. If a team member sees that the UX person is willing to do this and the outcome is positive, then it might inspire the member to behave the same way.

Another factor that can create challenges for an organization trying to embrace a culture of Agile are the logistics of the team and scale of the project. If a team is large, more than 10 people, or geographically dispersed, then scaling the method effectively is difficult but not impossible. The team should be aware of this and that it might need to modify its tactics to achieve the same outcome as a smaller, more colocated team. These particular obstacles can often affect UX people disproportionately, because they require extra effort and creativity to both collaborate on and communicate designs and to share research findings. Often, the project team responds to such a situation by asking the UX person for more documentation, a request that needs to be examined closely before agreeing to accommodate it. It is important for the UX team to use some of its resourcefulness in finding solutions to some of these challenges and the best answer to solve the problem rather than falling back on what might be more familiar, comfortable, or easy but does not really move the team forward in their Agile evolution. In this case, consider whether a document is really what is needed—Would an interactive prototype do the trick as effectively and with less effort? Would a video conference give you the most bang for the buck?

Working in an Agile environment can free you up to try new things; and if you approach the process from that angle, it will broaden your solution set. Moving to this process certainly is an adjustment, but it can also be a good excuse try new techniques and take more ownership of defining the UX role. If you were working with more traditional methods or the UX team had been in place for some time at your organization, you may not have had direct influence over how your role would integrate with other functional areas. This can be an opportunity to change that redefines how the UX team works. One thing to consider about Agile, however, is that, even if the UX role is broadly defined for the organization, each Agile team works in a slightly different way to fit its team members. Even if you do not get to define a new role for UX across the company, there is certainly room within Agile for your project team(s) to leverage your unique skills to great effect and with your direct input.

Probably the most important issue for the UX person to bear in mind is that out-of-the-box Agile methods tend to focus exclusively on the process of creating code and pay little attention to other functional areas. This is because, with the exception of Lean UX, they are intended to be development methods and not necessarily address the whole of what it takes to release a product. While this is such an obvious thing to point out, sometimes the reminder is necessary. I heard people dismiss Agile methods because they do not consider the UX team, the quality team, the documentation team, or any other team in the company. Well, it is true—and it is on purpose. Nor is it a bad thing. Most Agile methods are trying to tackle one problem—how to create high-quality, customer-centric code. If the development team elects to use this process, the burden is on the surrounding teams to define how they fit into the new way of working, keeping the Agile values and principles in mind. There tends to be little or no guidance for how a UX team can or should expect to fit into the cycle. This is an opportunity and should be embraced as such. We may not be the decision makers who control whether or not to use an Agile method or even which one to use, but we are completely in the driver's seat when it comes to defining how UX will fit into the Agile world. While a development team may have the luxury of picking a prepackaged Agile methodology and consuming it whole, the UX team has the responsibility (and freedom) to take a more thoughtful and targeted approach to writing the rules of engagement for working in an Agile way.

When I first started working on Agile projects and needed to figure out how my UX work fit into that picture, the common wisdom was for the UX team to work a sprint ahead of the development team on either design tasks or gathering user feedback. In fact, this perspective was so prevalent at that time and had so many enthusiastic adherents, that it did not even occur to me to consider working any other way. It also seemed very logical, given the pace of the sprints and my novice Agile status. While the development team worked out its infrastructure issues in the planning stages, I could conduct customer interviews and flesh out some of the user stories. Once we got underway, all of us could collaborate on design solutions before they reached the implementation stage; and once they got there, the developers would know what to do based on our discussions and the artifacts I put into a shared location. Transitioning away from traditional waterfall UX was daunting enough for me; and the sprint-ahead framework felt like a manageable solution for my first Agile outing. When working in advance of the development team, the UX team's deliverable of a design, lightweight spec, or customer feedback would be delivered to the entire team in the end of the sprint demonstration; then the design would be implemented by the development team in a future sprint. We chose to include the UX work in the demo partly because the spirit of that meeting for us was to show all the work that had been completed and it was the best way to reach the entire team without needing another meeting. The best practice for this style of Agile UX is to also to have a Stage 0 for the entire team to engage in planning and during which the UX team could conduct user research and do some high-level design to help guide future work, although that was not something I was able to do in this particular case, due to the timing of when UX was brought onto the project. Lynn Miller (n.d.) reported one of the earliest and most comprehensive examples of working in this way and describes her positive experience with this technique in "Case Study of Customer Input for a Successful Product," which can be found online at http://agileproductdesign.com/useful_papers/milller_customer_input_in_agile_projects.pdf. (This is just one of her papers, seek out more of her work if you are considering this approach for you or your team.) Quite a few examples are published on UX teams working in parallel sprints and achieving collaborative design results that provide great user experiences to their customers.

However, others express concern that working this way is tantamount to mini-waterfall. While this is not always an accurate description of what is happening for the teams who have been conscious, collaborative, and purposeful in their methods, it is a legitimate comment and a fair criticism. An inherent risk is that working this way might compromise the cooperative spirit of Agile. Since a typical sprint moves at a very fast pace, it may be challenging to get the time from developers to work collaboratively with the designers. This can be mitigated by having dedicated time from key team members or assigning tasks to the right developers to make sure they are given some slack in their schedule to work with the design team. But, if the development team needs to both support the work and its sprint as well as the work in the design sprint, what is the real value in parallelizing the work? The answer for your team may well be that there is a benefit to doing so, but some conversation around this question is needed to determine whether this is the right approach for your team. If the benefit is only for the UX staff and causes a burden for the developers, then the team needs to agree that it is the right trade-off. If everyone stands to gain, then work in parallel and reap the benefits.

When doing so, you should be aware of the danger in working in separate sprints, since there is less visibility and insight in to what the design team does. The design people end up being a bit distanced from the rest of the team and focused more on their own work. While one or two developers might be involved in the UX efforts, for other team members the design work certainly might become a black box. They might hear about it in daily scrum meetings (or not, depending how the parallel sprints are handled) and see the results in the demonstration, but beyond that, it is a bit of a mystery. To prevent this, create more opportunities to discuss and advertise the UX work throughout the course of the sprint. One of the benefits of working within a sprint can be a heightened awareness of what each team member is working on and a real sense that the team is working as a cohesive unit to achieve a common goal. Working in different sprints can affect some of the camaraderie and allow a design silo to be created. However, many teams happily and successfully used this technique and gave presentations on their experience—Lynn Miller has frequently reported on this topic, and her work is a great resource for insight into how to make this style work for a team while avoiding any of the dangers. As with any Agile method, it is important to keep reflecting on your process and seeing how you can become more efficient.

In interviewing different UX team members and managers, it is clear that as some UX teams spend more time in Agile environments, they evolve new ways of working with the process that do not necessarily match the parallel sprint approach. This evolution is a very healthy thing and can look different for each team. While working within a sprint might sound like the UX team works at breakneck speed, it can sometimes actually result in a more manageable pace. This is because it is easier to work collaboratively with the development team members, as they will be tasked to the same user story that UX supports. Since the work is being done in tight coordination, it is not likely to require much in the way documentation or the production of deliverables. The UX person will hash out the design issues with the development team in real time as the code is developed. It will be a very concentrated effort, but since it requires less time spent on manufacturing an artifact, it may be a more efficient use of UX time. It also relieves the UX team of trying to get it all done ahead of time, a smaller-scale version of the big up-front design burden that occurs in more traditional methods. One challenge in working ahead in an Agile environment is that things are much more unpredictable than in the traditional methods, where priorities and scope are fairly static. It is entirely possible to be working ahead on an item whose priority has changed before it gets in the hands of development, and it ends up being scoped out or deferred. The UX team cannot afford to waste that kind of time very often in an Agile environment. When working within a sprint, the collaboration tends to be more seamless and the design person works with the developer(s) to come up with a design solution as the developer is writing the code, and tweaks will be made along the way during the course of the sprint as issues are identified. This can actually be more manageable than trying to fill every moment of a sprint, front-loading design work so that UX is not a bottleneck to development, having the design ready for implementation, then finding out, a few sprints down the road, that the design has difficulties and needs to be reworked.

Working within the sprint does not necessarily mean that an earlier sprint was not dedicated to planning, high-level design, and design thinking or user research. Nor does it mean that time cannot be set aside during the release to do those things. It may, however, mean that the UX people have to estimate their efforts and track their velocity to fit their efforts properly into the sprint. Both methods have their pros and cons and may work better in some situations than others. If you are not sure which method suits your team or you can see the value in both, you can try to mix and match the two. They are not necessarily mutually exclusive; if you can find a way to strike a balance between the two approaches and it works well for your team, then that could be a good solution for you.

The pace of Agile development can be very fast and it can be easy to get lost in the work of the current iteration and lose sight of the big picture. Taking an iteration to conduct research and design or working a sprint ahead of development allows the UX team to maintain more control over the pace of its work and create the opportunity to take a breath. After a few projects or a few years, the UX team might want to work differently and feel more comfortable working within a sprint with the development team, once the UX team better understands the rhythm of the Agile cycle and establishes a good rapport with the project team. Or working so separately might feel awkward to you, and you would prefer to be in the same sprint as the development team from the get-go. Even among UX teams practicing Agile and effectively integrated in to the process, there is a wide variety of approaches and styles. Figure out what works best for your team and know that the only wrong answer is one that does not facilitate the production of a good user experience.

THE UX WORK

Regardless of how the UX team chooses to integrate with the development events, it can expect that some of the activities it is used to doing will need to be refined. The timing and the rhythm of a waterfall cycle is very different from the timing and the rhythm of the Agile cycle, even if the work that needs to be done remains the same. No matter how much Agile and UX values have in common, real work still must be done by the UX team. Simply understanding that people are more important than process does not provide enough guidance for the UX team to know which techniques should be used and when, which ones need to be modified (and how), and which tactics need to be dropped altogether. Development teams have a much clearer path for moving from one methodology to the other, because the processes are development centric. Since UX team does not have the same guidance, moving to Agile is a good time to re-examine the techniques the team uses to see where it can grow. Just like moving from Alaska to Florida, you need to get rid of your favorite snow boots and your heavy sweaters and start shopping for shorts and tank tops (but maybe you can hang on to your jeans and T-shirts). We start the inventory process by looking at the activities the UX team engages in and discuss what it means for the team to fit into Agile.

Resourcing and staffing

For the sake of brevity and simplicity, I have been generalizing as if the UX team is a part of traditional development environment moving wholesale to an Agile process and taking the UX team with it. I also speak in general terms as if one UX person supports a single Agile team. While this does happen, it is an oversimplification for the purpose of illustration. Realistically, it probably does not match the situation that you are in. I know that it does not describe any position in which I have been. It is certainly important to acknowledge that UX practitioners might find themselves in many other possible configurations, and each of these presents unique challenges.

Some organizations do not dictate specific development methods but have certain criteria in place, and as long as those are satisfied, a development team can elect to use whatever development method it wants. Other companies subscribe to a single development process but allow incubation teams to explore Agile and apply it to their release cycles as an experiment. In both situations, the UX team, or a single UX resource, might find itself straddling both Agile and non-Agile projects at the same time. This can be difficult, confusing, and a little bit exhausting. Instead of being able to mentally prepare for the switch from one method to another and really immerse yourself in an Agile state of mind, you may find yourself with one foot in both worlds. It can be daunting enough for a UX person to learn about Agile, sort out how to fit into that method, and get ready to work at a faster speed. To have your focus split between the old world and the new makes adapting to the pace of Agile even more challenging.

For those UX people who support Agile and non-Agile projects, I can say from experience that it is not easy, but it can be done without too much trauma if you have a good plan of attack going into it. The main reason you need a strategy in place before you tackle the work is that everything in Agile is very urgent and demands your immediate and undivided attention. Without a course of action laid out, you will get overwhelmed very quickly. Even if you have not yet experienced Scrum and are not sure what it will mean for you day to day, you can think about the practicalities of supporting two demanding projects, irrespective of the methodology they use. If you plan on supporting your Agile team on Mondays, Wednesdays, and Thursdays, how will you handle daily standups and requests for collaboration that come in on "off" days? Consider whether or not this is a team that you have worked with before and whether you have established a trusting relationship with them. If you need to invest in a certain amount of relationship building, then plan on being available for more (if not all) team events and meetings. Think about the level of experience the team has with UX and if it has a good understanding of what you do and how you do it. No matter what ther level of familiarity is with UX activities, you need to devote time to working with the team to define your role with it and understand what kind of support it needs. If the team is not familiar with UX activities or some of the techniques you are planning to use, you may also need to do some evangelizing and education to manage their expectations.

Also think about how you will handle unexpected requests for advice. If you ask a developer with a tight schedule to wait a day to talk to you because your Agile day is Tuesday, it is pretty likely that he or she will just move forward without your advice and not come looking for your input in the future. If you can at least hear the developer out with a commitment to thinking about the problem and getting back with an answer by lunch tomorrow, it will go a long way to establishing a healthy dynamic. It might also be necessary to make sure hours are dedicated to the Agile team every day, since it is not very collaborative to tell a team member that you do have no time until next week because you used up your Agile project time allotment by Wednesday. Being flexible and allocating hours of the week to each project could work well, as long as you are very strict about it. Since it is always very challenging for a UX person to say no to providing help and the Agile project always is in need of urgent help, the reality is that the non-Agile project that might suffer when time becomes tight. It is easy to convince yourself that there will be more time later on to do the necessary work for the non-Agile project, but if you trade off in favor of the Agile project every time, you will absolutely run out of time. Keeping a balance between the two projects requires more discipline than supporting multiple traditional projects. It can be very effective to allocate hours during the week, as is the idea of managing your level of activity in a given sprint. Some sprints are design heavy relative to others, and it may make sense to choose to focus on only the Agile project for that sprint. Similarly, if the non-Agile project has a spike in its need for the UX person, then it could make sense to take that sprint off from the Agile project, except for some maintenance, consulting hours, or time to attend team meetings. Perhaps, the non-Agile project needs intensive design activities, usability testing, or a solid chunk of time generating your specification. You could commit to not taking on any tasks for that sprint cycle and, aside from the agreed upon support activities, focus on your non-Agile project. This requires discussion with the team, but it is likely to be very understanding. After all, it probably feels overwhelmed with its one Agile project and very sympathetic to the fact that you are supporting multiple projects.

The same factors that you analyze for staffing Agile and traditional projects apply if you support multiple Agile projects. However, in this situation, you are less likely to have one project with more urgency than another, as both will be operating at a high level of urgency. Unfortunately, you may not be able to attend all the events for both projects, since balancing multiple daily standups, regularly occurring planning meetings, and retrospectives can leave you with little time to do any work. You need to be more strategic in how you spend your time and decide which meetings are valuable both for information exchange and team building. You do not want to be viewed as less of team member because of your split focus, as that could inhibit some of trust and collaboration you are trying to engender. Perhaps, attend only a few of the standups each week, but make sure that your status is communicated to the team even for the meetings that you cannot attend in person and work with the scrum master to be made of aware issues that arise in your absence.

If you do find yourself only supporting one Agile project, you may still want to do dedicate time to longer-term research projects in addition to your design work. In that case, treat the research as a separate project and manage your time and effort that way. The main difference is that, instead of it being an entirely separate piece of work, you may occasionally bring the results of your research back into your Agile project. Of course, the entire load balancing effort requires that your teams understanding what your commitments are, where you are spending your time, and why. It really requires that you keep the doors of communication open, so that your team can let you know if your strategy is causing them any concern. It is also possible that your first attempts to balance the load may not work very well in the beginning and require a bit of refinement. That is why communication is so critical to maintain, since the team may notice problems in your strategy even before you do.

Tactics

- **Communication**. This is a recurring theme for all UX and Agile activities. Agile environments can be pressure cookers, especially for teams that are not as experienced. Failing to manage expectations about the UX role and the amount of time you will spend with the team can result in tension and compromise your ability to be seen as a fully vested team member. This can compromise your ability to work collaboratively and really hinder your efforts. It is also important to provide the team with insight into your work and why it is important for you to spend time on a particular design issue or run a round of usability testing. While everyone might be content for the UX team to simply do its thing in a waterfall environment, there is a greater team investment in individual activities in Agile. Part of developing the desired transparency is not to just let the rest of the team know what you are doing but to provide them with an understanding of why it is important that you do it.
- **Planning.** The process is very fluid and there will certainly be a need for replanning, but it is critical to have a rough plan, so you can see when you start to deviate and need to look at a course correction or simply adapt your plan. Sorting out what your teams will need from you and when helps anticipate your peak demands times and whether you need to streamline any of your methods.

Specifications

In many companies, specifications is *the* deliverable created by the design team. These can range from a short brief describing a feature to a novel-length tome that describes every bit of the interactions in a product (Figure 2.1). The document may be created as an expression of the design intent, to support communication, as the design statement of record, or as the single point of contact between design and development. Once a team goes Agile, the need for heavy-handed documentation is replaced by frequent communication and collaboration. For the UX practitioners comfortable and skilled at creating

FIGURE 2.1
Specifications.

heavy documentation of their design, it may be a challenge to let go of doing so. Some practitioners may find it freeing to no longer have to labor long hours over documenting the minutia of their design intent, but others may be reluctant to relinquish the illusion of control that such a process imparts. It can feels as if the act of putting every detail into writing results in a process endorsed document of record, which of course means that the resulting software has to match the specifications. Unfortunately, this is rarely, if ever, the case. Despite the benefit of no longer having to spend days and weeks working on such a large effort of questionable value, it can be hard to move away from what might be the UX team's largest and most concrete contribution to the release. For managers who are transitioning an existing UX team to Agile, this is an area that may lead to skill-set mismatches. A staff member who prefers to plod quietly along on a design solution and spend a significant amount of time working through every design detail and documenting it, may be very challenged to work as quickly, collaboratively, and with more uncertainty as he or she must in an Agile environment. Replacing paperwork with real communication absolutely takes getting used to and may come more easily for some people than others. Some team members may also just not like the change in working style, which is fair—Agile is not for everyone.

For a colocated, highly collaborative team, where all the functional areas are well represented, there is no real need to create any kind of specification. Daily communication and intense collaboration should replace the need for any written document. If the team is working well together and focused on a given piece of work, then all the members should be on the same page and have a common understanding and shared vision, which is realized in the implementation and the documentation. Since Agile is so focused on the creation of working code, the software should be produced relatively quickly and can be reviewed in short order to verify that this assumption is true. With a faster turnaround of the design, the team finds out sooner if there are any misunderstandings, and if there are, these can be corrected in fairly short order.

In practice, teams are often spread across time zones and countries, and some resources may straddle multiple projects and be less able to participate in the necessary conversations to achieve mind share. When practical issues such as these arise to slow down the speed of communication, it is not uncommon to produce some artifact to help speed things back up. Wireframes, .html prototypes, and screenshots are all fair game and likely being produced by the UX team anyway as part of the design process. Even producing lightweight specs that contain sketches or screenshots with callouts and a small amount of text (I like to call them *speclettes* to reflect their diminutive nature) can be a great solution in many situations. The benefit to these, if they are needed, is that they are no burden to produce, can be done as needed, and can pay off huge dividends by ensuring that everyone on the team is on the same page, even if they cannot be in the same room together. Any artifacts that are created should live in a known shared location, team members should be aware of when they are posted, and finding them should be effortless. The system used to create and track tasks, if there is one, can be easily leveraged for this purpose. If the team does not use such a system, a commonly accessible location like a Wiki page or a SharePoint folder works well, too. One caveat to bear in mind is that, before producing any kind of documents, even speclettes, the UX team should examine why it is being done and if it is the only or the best solution. If one part of the team is located in Boston, another part in Shanghai, and yet another in San Francisco, then it is probably reasonable to have a Wiki page or shared documents to gain a common understanding, since face-to-face communication is limited. International teams often appreciate the ability to view some kind of screenshot or sketch before having a conference call, to give them the opportunity to digest the information and formulate their questions. This is a best practice for any kind of remote collaboration, as it can help make a conference call more efficient. However, if the UX team posts documents because the colocated documentation staff or quality team is not brought on to the project until late in the process, it would be better to consider options such as bringing them on earlier, even if only part time, or having on-boarding meetings to bring them up to speed with the state of the project and the design. Direct communication is always more effective and usually more efficient than even the most interactive prototypes. If the team is completely colocated and all the functional areas support the project, but there is a request for documentation, this should be considered a red flag. It is natural to look for a document to replace or supplement communication, because documents served that role in traditional methods. But, if a team is looking to lean on documents when there is no logistical reason for doing so, this can be a sign of a process or communication breakdown and the team should most definitely look for a solution beyond just creating a document, since that will likely only be a quick fix that may not really address the root problem.

When replacing this particular deliverable, the UX team should think about communication and how to facilitate it better and without creating the overhead a large, single-purpose document requires. Before it became a bloated item on a checklist for release criteria, the specifications were intended to let all the functional areas know what the design should look like and how it should behave. Anything that replaces the specifications should serve that purpose while addressing the needs of the team and being lightweight to produce and to consume.

Tactics

- **Conversation and collaboration.** Engaging the entire team in design exercises greatly reduces the need for any design document. The team members know what has been designed because they were a part of the process of creating it. Having white board sketching sessions, conducting card sort activities, and engaging the team in participatory design sessions can help the UX person generate a lot of ideas very quickly, serve as team building exercises, and educate everyone about what design is.
- **Coding.** It is not unheard of for UX teams to have someone on the team who can write code that defines the front end and pass that to the developers to use. This is a more common occurrence for website or web applications than desktop applications, where the code base may not lend itself as well to doing this. But, what better way to influence the design than to code the presentation layer? Doing this not only ensures that the front-end interactions are implemented as intended but is an effective way to increase consistency. If styles and standards are built-in and the development team simply has to code the back end, there will be significantly less low-hanging fruit to deal with later.
- **Prototypes.** While it does not always make sense to have the UX team writing production code, it can still produce reasonably high-fidelity .html prototypes with very little investment. This allows the interactions of a screen to be shown, instead of the flat layout captured in screenshots and sketches. Illustrating the interactions provides clarity and eliminates the need for interpretation that often happens with a static picture. Not only is this a great communication tool to use internally, it can be reused for a usability testing session. The prototypes can be done witn a tool like Axure or simply be a set of screenshots pasted into PowerPoint with a few hotspots to simulate interactions. Regardless of how robust these items are, they may be worth the investment if they help remove communication obstacles.
- **Wireframes and sketches.** Certainly, these are the most lightweight kind of documentation and, since they are often created as part of the design process, might not require additional effort to produce. The sketches can be

paper and pencil drawings, whiteboard sketches photographed by a cell phone, Balsamiq sketches, or Photoshop masterpieces, but the important thing is that something is captured in a visual way. It very easy for a group of people to discuss a UI and come to agreement without realizing that all of them had very different visions in their head. Sharing an image grounds the conversation and gets everyone on the same page, so the proposed design can be discussed productively. It is even better if producing these items is done with members of the team, so it becomes not just a document but a collaboration exercise. When that is the case, sharing the item reminds everyone of the agreed-upon solution. If a few words are added to it to provide some explanation, then it can inform members of the team who were not present for the discussion.

- **Speclettes.** These should be used only as a last resort; and even then, it is best that they be used only with teams that are spread across time zones and have a limited amount of direct interaction. A speclette is a document that might contain a few screenshots, some callouts describing elements of the UI, and a few explanatory sentences. They should require no significant effort to produce and be used when the recommended methods of communication are impossible due to logistics. They should be no more than a page or two in length and specific to a particular task or user story. They should have as little as possible in common with their more formal relative, the specifications. They should contain the least amount of information necessary to convey the appropriate information to the intended audience and no more than that. They need not be polished or fancy, but they must be easy to find and access and clearly mapped to a user story or task.

User research

We consider two main types of user research (Figure 2.2), each of which fits into an Agile process in a slightly different way. Design research is done during the release to validate the design and general product direction. The solicitation and use of user feedback during the design cycle tends to fit fairly easily into an Agile rhythm. With its focus on iteration and support of refactoring, tweaking the design based on customer reaction is a natural part of the cycle and well accommodated by the process. Longer term research is used to determine user needs, define personas, and may contain other more significant efforts that take a bit more time and effort. These larger, more extensive or more formal pieces of user research can still work in an Agile process but may happen in a different way and with different timing than in a more traditional environment.

Integrating customer input regarding the design into an Agile cycle is very doable. It is advisable to come up with a strategy around this before engaging in the project life cycle, just as when working on a more traditional project. Many

FIGURE 2.2
User research.

teams have adapted to the rhythm of Agile can accommodate predictably recurring testing events, often weekly. A certain day of the week (or month) may be set aside for gathering user feedback. When that is the case, users are constantly being scheduled and whatever is ready for feedback is shown. Anything can be put in front of the customer—a concept, a sketch, a paper or digital prototype, or working software. One benefit of Agile, though, is that you might very well have working code to put in front of the customers and are more likely to have access to a development prototype early on than in a more traditional process. Bear in mind that such frequent testing is an ideal state, as it represents the (literally) continuous feedback and customer interaction valued by Agile, but it is not necessarily achievable for every situation. If you have easy access to customers, then it is worth building that into the schedule and seeing if it can be achieved. Not planning for it in on the schedule ahead of time makes it highly unlikely that weekly or even biweekly feedback sessions will occur. Having such a constant flow of customer insight might transform the designs in a way that results in a more powerful user experience. However, if this does not feel like a reasonable option for your situation, another choice would be to identify key milestones and perform usability testing around those dates, gather user research ahead of the sprint cycle to drive early design, or simply squeeze in the testing when it makes sense. While being a little more sponta-neous about scheduling the usability testing is unlikely to result in weekly test sessions, looking for opportunities and sprints where time can be set aside for them is not entirely unrealistic.

Many techniques can fit easily into a more streamlined timeframe, so you may not be as limited in your choices as you might think, even for more high-level research. It might mean thinking beyond the methods and techniques you are most comfortable using and exploring different options. For defining user stories or influencing the design, it might be worthwhile to investigate using a technique like Indi Young's mental models, which she discusses in *Mental Models: Aligning Design Strategy with Human Behavior* (2008). This technique allows a researcher to collect information about user behavior and visualize it in a way that it makes very accessible for team members. Card sorting, especially if it is done using an online tool, can quickly yield results that assist with design decisions relating to information organization and terminology. The online version can even be done with remote users and, since it happens without moderation, have a very low overhead in terms of the UX team time required. Surveys also have an extremely low cost to the UX team in terms of the time required and can quickly yield actionable information about the users or the features from a large number of participants. Information from web analytics can be brought to bear on the design or feature definition without extra work by the UX team beyond reading a report. Unmoderated remote testing can fit in at any point, since it requires no administration. While it does not yield as much rich data as classic, face-to-face usability testing, it might help supplement efforts during the release cycle. Kyle Soucy's "Unmoderated, Remote Usability Testing: Good or Evil?" (n.d.) takes a look at the pros and cons of this type of effort and some of the vendors of this service. If you consider using remote testing, it would be worthwhile to review her findings. Her article can be found online at www.uxmatters.com. Moderated usability testing, either remote or in person, can be made to fit within the cycle as well. It might simply require working with a smaller sample size than if there was more time. Another tweak might be to run shorter sessions that have a more narrow focus than you typically do. It is also possible to make the testing more efficient by simply running the sessions over a shorter period of time and turning around the results more quickly. Usability testing can certainly be done within the sprint cycles with minimal refinements, and the information gained from these sessions are well worth the effort.

For iterative design and customer collaboration consider RITE (Rapid Iterative Testing and Evaluation), a method that applies user feedback to the product immediately and proceeds to test it again, change the design, and test it again. This technique is gaining popularity in Agile circles, because it can drive significant change in the design very quickly and really uses the customer as a collaborative design partner. A case study written by Jeff Patton about salesforce.com's use of the technique can be found in the article "Getting

Software RITE" (Patton, n.d.). Another, more detailed source for understanding the technique can be found on the Microsoft website in t "Using the RITE Method to Improve Products: a Definition and a Case Study" (Mollock et al., n.d), which fully explains the method.

If this is your fist time working with Agile, be prepared that the pace of Agile can be overwhelming at first. Because of this, if you have no plan for what kind of techniques you will use and how you will use them, you will find at the end of the release cycle you have done little or no research. Taking a proactive approach to ensure that user feedback is part of the design cycle by looking at the schedule and finding where it can fit comfortably makes your life much easier in the long run. The reality is that the need for research does not change simply because the schedule moves faster, it still needs to happen and it might take a little more creativity to do it. However, including user research somehow in the sprint cycles helps keep the user perspective at the forefront of the product design, and that is what Agile UX is about.The more significant research efforts need to be handled more carefully, since they require more time and effort, neither of which is in large supply in an Agile release. It is not impossible, but it will require even more planning and work to incorporate into the release than the design research. This is one of the few places where Agile might make you long for the waterfall method, where the slower pace seems to allow an easier fit for this kind of research. Unfortunately, this is also the area about which there is the least amount of guidance for UX practitioners. This is not because research is not happening but because so much of this work is happening outside the sprint cycles and does not always make it into the discussion about Agile UX. Just as the importance of design research exists regardless of whether a team is Agile or waterfall, the need for customer interviews and quantitative usability tests does not go away just because a team changes its development practice In fact, it might be fair to say that this type of research is even more necessary when engaging in Agile. Since the teams move so quickly once a release is kicked off, it is very important to have a clear vision and direction before the work starts. When testing is done in a sprint, the work is treated, from a process perspective, like any other task the UX person might do. The UX person reports on it in standups, tracks the effort, and fits the event within the boundaries of the sprint.

This kind of work is challenging to fit into a sprint cycle, not just because it can take longer than a single sprint but because the type of information it yields may not be easily fed back into the process. With design feedback, it is easy to turn issues into backlog items, prioritize them, and get the changes into the product. Larger research efforts yield bigger results, and these findings lend themselves better to being incorporated into the planning stages, even in traditional environments. Many teams have some kind of planning period, it may be called *Sprint 0*, it may be a time when the development team is working out infrastructure issues and is not ready for design feedback, or it may be a window of opportunity before the project is formally kicked off, where some research can be done. All these moments can be used as opportunities to do research and allow the UX team to deliver findings that will influence the release cycle.

It is also possible to work outside of the sprint cycle altogether and treat research as if it is a completely separate project, in the same way you would carve out time to support multiple products. Another option, which may not be available to everyone, would be to resource it to a different person, who will manage the research work based on the project's needs. In both cases, these tasks are not tracked by the scrum master, they are not necessarily reported on in daily standups, and they need not be constrained to occur within a sprint-based timeframe. However, even when gaining a little more flexibility by working outside the sprint cycle, it is likely that the time for research will be shorter than in a non-Agile world, since the findings still need to be turned around quickly enough to be used to inform the release cycle. Less time does not mean that the quality of the research needs to be compromised. To work with shorter deadlines, and in keeping with the lean spirit of Agile, the UX team needs to look for opportunities to reduce waste and streamline the process as much as possible. This might mean spending less time on the recruiting phase, working with more participants in a shorter time span, and producing analysis more quickly. There may be no need to change the actual methods or techniques but rather fit the entire event into a smaller time frame. Also consider which methods to use when trying to decide on how to handle this work. Both usability testing and customer interviews can be accommodated within the sprint cycle, if necessary. However, working with larger user groups or investigating broader topics is best saved for a separate effort. Contextual inquires, diary studies, and any kind of ethnographic research requires more time and attention and should not be attempted to be fit into sprint cycles.

When the designer and the researcher are the same person or people, much more out-of-the-box thinking is required to find opportunities and make time for research. This is a challenge because the UX person hase to be heavily involved in the day-to-day operations and rhythm of the sprint cycle as well as produce the designs and accommodate user research when it can fit. If the heavy lifting is done by a researcher or consultant, then making it a part of the cycle without overloading an already maxed out staff member can be a little easier. While the designers have to be involved in sprints, because they are responsible for the production of the user experience for the product, researchers or consultants can work more independently because they are provide information that the designer or product team then feeds back into the cycle. Dedicated researchers still need to move more quickly to get their analysis into the process in a timely manner, but it will likely be easier for them to carve out time to focus on more significant user research.

Tactics

- **Right method, right time.** Discount usability methods that require less effort can fit easily within sprint cycles. Surveys, web analytics, unmoderated remote tests, and unmoderated online card sorts can happen without much investment or effort on the part of the UX staff. Usability testing, customer interviews, mental model development, moderate card sorting, and RITE sessions require more dedicated time and may need an entire sprint to support but can be incorporated with a just little more effort. Contextual inquiries, ethnographic research, broader usability test, and customer interviews are challenging to handle in a sprint, unless Sprint 0 is long enough to accommodate the work. Otherwise, these are probably best done outside the sprint cycle and managed as an independent piece of work.

- **Plan ahead to execute successfully.** Of course, we always try to plan our time; but with much less slack in the Agile schedule, it is critical to have a good, realizable plan in place. It might be easier to be more flexible when it comes to in-cycle usability testing, but larger research efforts require careful forethought and execution. A single, central research resource is one way to have someone doing the planning and the investigative work outside of the Agile production cycle. This allows the team to worry about syncing up the timing of only that resource's efforts with sprint planning activities. If no central resource is available, as is often the case, research work needs to be coordinated so that it occurs during lulls in the production cycle. Since the planning cycle, if there is one, might be too short to do the necessary research, it might be helpful to use the endgame stage of the current cycle to begin research efforts. There is likely to be less of a need for design or usability testing in the final sprint(s), so that might be the best opportunity to focus on research in support of future work. It that does not allow enough time, and it very well may not, then it might be necessary to carve out more time to do research. If it is too much of a challenge to set large pieces of time aside for research, consider setting smaller bits of time aside throughout the release cycle as you work on day-to-day design and testing efforts. Consider dedicating a set amount of time each week to ongoing research and consider that a separate project you are supporting.

- **Target user stories.** When any kind of research is done, it should be used to inform and define the user stories. This is one of the most powerful ways to get the user feedback into the cycle and influence the direction of the product. Since the user stories are the basic building blocks of the release, this is your best opportunity to affect the entire team by describing the work that they will be doing in a way that accurately reflects the user's needs. Influencing the language used in and the content of these stories influences the entire direction of the release.

Usability testing reports

Regardless of how user research is integrated into the process, it is highly unlikely that the research will culminate in the generation of any kind of formal report. The purpose of a report in more traditional methods is to serve as a record of what was discovered. It can also be used to stamp the findings as being "official," because they appeared in a document of record (Figure 2.3). It also serves as a mechanism for communication, although this is often the least of the motivations for a formal report, since the key findings are often distilled into a presentation to communicate them to a broad audience that may not be motivated enough to wade through a more structured document. In an Agile environment, any kind of formal documentation is meant to be replaced by communication and human interaction. There is no need to record findings simply for the sake of posterity on behalf of the project team, since the findings and necessary action items are immediately discussed by the team and their disposition resolved. In the case of frequently recurring testing, gathering the data and feeding it back into the product is a seamless activity that requires no documentation beyond the backlog items created as a result. Since sprint tests tend to be fairly narrow and focused in their scope, conducted with a small number of users, and qualitative in their analysis, analyzing the results and presenting them to the team should require little time. Ideally, representatives from each functional area observes the test sessions and the test team debriefings over the findings at the end of the day or on completion of the sessions. They could then bring back the key findings to the team and work together to identify feasible solutions and prioritize these efforts to fit within the sprint schedule and defer items that cannot be addressed in the time available. In the real world, the UX person might be on his or her own participating in the sessions, since other functional areas may not be able to find the bandwidth to attend all (or any) of the sessions. Even without full team

FIGURE 2.3
Usability testing reports.

participation in the sessions, the group can still follow the same workflow; it just might require a little more context given to describing the results. Stopping to create a deliverable around the testing results could interrupt the immediacy of the activity. The speed of the testing and quick delivery of results to the team should not mean sloppy research. While it is okay to test whatever is available at the time of the testing, the sessions should still have clear goals and objectives and the feedback from the users must be analyzed and presented in such a way that it can be translated into actionable tasks. While the research may be a little more ad hoc and evolve a bit organically, it is still research and needs to be treated as such.

It is also important to consider what will happen with the results when the testing is done. Producing a set of slides or a high-level summary report, even if they are fairly lightweight, serve sas communication tools but does not guarantee that the information will influence the design. It might be a great way to communicate the findings to remote team members to make them feel more involved with research activities or as a method of distributing information to internal stakeholders, but a simple presentation is not really a consumable format for the project team. Bear in mind that any document created should be done with the intention of supporting communication and distributing information rather than serving as a report of record. Since the broader product team will not necessarily be a part of the research effort but will be affected by the findings, it is important to share the testing process with the team so that it can appreciate the value of the feedback and become more engaged in a user-centered design process. If this means writing key findings on a whiteboard and working together to write out user stories or create personas, that kind of processing of the results is much more powerful and "Agile" than posting a 20-page document online and hoping that team members read it. The intention of this is not to minimize the importance of user research but to encourage a new way of thinking about how to more effectively work those findings back into the process and influence the product. Instead of leaning on the old way of working up a set of slides or producing a document, we should be thinking of how to make the feedback more tangible and the delivery something that results in concrete actions. At a minimum, the information should be presented to the product team in a meeting that allows for questions and not through an email informing the team members that the results have been posted. If the researcher is a separate resource than the UX person supporting the team, then these two people need to work together to translate the results into user stories, UX tasks, and preliminary sketches to put the information into a format that the Agile process can consume. The only time when a more formal piece of documentation or reporting should be produced is if a larger research effort is occurring outside of the sprint cycle and the intended audience is broader that a single project team.

Tactics

- **Create personas.** Personas are a great way to feed complex information back to the team, especially if it is the result of larger research efforts and poised to drive the direction of the release. If you used some of the usability test sessions to flesh out or validate personas drafted earlier in the cycle, update them, and recirculate the personas. Considering using the end of sprint demonstration for delivering the updates or turn the delivery of the updates into an activity for the team. If you uncovered new personas during the course of testing, write them up and share them. Personas are very helpful in reminding the team for whom you are designing and making the users less theoretical and more real. If the word *persona* is too loaded of a term to use in your organization, call them *profiles*, *customer snapshots*, or whatever helps get them accepted into the culture. Do not just leave them as something that is discussed at the beginning of the process; find ways to weave them throughout the release to make them most effective. Have the user stories reference them, put them up on the walls, incorporate them into the sketches, frame research findings in terms of the personas, and do what you need to make them a living, breathing part of the development process.

- **Inform user stories.** Yes, user stories again. They are so central to the Scrum process that any opportunity to create or contribute to user stories should be used to its fullest advantage. Leveraging this mechanism to also communicate findings eliminates a barrier to getting the research results back into the process. Since user stories are the basis of the development effort, translating feedback into this format makes it that much easier to settle on priority, identify related tasks, and assign the work to a sprint.

- **Present findings in person.** It is always good to give the team an overview of how the testing went, and the act of creating or discussing the resulting user stories serves to drill down into more specific issues. When team members are unable to attend the test sessions, an interactive meeting gives them a chance to hear the big picture of what happened during the sessions and a sense of the general reaction (both the positives and the negatives). It would be great to also have a separate brainstorming session or design discussion to resolve the issues that came up, but delivering an overall report verbally to the team should be the minimum done following the testing. Delivering the results verbally removes the barrier to common understanding that can sometimes be created by a written document, which can be interpreted differently by each reader. While listening to a presentation on research findings is no substitute for attending the actual sessions, it is the next best thing for teams that are sure to be very strapped for time.

Design activities

In some organizations, the design is "owned" by the user experience staff. However, in Agile, only the product owner role is recognized as having any kind of ownership and ultimate authority, while the rest of the team members are contributors. The team is intended to be empowered to make its own decisions, so the product owner should need to exercise power only on the rare occasions when the team cannot come to an agreement without intervention. It is also important to remember that team members are meant to work to their skills and not their titles. In some cases, this might mean a team member who does not have a UX title might execute some design work. The idea of ceding territory might be frightening, but it also has potential for increasing the general awareness of design issues across the team. Design divas or UX rock stars will prefer to capture the spotlight and the glory by swooping in with a genius design solution, and they feel very uncomfortable with this idea. There is no room in Agile for people that are not interested in working as a team, so if you are struggling with this concept, then you might want to consider whether you are concerned with moving the product forward or about not being recognized for your genius. When small design tasks are supported by people with good design skills, regardless of their functional area, then the user experience staff can be freed up to focus on the larger design issues and user research. Schedules tend to be fairly tight on Agile projects, so a given UX person is unlikely to be able to address every detail of everything that appears in the user interface. Being open to allowing other team members to contribute in a substantive way to the design can improve the overall design and result in a better product. It also gives the broader team a greater sense of ownership of the design and acknowledges the contributions that they make to the user experience.

The idea of pair programming that evolved from Agile methods can also be co-opted to pair a designer with a specific development person as a partner. This kind of real-time collaboration can speed up the process of design and implementation considerably, just as pairing two coders increases the quality of the resulting code and the time it takes to produce it. Leis Reichelt explores the application of this technique in "Pair Design Pays Dividends" (2006), in which she discusses her experience with this method and the value that it added to her work as a consultant (Reichelts's article can be found online at uxmag.com). It may not be necessary to engage in a fully paired approach to reap the rewards of this technique, but having a specific development person responsible for large portions of the UI and working in concert with the UX designer could be a very transformative experience for everyone. This may not be a good fit for every project; especially if multiple people work on the UI elements, pairing closely with one person might be counterproductive.

In addition to relying on the team members to be collaborators, using customers as design partners is well supported by the Agile values and principles, which encourage working with customers collaboratively. Leveraging the research sessions to actively work out design issues with the customers using techniques like RITE, card sorting, brainstorming, cognitive walkthroughs, in addition to usability testing can provide the users with a chance to directly influence the design process and express their needs. This might also be your chance to explore participatory design methods, if you have not done so in the past. Participatory design encourages customers to completely immerse themselves in the current context, imagine an ideal future, and create a representation of the ideal. A great introduction to the technique can be found online at boxesandarrows.com in "Making Emotional Connections through Participatory Design," written by Marty Gage and Preetham Kolari (2002). Participatory design can yield really interesting results and is great technique to get the customers to think in terms of their experiences and needs and not be constrained by their understanding or expectations of the software. Another benefit to this technique is that it requires no working software and so can easily be done at the beginning of a cycle to inspire the design.

The goal for any design activity in Agile is to identify the best solution as quickly as possible and refine it so that it meets the customer's needs and creates the best user experience possible. The most efficient way to do that is to involve as many internal and external stakeholders as possible in the design process, so they can contribute their unique perspectives and help move the design forward. This should be done without creating a chaotic environment or a design by committee mentality, however. Using techniques that allow this the collaboration to occur within a specific framework, so that the process does not spin out of control, can help to keep the conversations on track and moving forward in a productive way.

Tactics

- **Teammates are codesigners.** This can be made explicit by using pair designing and collaborative design techniques or assigning certain design tasks to capable (and interested) teammates. It can also be more implicit by simply involving the team more frequently in conversations about the user stories. It is also powerful to solicit team members' opinions in design reviews, especially if you show that you are genuinely listening to their ideas and incorporate the best comments into the design.
- **Customers are codesigners.** In addition to user research activities, consider working some of the participatory design methods into your repertoire, especially if you are having regularly occurring customer sessions. Getting their feedback is great; getting their design perspective can be even more powerful. Use one of the techniques meant to support this, since unless

your customers are software designers or UX professionals, they are unlikely to sit in front of a blank piece of paper and generate anything terribly meaningful.

CASE STUDY—CATHERINE ROBSON, SEACHANGE INTERNATIONAL

While there is often trepidation around the change from traditional to Agile methods, the reality is that it can actually be very beneficial to the UX team. Not only is it an opportunity to be in control of defining the team's process, possibly for the first time, it is an opportunity to become a more cohesive team. Catherine Robson's story is that of a team that not only excelled in an Agile environment but has been innovative in their approach. The result is that they are able to be very effective and now have a way of proving their value to the organization.

Catherine is the manager of user experience at Seachange International, a software company that specializes in multi-screen video. She was a part of the original adoption of Agile at the company. Overall, the company weathered the transition fairly easily but the UX team had to change its approach along the way to better support the production efforts.

A few years ago at Catherine's company, a team on a separate code base was working on a forward-thinking project and picked Agile as their process. The team was successful in its project, and the use of Agile was credited with its ability to react quickly to changes and improved communication. As a result, the director of engineering chose to roll the methodology out to the entire organization. As a part of the new initiative, the managers were sent to Agile and scrum master training. Additionally, the initial team members that piloted the process were spread across the company to other teams to distribute their knowledge. At the time of the interview, they were two years in to their adoption and Catherine is really enjoying it. She feels it has created a more organized environment for UX. Historically, team member had their heads down and were focused on their individual projects, but Agile has allowed them to become a closer team. It is interesting to hear her make this comment, because many UX teams feel that the pace of Agile increases their individual focus and reduces the sense of UX community. The fact that Catherine's team had the opposite experience is a sign that the UX efforts to become Agile were done with great forethought and in a way that created a more cohesive team.

Catherine and her team were asked to guide how UX would fit in to the process. One of the pilot team members was a UX person, and she was able to share her experience. This helped the team as they tried to sort out how to come up with a generalized approach. Catherine did some research. She invited folks from IBM to share their experiences with the team. She also attended some user interface engineering seminars, which really informed her opinion of how the sprint process should work. Additionally, she participated in Scrum training and found it helpful to understanding the point of the Scrum methodology and where it was okay to bend the rules. This type of training and the confidence can provide is invaluable for someone just starting out with Agile. You have to make many adjustments along the wa, and it is important to know when you are making an adaptation and when you are compromising the Agile method that you support. For her, the point of Agile is to *be* Agile. She suggests being comfortable with the idea that, if the first sprint does not work, we will fix it; it does not have to be perfect the first time around. Refining the process is fine and healthy, rigidly sticking to something that is not working is not.

Retrospectives were uncomfortable at first. Seeing change happen as a result of the meeting—even just a small change—built up confidence in the process and made it more comfortable. It is really important that the team members see that their feedback is being taken seriously. Sometimes, being responsive to the small things is the most important action, because this builds the trust and creates an environment where the team feels safe raising bigger issues. She feels that, if you can get the team to buy into the idea that you are creating your own environment and are not just mindlessly implementing a process, you can be successful. The executives may have mandated that the organization go Agile, there may have been formal training activities, but ultimately the team members decide what Agile means for them, and the retrospectives are the main vehicle for this. She cautions that, if you have a scrum master who is closed off, then this really shuts down the discussion. This can cripple the process and inhibit growth.

At first, the adoption of Agile was messy. Sprints were three weeks long and each project team had its own starting point. The UX team did not have its own sprints, and its work was not centralized. One UX person might have two Agile projects to support, and this was hard for everyone. Engineering did not want to do story-point estimations on the UX stories, and the UX people did not want to sit through detailed architecture discussions. They changed things up so that the UX team had its own separate schedule. Catherine gathered requirements from each team. She is the UX product owner and scrum master. All UX requests are in one backlog. This is very helpful for load balancing, and she was much better able to resource the requests based on skill sets and availability. This is one of the changes that helped contribute to a stronger sense of team for the UX people.

User testing is done as a story that occurs within a given sprint. When the product is ready for tech support and customers, the UX team solicits feedback on it. Two people work on the story within a sprint and do the planning, testing, writing the report, and meeting with the team to discuss the results. Then, they negotiate to get any additional stories resulting from the testing into the backlog. They also work to get informal feedback as often as possible, but those activities do not necessarily require an entire sprint dedicated to them.

They use Rally for tracking tasks and monitoring work. They schedule the UX sprints a couple of months ahead of time. They make changes along the way, but work off a soft plan. They assign UX stories as a requirement for the engineering story, so development depends on the UX work being done first. Timing of the UX work is based on the complexity of the design effort, the task dependencies, or where it is planned for implementation in the engineering schedule.

The most important thing in moving to an Agile environment is a focus on communication. There are improvements on this front within the project teams, mostly supported by the daily standups. Having an opportunity to discuss problems daily and not wait until something blows up to raise an issue has made it easier to manage issues. However, since Scrum focuses on the communication within a team and not across teams, projects, or products, there is still a struggle to improve the sharing of information more broadly.

A UX person who supports multiple teams still invests in meeting time, because it fosters discussion that might not otherwise happen or might not include the UX person. It is expected that not every piece of information discussed is relevant to the UX team, but being present ensures that if something comes up the UX team is there to speak to the issue. The presence at these meetings also signals the commitment to the team and an interest in being fully engaged in the process. The team has four UX people spread across 5–10 big projects. Each UX person takes on two projects per sprint, at the most. If the people try to take on more than that, it is not possible to support all the meetings. They work together as a team to review each other's work. This increases efficiency by introducing multiple perspectives, increasing awareness of other projects, and making it easier for team members to swap projects, if necessary. The team has also made an investment in spending a lot of time speaking to engineering management and product management to see where the UX team should spend its time. This allows the members to be as strategic as possible in their efforts and to make sure that these efforts are in line with what the other teams consider to be a high priority.

The team's deliverables are the Axure prototypes. It is working toward a unified UI and has a prototype that shows all the teams' contributions to the UI. It uses Wiki pages (Confluence) to post screenshots with a brief description to provide additional detail on things that might not be clear. It is definitely not a specification. The pages are there more to support and complement the existing team interactions and discussion and provide only what is necessary for clarity. The QA/QE (Quality Assurance/Quality Engineering) is integrated enough that the team can rely on Wiki and know who to ask if it needs any additional information. It is harder for the documentation team, but the UX team mitigates that by meeting with documentation team members and walking them through the prototype. Since this tends to come late in the cycle, it is easy for the UX team to accommodate the other team's members because it is not as entrenched in design activities. This is allows the UX team to produce only what is necessary; an interactive prototype that not only illustrates design intention but also promotes consistency across applications. For the team members who need more information because they are not as heavily involved in the design cycle, the team does not produce a more heavyweight document but meets face-to-face with them to help bring them up to speed. This shows that the team is not just doing things the way it used to do them but is trying to be as Agile as possible.

The UX team is located in Acton, Massachusetts, but many of the functional areas are around the world. A development team is in the Shanghai office, and for that group, it does more documentation than it might for a team that is colocated. For this group, the UX team creates Illustrator pictures, fully detailed, in their design documents. For the teams in Manila and Europe, it tends to communicate in the same way as with local teams. This reduces some of the burden of working with geographical distributed teams, since only some of them require more written communication than is typical.

The hardest part of the transition was figuring out the time management at the beginning. Once you have experienced everything, you can better identify what is valuable and what you can trade off. But, you have to go through the initial period first to figure that out. This is very true for teams that have been working in waterfall and cannot really wrap their minds around what it means to work in a three-week sprint. You can plan for how you might need to adjust to accommodate the new work flow, but until you have actually done it, you do not know exactly where the pain points or the easy parts lie.

The most important piece of advice that she would pass along to other UX practitioners is to get the company bought in to having a UX backlog. It is a way of positioning the UX team and establishing that teams come to UX for help and the UX team provides value. It was possible to make that statement and prove it, because the team established its value and can use the product backlog to prove it. She acknowledges that this tactic might not work in every organization or for every team. Still, she finds having a backlog of requests useful to prove that engineering has a need that the UX can satisfy. There have been management changeovers during the past two years, but having a body of evidence of what the UX team has done and what the engineering teams would like it to do helped prove the worth of the team.

In this story, we can see a UX team that not only thrived in an Agile environment but even benefited as a team from making the transition. The move to a new process allowed the UX team to become a more tightly knit unit and work in a more organized and efficient way. It also inspired Catherine to build UX backlog that not only organizes the efforts of the team and assists in load balancing but provides high-level visibility of the UX effort and a clear record of its value add to the product.

Key points

- A culture of open and honest communication can grow along the way. People who are initially inhibited during retrospectives can work through the problem if they see that feedback is well received and taken seriously. As long as somebody is modeling that behavior, change will occur. The more people who model it, especially if they are in leadership positions, the faster that change will occur.

- Showing up to meetings is a drain on time, but it can be worth it. Often, the discussions may not directly bear on the design, but showing up and being present goes a long way to reassuring the team that, no matter how busy or hectic things are, you are going to be an active and collaborative team member. If this means supporting fewer projects to be able to support these events, then that might be the right trade-off to make.

- Consider a common UX backlog of tasks. This is not a common tactic, but it can provide very clear evidence of where and how the UX team adds value without trying to tackle complicated metrics. It will require that the team is somewhat centralized and that one person is responsible for the distribution of work, but it can provide benefits beyond simply dovetailing into the Agile process.

SUMMARY

These recommendations and modifications to UX techniques assume that an organization or team has fully embraced the spirit and values of Agile and the whole process has been undertaken in a thoughtful and supportive manner. If this is not the case, these activities are still worthwhile but may meet with less support or enthusiasm than if the organization had genuinely adopted Agile values. For those situations, your priority might be on simply fitting your work into the time it has been given rather than doing so in a way that also embodies Agile values. This does not mean that you should not try to be as Agile as possible, but you should be realistic in the expectation of how much traction that your Agile UX efforts will have. However, do what you can to stay on the Agile path, because you never know when the culture might change to be more receptive. In the next chapter, I share some case studies of teams that fall on both ends of the spectrum and one or two that land somewhere in the middle.

References

Gage, M., Kolari, P., 2002, March 11. Making emotional connections through participatory design. In: Boxes and Arrows: The Design behind the Design Retrieved April 2, 2012, from. http://www.boxesandarrows.com/view//making_emotional_connections_through_participatory_design.

Medlock, M.C., Wixon, D., Terrano, M., Romero, R., Fulton, B., n.d. Using the RITE method to improve products: A definition and a case study (Playtest Research). Retrieved April 2, 2012, from http://www.microsoft.com/en-us/download/details.aspx?id=20940.

Miller, L., n.d. Case study of customer input for a successful product. Agile Product Design. Retrieved April 2, 2012, from http://agileproductdesign.com/useful_papers/miller_customer_input_in_agile_projects.pdf.

Patton, J., n.d. Getting software RITE. Agile Product Design. Retrieved April 2, 2012, from www.agileproductdesign.com/writing/ieee/patton_getting_software_rite.pdf.

Reichelt, L., 2006, November 20. Pair design pays dividends UX Magazine: Defining and Informing the Complex Field of User Experience (UX) Retrieved April 2, 2012, from. http://uxmag.com/articles/pair-design-pays-dividends.

Soucy, K., n.d. Unmoderated, remote usability testing: Good or evil? UXmatters: Insights and Inspiration for the User Experience Community. Retrieved April 2, 2012, from www.uxmatters.com/mt/archives/2010/01/unmoderated-remote-usability-testing-good-or-evil.php.

User Experience: Our Definition, n.d. Retrieved April 2, 2012, from www.nielsennormangroup.com/about/userexperience.html.

Young, I., 2008. Mental Models: Aligning Design Strategy with Human Behavior. Rosenfeld Media, Brooklyn, NY.

CHAPTER 3

Case Studies

CONTENTS

Introduction 72

Suzanne O'Kelly, AppNexus 72
Key points 76

Thyra Rauch, IBM 77
Key points 79

Archie Miller, Snagajob.com 79
Key points 83

Carol Smith, Perficient 83
Key points 87

Kayla Block, PAR Springer Miller 87
Key points 91

Anonymous 1, at an Enterprise Software Company 92
Key points 94

Christina York, ITHAKA 94
Key points 99

Anonymous 2, a Large Desktop Software Company 99
Key points 104

Austin Govella, Avanande 104
Key points 108

Josh O'Connor, National Council for the Blind, Ireland 109
Key point 110

Adrian Howard, Quietstars 110
Key points 112

Elisa Miller, Senior User Experience Engineer GE Healthcare 112
Key points 117

Summary 118

References 118

Agile User Experience Design. http://dx.doi.org/10.1016/B978-0-12-415953-2.00003-0

INTRODUCTION

When I started interviewing people, I hoped to be told that the magical sprint number was precisely *x* number of days, the best tool for managing tasks is this one, and the secret sauce to making Agile work is as follows. Turns out, there is no magic or secret sauce. What I learned was that the successful teams, the middle-of-the-road teams, and the teams still struggling all talked about the same issues. There were no discussions that did not touch on the importance of communication, transparency, culture, and training. However, everyone described an experience that was a little different and the way that each group approached the problem reflected its unique situations. Techniques used in one company may not apply to another, but hearing their stories proves that the road to Agile is not always smooth. But, the trip can certainly be worthwhile. It also illustrates that if your adaptation of Agile methods is different than those of someone chatted with at a conference, it does not mean that you are doing it incorrectly. Keep the values of Agile present in your mind and visible in your work. If you do that and your team is successfully delivering a good, or great, product, then what you are doing is working.

As you read these cases studies you will recognize some names, either the person or the company might be familiar to you. Quite a few of the people I interviewed are active in the discussion of Agile UX and have given presentations or dedicated blog posts to the subject. You will also see a few anonymous case studies. Many people were willing to share their stories, but not everyone is on the record. It can be difficult to being so open and honest about the experience in a public way, especially when your story is not all rainbows and sunshine. While I am grateful to those who were able to speak on the record, I am equally appreciative of those who would only speak if they had anonymity. I felt that their stories were incredibly valuable, in part because it can sometimes be more helpful to hear about teams that are challenged or struggling than only the success stories. Some comfort can be taken in knowing that you are not the only one having difficulty finding your way. I believe that these case studies help present a broader picture of the Agile universe, because we can include tales about where Agile has not been successful for a team. I am thankful for all of my colleagues who shared their stories, and especially to those who did it simply to help others learn from their experience without receiving credit for doing so.

SUZANNE O'KELLY, APPNEXUS

Suzanne manages the UX team at AppNexus, a platform for real-time advertising. She was able to receive the most intense formal training of anyone with whom I spoke and was able to apply the training immediately to the project on which she was working. Suzanne's story provides a good illustration of a small

UX team given very solid Agile training and rolling out the methodology in a focused way, starting with a single project. Often, the discussion is around wholesale changes and entire organizations moving from traditional development processes to Agile, but Suzanne's story reminds us that it is possible to concentrate deeply and thoroughly on one project and leverage that success to influence a bigger change.

Suzanne test drove Lean UX on the development of the AppNexus's "Autotagger" feature. This project required that the resulting design be simple to use and transparent in its behavior as it executed its functionality. Suzanne kicked off the project with the product manager then worked with the UI developer, the API (application programming interface) developer, and one other UX person to realize the project.

The development team had been agile for quite some time, but an element of the UX work was still a bit waterfall, and it was not really working to throw the designs over the wall. In her research, Suzanne found lots of information about how different teams were doing UX with Agile. Taking the time to do this kind of research helps make the UX team well-informed about its options for adopting Agile UX. This is fairly critical to success, since the development teams most likely understand Agile only as it affects their process. Unless they had access to a coach who specifically raised the issue of bringing UX into the process, the UX team will be responsible for defining this interaction. Suzanne also wrote a manifesto, to help guide the UX work. This is a really interesting idea and not something commonly done. The Agile Manifesto is so central to all its methods, it makes sense to write a manifesto for your UX team to define the values and principles of how the team will practice Agile UX. While Suzanne did this herself, the creation of a manifesto might be a very interesting group activity. It could be very empowering for the members of a larger UX team to craft a statement of their intention for becoming Agile UX. This is something easily shared outside the UX team, and can help create a much better understanding for everyone about how UX activities fit into an Agile development process.

In addition to Suzanne's efforts, the company sent her team to LUXR (Lean UX Residency) and they used real projects as homework, so they were able to get coaching on the actual project as they went through the 10-week program. The program was a great training, but it did not yield immediate results because the team still had to do the background work of defining personas, engaging customers, and so forth. However, the goal was to have good results at the end of the project and to be able to make traction with the UX integration into Agile; and the training set the team up for that. This approach has a lot of appeal to it.

Suzanne was working with a small amount of UX resources and needed to be strategic in her efforts, so it made sense that the effort to integrate into an Agile environment be done one step at a time. This tactic could work well for larger UX teams and bigger projects, because it gives the UX team an opportunity to test drive a well-informed approach and leverage its subsequent success, rather than making a big statement about how the UX team will work then needing to refine it. While nothing is wrong with the second approach, if it is done in an organization where not everyone is fully bought into UX, the act of refining an approach may be viewed as a failure rather than a healthy evolution. Starting with a success, of any size, makes for an easier sell of the UX team's approach to Agile.

The whole Autotagger project took about three to four weeks, which was about how much time the team would have expected it to take without using Lean UX. Originally, some had been concerned that the UX team could slow down the development speed. That the UX team had no negative impact on the overall schedule was a big win and recognized as such.

Suzanne was the only permanent full time UX person on her team. She had one full-time UX contractor and two engineers, one of whom had gone through the LUXR training. Additionally, one of the engineers worked remotely and was on site only one week a month. The small team size might be ideal for an Agile process, but the lack of colocation is certainly less than ideal. On the other hand, one benefit of not being really formal in their Agile application is that the members had no specific stages or sprints, which allowed them to follow the natural rhythm of the project. some loose Omnigraffle functional specs were developed to facilitate communication. Suzanne acknowledges that, if the whole team had been local, they might have been able to just whiteboard many items. But, since that was not the case, they chose to produce fully interactive prototypes. She and her remote developer would plan together. They managed remoteness by making sure there was a lot of communication. They did informal daily check-ins, constant emails and phone calls bridged the distance and fostered team dynamics. Sometimes, the engineer had questions, because he was working off of a more lightweight spec, so he would reach out to Suzanne and ask which solution to go with. Sometimes, Suzanne would ask him to implement a few solutions, and they would test them to see what worked better.

She was doing UX testing every day or two. Often, it would be done with internal users. In the very early stages, they did the testing this way while they worked out the big kinks. This high frequency of feedback might be more challenging to manage on a larger project, but it allowed this team to function as if it was bigger, since many more sets of eyes were on the design than the handful of people directly supporting the work. When there was a consensus that the overall design made sense, the team began to take it to customers' sites and gather more robust feedback. Having this level of engagement with the customers really allowed them to build stronger customer relationships. Asking for feedback from the customers earlier in the process also instilled a sense of trust and confidence in the process for the end users. Suzanne found a lot of value in this activity, beyond just getting direct customer feedback. All customers enjoy having their opinion solicited, but on this project, customers were often able to see the impact of their comments on the project and really know that they were being taken seriously. This gives an end users a new kind of appreciation for the company and allows them to see the relationship as being more of a partnership.

In looking back at her experience, Suzanne felt that communication was a critical factor for the success of the team. They were very informal in how they handled the avenues of communication and the developers were proactive about reaching out to the team. She was not sure that the type of collaboration they experienced was necessarily something that could be formalized and repeated more broadly across different teams. She noted that they were very casual about daily standups, since the team was so small and in such constant communication with each other. Skipping a daily standup would be less viable in the context of a larger team, where it could actually contribute to a communication breakdown. It is true that when a team grows, it can often necessitate formalizing team interactions and more closely following events like those prescribed by Scrum. However, it is important not to lose some of the natural rhythm, and create a camaraderie that makes it comfortable for a remote worker to reach out or, even better, have your voice in the back of his or her head while doing the work. A smaller team, especially one that attends training together, is better able to connect with each other and facilitate collaboration. A larger team should look to see what it can steal from these smaller groups to create the same feeling. Encouraging frequent emails, IM chats, and screen sharing sessions to review work—any of the things that small teams do naturally can be leveraged by a bigger group.

Having gone through the process, Suzanne acknowledges that she is still in the early stages of Lean UX. Despite her formal training, she feels that tackling Agile does not have to be a really formal process. She recommends engaging in Agile in any form, even if it is by the seat of your pants; doing a little piece of Lean UX is better than not doing any Agile at all. This is a very interesting thought, since so much of the discussion around Agile is very all or nothing. However, the idea of getting leaner is just as valid, as being Lean UX is very powerful. It also might make it less intimidating for teams to move in this direction if they approach it as something that can be tried on a per-project basis or on a small scale rather than adopting it across the board. And she is right; it is better to try to get more user feedback into the cycle or spend some time discussing the design rather than focusing exclusively on producing the specifications. Taking those baby steps does not qualify your team as a Lean UX, but they may reduce some wasted effort and possibly encourage a move to a different process.

While Suzanne's experience is certainly a testament to the power of strong training, her ability to work well with her colleagues and customers allowed her to be effective in such a short amount of time. She was truly able to treat her team and her customers as design partners and produce a better user experience because of that. To read more about Suzanne's experience (O'Kelley, n.d.), expressed in her own words, check out the AppNexus tech blog online at http://techblog.appnexus.com/2011/autotagger-a-case-study-for-lean-ux/.

Key points

- The communication strategy needs to fit the team dynamics. It does not need to be formal for the sake of being formal, but if the team chooses to skip standups or another Agile event, then it should be done consciously and only if there are no negative consequences. The team must find opportunities to speak frequently outside formal meetings and use whatever technology is available to support that—video calls, chat clients, online workrooms, Wiki pages.
- Formal training can be a fantastic opportunity to learn and get coaching on a project. It can also encourage team bonding and getting the team on the same page. Funding for such training also indicates organizational support for the effort and creates more of an investment in the process in general. It should be pursued within your organization, as much as possible. And, if there is no budget for these things, be creative in seeing what you can do to replace it.
- Engaging in Agile does not have to be intimidating. While corporate initiation of the process can contribute to a broader, more successful adoption of the process, introducing Agile into the process a little bit at a time or in a more grassroots manner can create interest in taking bigger steps and help introduce Agile concepts in a nonthreatening way. A little

FIGURE 3.1
Lean UX.

Agile, when it contributes to the success of a project, can go a long way in creating interest.

THYRA RAUCH, IBM

Thyra is a user experience leader at IBM, and her story gives insight in to how a practitioner can manage to support an Agile project that faces the challenges of multiple locations and time zones. Her approach is an example of how to adapt to fit without compromising the process.

On her first Agile project, none of the team members really knew what it meant to be Agile. Then, the entire team went to Agile training together. They were able to use their real project as the in-class example and get coaching as they did their training. (This was seen as a success and has been done for other teams since then.) Once they were done with training, they were very strict about their application of Agile. Thyra says it was a bit awkward at first, as is any new process, but it worked. Successfully releasing the product in three months also made people feel very positive about the experience. At the next release, they made some minor adjustments to the process, based on brainstorming sessions they had during the postmortem about how to make the process work even better. As a UX person, she had not come into the process with great expectations but was really surprised at how much she liked it. She was additionally surprised to see how much more effective she was. Previously, Thyra found that she was hung up on all of the work around the up-front design. With Agile, she was able to put that aside and keep an open mind as she engaged in the design process. She describes the process as more fluid but feels it gives her more control over what she is producing. Every sprint you plan again and can feed all the user research back in to the cycle rather than waiting months or years for the next release because it was too late in the cycle to react.

Thyra feels that the Agile environment changes the dynamics so that the place no longer feels as though development's voice primarily gets heard. Everyone, including those in UX, is an integral part of the team. There may not be an opportunity to do big research ahead of the cycle, but UX people create scenarios, refine them, and check in with customers as they go along. She acknowledges that it is not necessarily going to be comfortable to go Agile at first. The team has to believe it is the right thing, and management needs to support it for people to really invest in making it work.

At the time of the interview, Thyra was working on a text analytics product, which provides visual representations of a large amount of structured and unstructured data that the user can explore. Unlike most Agile teams, the makeup for this particular team is not colocated. Development is in Japan, QA (quality assurance, testing) is split between Japan and North Carolina.

Documentation is in Maryland, the visual designer is in Vancouver, while the product manager is in southern California. She is either in North Carolina or northern California. There are few convenient common time zones, so daily standups for the entire team are not a practical option. Communication is very critical to any Agile team, but they had to approach this in a nontraditional way. Thyra works with the visual designer, and they post their work on a Wiki page. Designs get linked or attached to individual story items and can be viewed 24 hours a day. The group tried to have a weekly scrum meeting with the whole team, with development having a daily scrum meeting, but they have since refined the process to eliminate the weekly get together. Development still meets daily, and the scrum master takes notes on the discussion and posts them to the Wiki page. If other functional areas have anything to share, they post it to the Wiki page.

To facilitate communication, she posts a variety of visuals, such as scanned pencil sketches, screen captures with callouts, wireframes, and high-fidelity prototypes. The development team does prototypes and end-of-iteration prototypes and keeps them up on a server. This is critical to communication, as she can access the server any time and see if the interactions are what they need to be. She can also use these end prototypes for user testing. Thyra notes that many methods of communication are available now and the communication itself is more important than the event of a face-to-face meeting. While Thyra is the only official UX person, she describes herself as being on a UX team. The team is composed of the visual designer, technical writer, product manager, project manager, QA leader, development manager, and UI lead developers. This group of people meets once a week for an hour, more if necessary. They might discuss the items one iteration ahead of when they will be worked on. The meeting topics and prototypes are usually distributed ahead of time for easier communication and a more effective working session. Using this forum, all the stakeholders are able to provide their feedback

Incorporating user feedback has been different on each Agile project. On brand new products, where she was less familiar with customers, they were able to test every sprint. That worked well for her when she was trying to understand the problem space. With her current project, frequent rounds of usability testing allows them to identify the most successful features and quickly identify issues, such as the need for the users to access "Help" despite their reluctance to do so. As a result, the team was able to build more help into the design and create mini-tutorials that facilitated the end user's ability to navigate through the product.

When supporting a more mature product, she can cut back to one user session every other sprint. She has more design partners, which are critical, since she needs a certain amount of feedback from expert users on what works for them and what needs improvement. She will continue to test with novices as well, because making it easier for them makes functioning easy for everyone. All user feedback is extracted into requirements and put into the backlog.

Thyra thinks that it is possible to take some of the Agile nuggets and drop them into any process. If you learn something in Month 3, you should be able to react to that and incorporate into a release. She notes that there are many Agile methods and not really one way to do it. The important thing is to consider the best way for a team to work given the cost, speed, requirements, the like to which they are beholden.

Key points
- Be adaptive. Part of going Agile means working more collaboratively with the team, stakeholders, and end users. Do not get hung up on having a particular event, like a daily standup, if it is impractical for the team. Instead, be creative and find a way to use technology to replace the communication that the event is intended to support.
- Get comfortable with things being more fluid. It is unlikely that there will be opportunities to have huge research projects or to do massive amounts of up-front design. On the other hand, it is more likely that user feedback need not be tabled until the next release cycle because it was received at the wrong stage of development.

ARCHIE MILLER, SNAGAJOB.COM

Archie's experience is a little different than the other success stories. Rather than being the initiator or on the first wave of a UX adoption of Agile, he came into a company that was already using Kanban quite successfully. This case study is not only a study of a culture that is a perfect fit for Agile, but of what it means to fit in to that culture after it has already been defined.

When he first arrived at the company, an online job site for hourly workers, he did not even know what a Kanban board was. This is not unusual, since most UX people are not exposed to Agile methods until they find themselves on a project that uses them. It can also be unsettling to be on such unfamiliar territory, especially if you are well into your career. Adding to the learning curve for Archie was that each team also had its own interpretation, so he had work hard to orient himself to the process quickly as he worked on the job seeker part of the site. In a situation like this, the best thing to do is first understand the lay of the land and how you can contribute to it. Once that has happened, it is important to get training or education on the process, so that you can be part of identifying potential opportunities for improvement. If you are coming into an existing Agile project, the way Archie did, you are likely to receive your training later anyway, since the company might wait until its coach is available or there

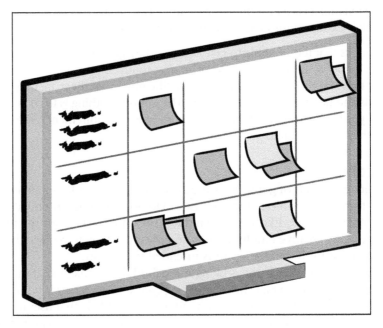

FIGURE 3.2
Kanban.

are enough new hires to put through a class. This is not necessarily a problem. While it is important to get a handle on the process itself, the most critical thing is to understand how your team or teams are working and how you fit with that.

The transition for Archie was undoubtedly made easier by the fact that Agile principles dovetail very well with the corporate culture at his new company. Their culture is so strong, that it practically radiates from the pages of their website. Instead of the typical dry content that one often finds in the "About …" sections of a corporation's website, the Snagajob site has a culture blog, a "How We Roll" page and stories that embody its corporate values. The company defines itself as "Collaborative. Accountable. Passionate." Just from looking at the website, it is very clear that it is intentional in creating a certain environment and wants that to be known. In comparing its site to other job search sites, it certainly has much more content describing the company and giving insight into what it is, what it does, and how it does that. Obviously, this is a great recruiting tool, but it also humanizes the company for anyone who will be doing business with it. The description of what it is provides a certain transparency into the workplace and creates trust with potential customers. Archie describes the culture as being carefully curated and intentional. The recruitment process is geared toward identifying candidates for fit. Once you are an employee, the company establishes a balance between personal growth goals and specific project goals that recognizes and supports the needs of the individual and the needs of the work that individual supports. If ever a corporate culture was best suited to adopting Agile practices, it is this one.

On its Kanban board, Archie's team typically has the columns "Not Started," "Discovery," "Clarify Context," "Design Solutions," "Plan Delivery,' and "Done." The "Context" column represents tasks in which problems and goals are still being defined, target users are being determined, and so on. The "Design Solutions" column includes sketching, prototyping, and testing activities. It is important to have this column, as it creates an awareness of the need for these activities and helps teach the team how long these efforts might take for a given feature. The "Clarify Context," "Design Solution," and "Plan Delivery" columns each have "To Do" and "Doing" subcolumns to identify the items ready to be acted on and those that in progress for the given activities. This allows the team to differentiate between items that have moved into this phase but not been worked on and items in progress. Not all teams might find such notation necessary, but it is a great idea for larger teams and larger projects, as it makes it easier to track the real state of a card and identify slow moving or "stuck" items. The rows of the chart large represent chunks of work like "Active leads with job tips" or similar higher-level task. The granular tasks within that row are the ones that make their way across the board until they hit the "Done" column.

Archie's team is responsible for the seeker portion of the site and is made up of a core team of 20 or so people, with a handful of those people working on maintenance projects. The team is colocated, or as Archie describes "extremely colocated," which is a function of both the culture and the company growing at a rate causing it to reach capacity in its office space. Other teams in the company are larger and more dispersed, so those teams rely on tools like Trello to replace the physical Kanban board and help track the work.

The rhythm of the cycle can vary, but the company tends to release every week once the site is up and averages around two weeks during the discovery phase. Archie works a sprint ahead of the development team and his deliverable during the discovery phase is to populate the backlog and create the tasks. This is a great role for a UX person n the process. Not only will you have a great understanding of all of the items in the backlog, you can ensure that the items are customer centric. During the production cycles, he creates Axure prototypes and distributes them to the developers by sending them .urls using AxShare. Archie describes the delivery of the prototypes as organic. The developers can easily access the interactive prototypes that communicate Archie's design intentions. The team is also able to incorporate user feedback into the process as often as it wants by recruiting users, using Ethnio, to do remote testing. This means that a user who visits Snagajob.com might see a screener from Ethnio to be recruited for a remote usability study. The team has also been able to conduct larger pieces of research via diary studies and site visits with users.

Retrospectives are conducted faithfully and taken very seriously. Archie describes them as being like a religious experience. Someone who cannot attend in person makes sure to communicate input via email. This kind of dedication to self-reflection and process improvement supports Agile but very clearly comes from Snagajob's corporate culture. It is also a clear part of the success of Agile in the company. A sprint or even a project can always go wrong, but if the team discuss it in a retrospective and can make course corrections or learn something for next time, then the process and the team have succeeded. It is also important to note that, even with such an effective process in place, the company continues to invest in training and coaching. It works with Jeff Patton to provide training and coaching to new hires and experienced teams, and he comes in on a recurring basis to work with everyone. This is essential for the newer staff members, because it means that they get the same understanding of the process as the rest of the team and can get some insight into the specific implementation at their new company. It is also very helpful for the existing team members, as it keeps them active in re-evaluating and refining their methods and techniques as the work and the team evolve.

Archie enjoys working in an Agile environment because he feels that he gets a better design more quickly than if he was just working by himself, because he is forced to collaborate with more people earlier in the cycle than he would in a more waterfall process. It is certainly true that, in waterfall, you can go months without showing your designs to anyone, but it would be nearly impossible to go more than two weeks without sharing the work in an Agile workplace. Archie acknowledges that learning to work more collaboratively was a process. He majored in fine arts as an undergraduate and considers himself to be an artist. He is also used to coming up with all the answers, which is typically the role a UX person plays in a non-Agile setting. Having successfully made the transition to Agile, he is a convert. Waterfall feels clunky to him now, and he says that the word *handoff* is not even in his vocabulary anymore.

Archie's story is an example of a culture and a process that fit together l hand in glove. Obviously, corporate culture can be slow to change, and the Snagajob. com environment is fairly unique. Depending on where you work, it may not be a realistic goal for your corporate culture to be as carefully cultivated as that one is. However, an organization that is genuinely adopting Agile values will move in that direction by fostering communication, engaging in healthy retrospective, valuing the contributions of individual people, and fostering an empowered team environment.

Key points
- Everyone needs a little help. Even in a company with an exceptionally Agile-friendly culture, there is still room for coaching. There is always an opportunity to refine and evolve your approach. Having the coaching available to new hires makes their transition much more productive.
- Agile changes the UX role. Archie is not the only to mention this, but being a UX practitioner in an Agile process requires you to think differently about your role and work more collaboratively. If your mind is open to that, the transition is easier.

CAROL SMITH, PERFICIENT

In her role as a lead UX business consultant, Carol has the opportunity to see Agile implementations at many companies and cultures. Carol says that she has not worked with any groups that are doing ideal versions of Agile, but she also points out that she has not worked with anyone who is practicing an ideal form of UX either. Because of her role and expertise, she tends to be involved more in research and usability testing and experiences the companies' Agile experience from that viewpoint.

She recalls one project where she was working for a large insurance company in the Midwest that had a team of 60 UX people. This team comprised the interaction, visual design, and research groups. Carol's project was for the research group. In that company, most projects used Agile. The UX group was also well established, very strong, and played a well-defined role within the organization. However, the level of UX integration into the Agile projects varied by team. This is not uncommon with big design teams, as it can often be hard to standardize across such a large number of people. The UX team members themselves were very open to practicing Agile, but their ability to do so successfully tended to be specific to the team with which they worked.

She noticed that, to fully adopt Agile, the organization has to be at a point where it sees that what it is does not work. She feels that this is fairly analogous to the successful adoption of UX practices in a company. This insight raises an important point about the motivation of a company in engaging in Agile. If the company is doing it because Agile is the new and modern thing or to make things happen faster, the problems that require correction have not necessarily been acknowledged, implementation of Agile may move forward while keeping broken things "as is," and no real change will occur. However, if any organization recognizes that it could be more efficient or relies on a process that has become unwieldy, then it may have an engagement with Agile that is more focused on shifting the culture and have a sense of where things are or are not working well in the current environment.

FIGURE 3.3

Agile.

She finds that there is a still a huge amount of ignorance about Agile. At a recent conference on computing, she was surprised that no one she spoke with had even heard about Agile. For those of us in the midst of Agile, it seems like it is all anyone is talking about, but the reality is that, while Agile has gained significant traction over the years, it is not quite ubiquitous. Within the UX community especially, many practitioners have not experienced Agile in their careers and do not see it on their horizon. Carol never encountered any resistance to Agile processes but found plenty of ignorance. When she mentioned this, I wondered if there were geographic clusters in which Agile has been adopted. As someone who lives on the East Coast, I can say that it seems to have taken longer for the conversations about Agile to begin happening out here, and even now Agile methods may not be as commonly used here as out West, where Agile was born. It is also a great sign that Carol says that she has never encountered resistance to Agile, because I can recall quite a bit of resistance or fear of the unknown among UX teams when they started to realize that this development process would have impact on them. It seems that enough UX people now have had direct experience with Agile that the conversation has gone from being based in irrational fear to trying to figure out how to make it work and sometimes about how to make it work better. This really indicates a maturity for both Agile processes and UX practitioners.

Carol acknowledges that ideally you would need a running start to get the research done and ramp up on background information. She suggests that this could be done while development is coding the architecture. She thinks that, once this is completed, UX team members can set up regularly occurring usability testing and do activities like a card sort to hash out the big questions, then just continue the design as they go. Using collaborative techniques, such as a card sort, is a great way to involve the team in early design activities and get everyone to agree about the design goals. It can also be done without investing significant time into the activity, which is critical in the fast-paced Agile environments. It can also serve as a team building activity, thus supporting another element that contributes to a team's success.

Carol points out that, "Agile doesn't mean you aren't planning. You have to know what the user needs and what your goals are, so you know when you done." Sometimes, this message gets lost as teams put their heads down, work from sprint to sprint, and look at only the next step they have to take. This breakneck speed can even affect designers, as they focus on producing all the work they need to for a sprint and forget to take a breath and seek out customer validation. Because it seems like the work can happen without it, some teams do not document a vision or an overall strategy, but this is a mistake. Even though the work can happen, the outcome may not adequately meet the customer's needs. As Carol's comment illustrates, if you do not know where you are going, then how do you know if you have gotten there? A list of features that need to be in a release is not exactly a plan or a product vision. While the team may be able to execute pieces of work, there is a cost to not having an overall vision, goals, or plans. Throughout the cycle, formally or informally, priorities must be identified and trade-offs made; without a plan or guiding principles to use as a touchstone, these efforts may not result in the most strategic decisions having been made.

Carol likes to use RITE as a usability testing technique. She feels that it works very well and gets everyone really involved. In her experience, you can bang out the prototype, and by the third day of testing, you have something close to being on the right track. This is technique allows the team to really embody the value of having customer collaboration as part of the production cycle, since the design work is based on sessions with the customers. The technique adds value, since it is quick and easy to do, which makes the RITE technique a good fit for an Agile cycle.

Carol also values the use of personas and thinks that the group should at least define the users at the beginning of the project, and the creation of personas is the most appropriate way to do so. She does not feel that the group necessarily needs to define fully fleshed-out personas, just discuss them and get to some initial agreement. The UX team can use that outcome to create draft profiles, which gives the development team something to hang its hat on. She feels that this activity also gets everyone on the same page. Carol points out that if we all are not thinking of a customer in the same way, then we are not really working as a team. Some organizations may be reluctant to have visions and high-level goals in their version of Agile, but there is likely to be little resistance to the creation of personas or user profiles. These can s keep the team working toward a common goal without stepping on any toes and, in most cases, with very little effort required. Although she will often work off of the draft personas, if more time is available, Carol might flesh them out a bit more. When she does this kind of work for teams, she makes sure that the main customer gets a persona, but a secondary user might get a more lightweight profile. Sometimes, she relies on profiles and flesh them out in more detail during the usability testing. Also, she likes personas posted on the walls. She feels that is important for them to be visible and accessible. Showing them is an important part of the process. One of the most powerful tricks a UX team has is putting its work on the wall to show what it does and spark conversation. It can often be important to create awareness around UX activities to help different functional areas better understand what the UX team does and how it contributes to the product. Carol's idea of posting the personas not only makes sure that everyone is constantly reminded of who their customers are but is a tangible representation of the work done by the UX team.

Now that Carol has spent some time working with Agile, she finds that she likes that it is so focused on users. She recognizes that, with technology changing so fast, designing ahead does not work, even within a six-month project. She sees that you risk not being relevant by the time that you are done with a release. She also likes that an Agile environment makes things transparent. She thinks that, in general, when you are doing waterfall, you go off and it becomes a black box to the rest of the team. This not only inhibits collaboration but reduces the amount of moments to educate the team about good design. The job is not to just produce research or designs; it is to help create an understanding about our customers and what good design is. She sees some challenges and acknowledges that the pace can be frightening. She realizes that, for some UX practitioners, not knowing what you are designing up front can be frightening. She likes deadlines, so it does not bother her. The one piece of advice she would give to a UX person who is about to go Agile is this: Try to become very close to the project managers and influence how UX gets incorporated into the process, especially if it is Kanban. This influence is critical because the UX team is in the best position to identify the work it needs to do and figure out how to work that in to the proposed process. It also affords an opportunity to create visibility around certain key activities and ensure that they are accounted for in the timeline.

Agile is nothing to be afraid of and does not fundamentally change what the UX team needs to do to involve the customers and keep the development team conscious of the customer. It is really the speed at which things are done, the frequency with which they happen, and the amount of communication that occurs around those things that are different. Familiar techniques like research, usability testing, and persona creation can all effectively be put to use in an Agile environment. Additionally, techniques like persona creation and RITE can be leveraged, because they help achieve an outcome at a quicker pace.

Key points

- Research and planning are still necessary to provide a framework and guidance for the team's efforts. These activities can still happen, but UX people might find themselves having to try new techniques, rather than the ones they relied on in a more traditional environment. For more advice on this, check out Carol's presentations on slidehare: "Faster Usability Testing in an Agile World", (Smith, 2011) and "Getting Started with User Research" (Smithe 2010).
- Agile is increasingly common, but it is not so pervasive that there are no longer any software professionals who are unaware of it. Even among those who are familiar with the term, plenty do not know what it really means to "be Agile." This may include team members with whom you work, so be educated on Agile and prepared to educate others. Take any opportunity to express your understanding of Agile and how UX fits into it.

KAYLA BLOCK, PAR SPRINGER MILLER

When I spoke with Kayla, she was a user interface leader at PAR Springer Miller, a company that specializes in software for the hospitality industry. She faces the ever-more-common challenge of geographically distributed teams, often with team members across several time zones. Her team has seven or eight members in Las Vegas and four or five offshore. Since Kayla has a background in psychology, she examined the challenge of working remotely and its impact on team dynamics through that lens. Her intriguing blog post "Geographically Distributed Teams in Agile Software Development" (Block, 2012) can be found on her blog at http://kaylablock.com and offers a different take on what is lost by working remotely. We spoke about these challenges as well as the rest of the work of fitting UX efforts into an Agile environment.

She acknowledges that, as a UX person, working in an Agile manner brings with it a fair number of challenges. She feels that so much of UX design requires collaboration with product management and engineering and the most effective way to do that is with whiteboarding. The quickest way for any team to get on the same page is to sit in a room together, hash out design issues, and take turns grabbing the whiteboard marker. Not only will all have an opportunity to express their opinion, but the team will have a shared understanding of why and how a particular decision was reached. Kayla's team has been creative and tried many things to replace in-person whiteboard sessions. One method has been to use Skype with screen sharing, which allows interactions like reviewing a UI together and being able to say "can you move that a few pixels to the left." It is not as dynamic as working together in the same room, but it is certainly a more rich interaction that emailing back and forth over the changes to a screen. This also seems to be the best way of interacting with remote team members. The team experimented with aiming a web camera at a whiteboard for a remote colleague but it did not really work it and ended up being a fairly frustrating experience for the person who was not in the room.

The more time zones involved, the more complex things can get. The team was having a daily standup that would occur at 10 at night for the team members in the Kuala Lumpur office. Not only is this a challenge because it forces one location to work outside the rhythm of the normal workday, the remote staff often is taking the call from home, with all of life's potential interruptions, like crying babies in the background. Additionally, time zones that are further away often also come with cultural differences that need to be considered when attempting communication. In addition to the typical challenges of an average conference call, speakers need to be cognizant of language differences and the comfort level of remote teams in speaking up during a call. Kayla also worked with a developer who was based in Los Angeles and found that worked fairly well. Since they were in the same time zone, it was easier to be able to Skype and screen share during the typical business day. It was fairly easy to replace normal collaboration techniques this way, partly because they were dealing with only a single remote person in the same time zone.

In addition to location, Kayla sees that the ability to work collaboratively can be affected by team size. Her ideal team would be closer to three or four rather than seven or eight. Once there are more members on the team, facilitating the additional communication that supports collaboration becomes harder to scale. Skype and screen sharing work best when it is one to one, although it can be done with more people and still be beneficial. Conference calls can start to be challenging when they are too many people or just a few are on the other end. It is very easy for people to talk over each other and very difficult for someone on the phone to participate in a conversation or even completely follow the flow of conversation. When Kayla was working with a product manager (PM) based in Los Angeles, even though they were in the same time zone, the PM often felt frustrated on conference calls because it was hard to participate. The type of role may factor in to the ease of remote integration as well. The Los Angeles–based developer was likely a bit closer to the day-to-day project work and needed to have interactions on specific issues, which could be easily handled by a chat. The product manager likely needed to know and understand higher-level decisions and interact with the team as whole, which requires a meeting with multiple people and is harder to do as the only person not physically in the room.

Scrum itself can be an obstacle; it often feels as if there are so many meetings, that it seems like the team never actually gets to do any work. The rhythm of the Scrum cycle can present some pretty serious challenges in providing a high-quality, consistent UX. Kayla feels that you need to be consistent and methodical in your approach and not just constantly shooting from the hip. It is important to have a plan and a baseline. Kayla often worked one to three sprints ahead of the development team in what she refers to as *AgileFall*. She is not sure if doing so is in keeping with Agile values and finds that it often did not work. When you work ahead on something slated for a future sprint, things can change and the work either no longer needs to be done or might have changed in the interim. This can be one of the problems with AgileFall, in trying to keep some of the predictability and static planning of waterfall and interleaving it with the fluid nature of Agile, you can end up constantly shooting at a moving target.

One of her favorite tactics, which is very helpful in creating a baseline in a fast-moving environment, is to build a framework like a pattern or design library. Whatever its name, it documents what a combo box is, looks like, and how it behaves. She originally did some of those artifacts in Adobe Illustrator and produced a .pdf that she shared with the team. She would like to try doing a Wiki equivalent, but since that was not something her company was doing, she instead created a SharePoint list with searchable keywords. Each item contains a .png, .xaml code and any additional information she might need to add. This version was recently rolled out to the team and was received well. Not only do other people use it, she finds it to be a helpful reference for herself. She also uses other tools for communicating about designs to the team. Since her team uses Team Foundation Server (TFS) for the project work, she likes being able to add her deliverable directly into TFS. People need not go looking for the deliverables that way; they can just find them with the task or the user story. She produces lightweight specifications and images and simply attaches them to the user story. She does not want people to have to dig through multiple resources to find the information about the design, since it decreases the likelihood that they will actually see the artifacts.

In the first 18 months of the project, the work was done externally by contractors. This had two impacts on the project. The first was that there were often variations in the UI for similar tasks. This tends to happen when the focus is heads down on hitting deadlines and no pattern library is in place. A scrum of scrums can help manage some of that variation, as can a single UX person working on several projects. However, a reference of some sort that is easily accessible is probably the more effective solution. In general, the chaos of Agile and its schedule can make consistency a challenge. Even if you have a Sprint 0, the design is iterative and will continue to evolve throughout the release. If you have no vision to ground the work, then it can easily go in different directions. The other impact that it had was that, with other factors, it contributed, along to a cultural of literalness. When doing work with contractors, you must stay very close to the requirements and the spirit of the contract, especially if deviating means more work than the contractors agreed to do. This created a habit of the business analysts wanting to stick to the exact conditions of satisfaction in a user story, even when the work started being done in-house. Part of this may have been because the conditions of satisfaction are more vague when the work is done internally, leaving more room for interpretation. When the work is done by the contractors, the business analysts needed to be more specific, often creating functional specifications and workflows.

Kayla says that she would never want to go back to waterfall. Agile may be imperfect, but she feels that it is a better variant. She really appreciates that Agile provides the ability to react to changes in the marketplace and with technology. Warts and all, she loves an Agile environment. She cites an example that not everyone would see as a success. Her company recently had a meeting with a significant customer to discuss a potential large sale and, based on their feedback, the project needed to change direction fairly dramatically and the sprint fell apart as the team adjusted. Kayla rightly sees this as proof that Agile works. It is fantastic to be able to react to a customer request instead of having to say "not in this release." The sprint may be derailed, but when a significant sale is at stake, the development team's quick reaction creates a greater opportunity to close that sale.

Kayla's advice to UX practitioners beginning to work in Agile is to loosen up. If you are used to having every interaction nailed down before the developers get to them, you can let go of that and still get a good or better UX than you might have otherwise. She also recommends being okay with being imperfect and even taking advantage of the new way of working. She says to get your testing into the cycle and iterate away. She has even been able to make the process work for her and gotten buy-in to have user stories for "UX cleanup" as a part of a sprint that occurred before a trade show. She used this to create a punch list of the little cleanup items, set priorities, and get it in to the sprint. This advice can also help when you are unable to get everything done that you need. Kayla was not able to do any usability testing or site visits, for a variety of reasons. In her situation, as with most of us, competing demands for time and resources, so usability is not able to be a priority at all times. At the same time, Kayla recognizes that their product is so far ahead of its competitors that having an ideal design may not always be necessary, because the company's design is the best that there is. This is an interesting point, since as UX professionals, we are used to aiming for an ideal design or user-centered design process. In the end, we often have to compromise these ideals to fit into a messier real world. It might be more practical to look at the "ideal" design with respect to a product's competitive landscape and be as strategic as possible with those compromises. She notes that software is not perfect, so you have to pick where you want your imperfections.

Kayla also wrestles with the tension of producing deliverables that are very clear but lightweight and still work for remote teams. On the one hand, you want deliverables that are very clear and interactive like Axure. The need for communication is heightened in an Agile environment, since the documentation is so light and needs to be supplemented by a certain amount of immediate interaction to support a common understanding. On the other hand, you do not want to spend time producing documentation that works well only for colocated, collaborative team. She learned that, if the deliverable is sparse, you need to make sure that you had enough verbal communication around it to support that. You cannot expect to email a remote team a quick sketch on a napkin and expect it to walk away with a clear understanding of your design intention. There might not be so much tension between these goals if you can quickly and easily produce interactive prototypes. If creating these artifacts is not time consuming, they can satisfy the need to be lightweight in their nature, since they bear no resemblance to the heavyweight specifications of waterfall. Additionally, their interactive nature provides some of the clarity around design intent that would normally be communicated in face-to-face meetings full of hand gestures and whiteboard sketches.

Working remotely can present additional challenges in the already tricky Agile environment. Recognizing what is lost without constant face-to-face communication and experimenting with different ways of compensating for it is critical to building a cohesive team environment. It may mean stepping away from or supplementing textbook Agile techniques, but if the focus is on people over process, then you are heading in the right direction. It can be hard for remote team members to feel like a part of the team and even harder for them to "feel" the real difference between working in waterfall and working in an Agile way. Any effort that can be made to include them ultimately improves the speed at which the team can work.

Key points

- UX requires intense collaboration no matter what process is in place. With Agile and the increasing reality of remote teams, ther need to maximize the ability to collaborate under any circumstances and make that happen more quickly are more urgent, as the production cycle leaves little time to work out the kinks. Trying different tactics and adjusting as necessary as well as being creative about how to tackle the problem are skills that need to be in every Agile UX practitioner's toolbox.
- Even when it seems like Agile is falling apart; it might actually be working as intended. The sprint schedule may be blown up because you need to respond to a customer, but bear in mind the alternative. In a waterfall environment, regardless of the size of the customer or the severity of the issue, it might take an executive order to shift the release date or the course of the product development. Letting the schedule go where it needs because of customer feedback is a sign that the process is working.

ANONYMOUS 1, AT AN ENTERPRISE SOFTWARE COMPANY

Anonymous 1 is the manager of a small UX team at an enterprise software company. The development team had been Agile for quite some time, but the company started investing in UX a year ago and it was still sorting out how to integrate UX into its process. She is having a good experience with the teams tshe is supports, but finds that not all of the UX people are having the same success and is concerned about making it a more generalizable experience.

The company is Agile, teams have a lot of leeway to choose which method practice. Scrum, Kanban, and Scrumban are all employed, with varying degrees of faithfulness to the methods. This creates some confusion, as she thought her team was practicing Scrum but was recently told that it was in fact using Kanban. This can indicate a need for more consistent training across the teams so that the operational definitions of the methods, their differences, and their relative benefits are clear to everyone in the organization.

Overall, she feels that the process of integrating UX into the process has gone well. The teams have chosen to embed the UX person and make that individual a full-fledged member. Sometimes, the UX people may also serve as an on-call resource for teams that require less support. The UX people are doing well with the tactical UI work and are an active part of the team discussions; they create wireframes for the teams and conduct UX reviews of work. She is still working on building out a bigger, parallel track, where user research, usability testing, and strategic and high-level design would occur. Things are a little more ad hoc as they currently try to conduct research by piggybacking on preplanned events. If a customer visit is scheduled by the PM, UX people tag along. The company's customer advisory board meets several times a year, which allows for customer contact and research. Outside these events, it can be fairly challenging to get customers to participate in usability testing. Given their situation, the UX people are doing a great job of getting engaged with customers and finding out the information they need to inform requirements, user stories, and personas.

Originally, the product manager wanted to own the high-level design. Prior to the UX team becoming part of the process, the product manager had been running Sprint 0, but UX took over that responsibility. She feels that it is really important to have some amount of up-front design, so that the end result is part of a coherent whole and not just different-colored Lego blocks stacked together. This is especially true for large projects, where the seams of the product can start to show if every task is done as a separate piece of work. Not surprisingly, some politics have arisen, with the product managers wanting to be more hands-on and the development team wanting to keep them at a distance. Organizationally, UX is part of development, so these people are seen as part of the team and do not face the same challenge as the PMs. This is good for the UX team, but ultimately the issue needs to be addressed globally so that requirements and user stories are not caught in a tug of war over influence.

In her role as a manager, she serves as the UX architect and team leader but also supports product teams directly. She feels that she has done well integrating into her product teams but is starting to see that not every UX person is having the same experience. On other teams, the development managers are less experienced and may still be finding their way to managing an Agile process. One UX person is supporting a team that has the only development manager colocated with him; the rest of the development team is in China. Obviously, this presents different challenges in terms of communication and relationship building than when everyone is on-site. For her UX team members that are struggling, it seems to be that they are still working on some of the communication issues she has been able to avoid.

To plan her work, she meets with team leaders every week and discusses the stories that are coming up and what the guidance is from the product manager. If there is consensus that they need to write down what they talked about, then she authors scenarios or a matrix of features vs. needs, then the development manager will scope accordingly. If necessary, she may even work up some hand sketches to facilitate a shared understanding of the design intention. It the work is just a revamp of existing screens, she probably will not generate more than a screenshot with markups to call out the changes. For a large piece of new design work, she generates wireframes for the team. Having a discussion about the work allows her to set expectations with the team around what kind of deliverables or support they can expect from her for a given piece of work. Not only does this reduce potential surprises about what she will deliver, it can help give the team insight into what kind of UX work is necessary for what type of user story.

Once the design solidifies and people provide feedback, the developer is ready to execute it. While she has been fleshing out the design, he has been thinking about how to implement it. Once the design is firm, he completes coding and it is ready for review. The sprint cycle is not much of a driver for her teams; while each sprint is roughly a month, some stories do not fit well into that time frame, and they do not try to force it. While this may not match a textbook description of the methodology, she feels it works and that the team has found a good rhythm.

She thinks her efforts have been effective because the UX people have been willing to integrate with teams. She looks at another team in the organization, where the development people chose to be more closely aligned with the PM and they kept UX external to the team. She sees the UX people having a much harder time getting their designs implemented. She notes that, because they support multiple projects, the UX people do not go to standups and some of the other time-consuming events. This may not affect relationship building for them, because they are organizationally part of the team and are accepted as such without having to prove their commitment by attending these meetings.

The company continues to refine how UX fits in with the overall process. At the beginning, it used separate UX stories and tasks. But, this made the UX artifacts too separate and removed from the rest of the work. She would find that developers did not know how or where to look for the wireframes the UX people were producing. She thinks that it was helpful to start out this way; it allowed them to get their bearings and learn the process. Now that the development team understands how to include UX into its tasks, there is no need for separate UX stories.

One thing she did that improved the odds of success for the UX team was sitting down with the development managers and creating a diagram of how UX fit in to their Agile process. She then iterated on the diagram with the managers until everyone was happy with it. The diagram was both realistic and a bit aspirational, but in the end, it was something that all parties were comfortable with. Getting this kind of buy-in up front and at the same time managing expectations in a participatory way are tremendously valuable and eliminate many potential misunderstandings down the road.

Key points
- Recognize the variability within an organization. Different development teams within a company have different personalities and logistics, and the approach of the UX person needs to suit each team. She is very successful with her team, but her techniques might not work for other team members, so she must work with them to find the right tactics.
- An ounce of prevention is worth a pound of cure. Collaboratively defining the role of the UX team not only achieves buy-in for the agreed-upon definition and prevents future issues, it also shows in a very tangible way that the UX group is committed to being a partner in the process. It also creates a certain amount of comfort among the other functional areas, because they understand what to expect from UX, once they see the plan for how the UX staff will be working with them.

CHRISTINA YORK, ITHAKA

Christina is a UX manager for ITHAKA, a not-for-profit organization that supports the academic community to adopt and use new technologies. She has a team of two strategists, two interaction designers, and one researcher. She has been practicing Scrum for about two and a half years and has been able to integrate her team very effectively into an Agile environment.

The initial transition to Agile was a baptism by fire. The company decided to Agile and committed to a full-scale change. It brought in trainers, including Jeff Patton, to do training. Since there was not a lot of guidance at the time on how to integrate UX efforts into the process, the company specifically chose Jeff Patton because of his focus on user experience design. The organization continued its commitment to educating staff members, supporting their efforts to staying current on Agile practices, and encouraging them to be active members of the Agile community. The company even sent one person from each functional area to the Agile Alliance Conference, so that they could learn and bring these insights back to the company. When the transition first began, the UX team was able to get funding to attend a User Interface Engineering (UIE) online seminar featuring Jeff Patton. This was a fairly inexpensive training session and was run virtually, so the whole group could attend. As time went on, the UX people have been able to leverage their successes and get funding for the team to attend other UIE online seminars and to subscribe to online journals—all to help the team keep fresh and find new tools and methods without travel or significant expense.

Despite the organizational support and enthusiasm, there still were bumps along the way. There is a still amount of difficulty in estimating size and velocity. However, since the teams are, in Christina's words, "great at retrospectives," improvement in this area is likely over time. At first, sizing was a development-only effort, and it would just apply a ratio to the QE and UX efforts (e.g., if a task has a development velocity of three, then the QE effort might be one and a half, and UX one). Since a simple ratio to apply to QE and UX efforts relative to coding effort is not always apparent, this did not really work out. Some tasks might have a velocity of three but a QE effort of six, if it requires manual testing or rewriting automated testing. In the same way, that a velocity of three for the development team could be a ten for the UX team, if it requires significant design effort and user validation. The team also experimented with the Spike process to manage the design work. (A "spike" is a time-boxed piece of work, the outcome of which allows the team to define the user story and understand it well enough to provide an estimated effort.) The intention of spikes is to manage unanticipated development work that requires some up-front research and could work well to manage unforeseen design problems but might not work well to handle standard design efforts.

The UX team started with creating a one-year research plan and reviewed and refined it monthly but since evolved to revisiting the plan quarterly. Since the plan is fairly high level and the work is broad in scope, things do not necessarily change often enough to warrant frequent review and adjustment. The strategists constantly review the backlog and focus on high-level things as they move through the cycle. Additionally, the UX team works to communicate with the business owners who are not colocated. UX travels to them and does design jams to involve them in the design process, get their buy-in for design work, and increase the collaboration. The UX people generally pick one big or important item and get the business owners to contribute in a controlled way. They make these trips monthly, quarterly, or as part of the preparation for an upcoming sprint that has a lot of business logic associated with it. These efforts have been helpful in giving the business owners a forum in which they can get involved in the design and are fairly strategic activities for the UX team to engage in.

One really interesting innovation at ITHAKA is that, instead of having a single product owner, it has a product owner team. This team consists of a UX person, a PM, and a lead senior developer. There is no question that having a cross-functional perspective at this level allows the organization to make more-informed decisions than with a single owner, regardless of the owner's background. It may seem like extra overhead to have three people in a role that could be filled by a single person, but efficiencies are to be gained by doing this. Having multiple disciplines represented may eliminate the need for some team discussions and allow team meetings to focus more on resolving specific issues than hashing through every detail. The product owner team does planning ahead of the sprint and are also part of the scrum team. It breaks the epics into stories and the stories into tasks. It does all this work via sticky notes. It also uses JIRA and Greenhopper to manage the tasks, but it had a problem keeping the sticky notes in sync with the tasks in JIRA, so there is room for refinement. The interaction designer works with the owner team to identify the big issues, negotiate the timing, and distribute the effort. The designer is a member of the product owner team so he or she has insight into the decisions as well as the UX work. The process relies heavily on the UX team being highly communicative. While it is working very well for the organization, Christina thinks that it might not scale well, since it is so dependent on the communication abilities of the team members. Scalability is a very legitimate concern, especially in situations where the UX team is large or growing at a fast rate. However, if this skill is kept in mind during the hiring process or cultivated with existing staff, there may not be any problems extending the process currently in place.

For the most part, the Agile project teams are a colocated. However, the interaction person sits there only part time, because there is also a central UX team location in an open area, so that the members have a space and opportunity to work together as a design team. Spending time together as a unit allows them to create what Christina describes as "a hive mentality." The ability to sit away from the Agile team is also helpful, because the interaction designers also support non-Agile projects and need space to get away from the nonstop action of an Agile team. At first, the UX team tried to set up office hours but got rid of that. There is a facilities concern around having two spaces, so the group created a general rule that chickens (especially if they support multiple projects) can have two spots, but pigs cannot. The company is planning construction of a new space and planning to still have privacy cubes for phone calls, offices for ad hoc use, and lockers for personal items. A lot of investment by the company and the facilities organization made sure that these changes really work for everyone. Christina sees this as a real show of commitment by the organization to supporting an Agile environment. She sees their ability to continue to deliver as proof of the return on investment into this setup. It also helps that the QA organization really supported the idea of colocation and kept metrics to show its value. The organization was able to point to the number of bugs, the time to fix them, and the like as evidence that the colocation supports greater efficiency. It started making these metrics visible to customers, who in turn lobbied to support whatever was contributing to the metrics.

The team also did participatory design with customers and worked to define their mental models. When a customer was in town, they did F.I.D.O (Freehand Interaction Design Offline, see Tedesco, Chadwick-Dias, and Tullis, n.d., http://legacy.bentley.edu/events/agingbydesign2004/presentations/tedesco_chadwickdias_tullis_fido.pdf for more information about this technique) with the customer, discussed the results, and presented their findings. Previously, there was some tension between UX and the business owners, but using participatory design methods essentially made the customers the advocates for the designs and the publishers would negotiate on behalf of the UX and request UX involvement.

Since UX team members straddle both waterfall and Agile projects, it is left to the individual to manage a personal schedule and negotiate his or her time. The members tend to go to all the project meetings, the sprint planning, the retrospectives, and the standups. However, if they have a conflict or need to drop something, they will go to the team and say, "I have eight hours for your project this week, how do you want me to spend it?" The team decides if the time is better spent attending standups or skipping some other team event. Often, it will frontload the UX issues in a planning meeting so that the designer can leave once the conversation turns to development-centric issues. This is evidence of the trusting relationship that the UX people have been able to build with their teams. They have shown their commitment by constantly showing up, and they allow the team to help determine where the trade-offs need to occur when they cannot make it to everything.

The healthy communication that the teams established depends on having a stabilized team. One designer stays with a given team and that team is kept together although the projects that they work on might change. This improves retention and breaks down knowledge silos. This also allows each functional area to focus on hiring based on skills, because a process is in place to train people on the product knowledge. This speaks to the fact that the most important factor in going Agile is the people. Christina notices that there is a tendency to focus on the process, but there are so many different flavors of Agile and UX that the people end up being what really makes it work. This is as true for her as it is for every case study in this chapter. She points out that "People over Process" in the Agile Manifesto is right. Probably, the most frequently referenced part of the Agile Manifesto when talking to UX practitioners about how they are integrating into Agile is this concept. A team that does a really rigid, by-the-book adaptation might not incorporate Agile very well at all. A willingness to accommodate UX work shows a predisposition to the idea of "People over Process."

She feels an advantage to being Agile is that there are more shared decisions. She thinks that UX teams often stand alone because they want to. It can be easier to be the bearer of bad news and messages like "you didn't do it the way I wanted" than to put the effort into working collaboratively. This us vs. them mentality can often be made worse in waterfall environments, where the UX team ends up calling out where its designs were not implemented to specification. Agile does not really allow that kind of separation and distance, since it demands that everyone work together. She prefers solving problems together and sees that as the path to innovation. She says it is not about being right, it is about understanding. The team has no design divas; it is really a marketplace of ideas. Because of this, Agile is not for everyone. Christina can see how someone who is awesome at waterfall might not fit into Agile. Indeed, for many people, the transition can be a challenge, as it can require them to change the way they worked for many years.

When they went Agile, Christina added a section to the weekly UX meeting called "F*ckups and Wins" at the end. At first, only Christina would volunteer her mistakes, then it became a joke on the team, and finally other people started participating. Christina was really inspired by the UPA Munich presentation by Steve Portigal (2010), "Culture: You're Soaking in It" (Portigal's slides on this topic can be found at www.slideshare.net/steveportigal/culture-youre-soaking-in-it), and focused on creating a specific culture for her team.

Christina was conscientious in her approach to creating an Agile UX team and did a lot of research to inform her decisions. As a result, she could draw on a lot of inspiration as she navigated the transition. Just as important, she modeled the values that she wants to see and is able to influence change without being preachy. She does it from a leadership position, but her techniques can be equally effective when used by an individual contributor and can be used to change the style of dialog in planning meetings or retrospectives.

Key points

- Manage the culture of the UX team. Being conscious and deliberate about creating a culture of collaboration begins with your own team. Although Christina worked within an organization that was able to conduct effective retrospectives, her team would have been well-equipped to model this behavior and spread it throughout any organization. Embodying the culture you would like to see allows the team to model the right behavior and encourages others to do the same. It also creates a more uniform expectation from people about what it is like to work with members of the UX team. They may not know person A, but they know the UX culture, so they are better prepared for what to expect.
- Grow your Agile skills and your UX skills. While it is important to keep current on new Agile trends, especially as they relate to design, it is also critical to stay current on design and usability techniques and methods. Turning this into a team activity with design workshops and skill sessions not only allows the entire team to benefit from the knowledge but creates a more cohesive team.
- People over process. In the early days of a transition, it is easy to get caught up in the minutiae of the process. Some of detail is important, but the people and the culture end up having the greatest effect on the success of the effort. Learn what you need to about the process, but focus your energy and effort on coaching the people.

ANONYMOUS 2, A LARGE DESKTOP SOFTWARE COMPANY

This is a story about an adoption of Agile that is still struggling to find its way. In no way is it a case study about a complete failure. In fact, the company did many of the right things and even invested in training. In certain areas of the development process where Agile is working well. However, in other places, the organization is not really engaging in Agile values. This case probably resonates with many people for whom Agile is a mixed experience , neither an over-whelming success nor an abject failure. The UX person has chosen to remain anonymous to be as candid as possible.

Anonymous 2 has been working with Agile since 2006, after previously doing "heavy waterfall." When doing waterfall, she was writing huge specifications. After the move to Scrum, the company brought in a local person as an Agile coach. The organization also provided development training and product owner training. This taught people about writing user stories and being more user focused., which was not something they had previously been doing. These are certainly promising first steps on the Agile path and consistent with what many of the successful adopters do.

The motivation for the change was that the time between releases was too long, around two years. This is a legitimate motivation, as such a kind of gap in releases is not typical anymore, even for large software packages. Customers have different expectations, and even if they are not necessarily able to adopt more frequent releases, it allows the company to see the direction in which it is heading. Waiting upwards of two years can not only cause the company to miss important opportunities, it can also create some anxiety in the marketplace. Choosing Agile to address this particular issue is a sign that the organization had identified that its current process is not working, and it needs to make a change. Her company started out cautiously by beginning the efforts with pilot projects to test Agile. To minimize the risk, it used an independent project as the environment for the first test. She was happy to see some of the waterfall elements go away, especially the huge specifications that would take so long to go through approval that they became obsolete. They also did not really have an established UX process under waterfall, so the UX team saw this change as an opportunity to define the process. Even teams with years' worth of legacy at a company often have no formal process in place and a move to Agile can be a chance to put in place a thoughtfully designed UX process. Her team came to the table with a proposal about the UX process, suggesting parallel sprints. The members had done their research and thought that this would be the best approach for them.

Overall, the team has been pretty successful in integrating more frequent user feedback than it previously was able to do. The original plan was to have what she describes as "revolving door" testing. The goal was for every scrum team to test at the same time every few sprints. That way, the team would have a predictable opportunity for feedback and would know that testing would occur at the beginning of every other sprint. This is something many teams, especially teams that support websites, are able to do; and it seems like an ideal approach. The team found that it was not able to achieve that level of predictability and instead has been doing frequent ad hoc user feedback sessions. It is not the ideal it was aiming for, but tit gets feedback much more often and earlier in the cycle than before. During the time with waterfall, it would usually not get user feedback until a month before the quality testing phase, toward the end of the release cycle. The Scrum process definitely helped create support for including more feedback into the cycle, because it is an accepted part of Agile. The team is also able to show more features earlier in the process, because he sprint cycles produce workable features early on.

Something has not gone quite as planned is that the UX team has not been able to get on a parallel track and work ahead of the development team. The members found that they have been pulled into projects once the projects already have started, and it is very hard to get ahead if you start out playing catch up. This is a situation that UX teams often find themselves in during the first time out with Agile. In the rush to get all the work off the ground, it may not always be clear when and where UX fits in, and the UX team may often is brought in after the fact. When the work is already underway and the UX person required to produce designs yesterday can be an impossible position to be in and very difficult to change as the sprint cycles barrel ahead. Regardless of whether someone are working in parallel sprints or within sprints, it is never good to be behind. It may not always be possible to avoid these situations, but it is critical to minimize their occurrence. She notes that defining the big picture ahead of time is great, but that does not always work. She feels you can tell when it does not work, because the work is affected. The challenge with planning ahead is to plan to a finer level of granularity than is appropriate, given the level of certainty, or uncertainty really, around some items. You can also plan work that never materializes, which is fine if you have not made a significant investment and can easily change direction. As she points out, the real indication that time has not been well spent is if the work is compromised or derailed.

The company has over 30 Scrum teams and a UX team of six people to support them. As one might expect, the high-priority projects get attention and UX support. Any given UX person may have to juggle a few projects. She had once been assigned as a dedicated resource to a project, and while she liked it, this is a rare occurrence. On some projects of a sufficiently high priority, it was possible to give that focused attention, but on others, the UX team functioned more as consultants. Working like this can make it even harder for the UX team to fully engage in projects and figure out how to master their new process. So much of Agile is about building trust and transparency and being really involved with the day-to-day work of the team. If the UX people cannot do that, it might mean that they are taking on too much work. It may be hard to push back, especially since no one likes to say no to project work. Especially when the team is orienting to a new way of working, there needs to be some space to take a pause and reflect on how things are going and where changes need to be made. Supporting too many projects and working at a very fast pace can prevent the necessary self-reflection from happening.

The UX team was excited to make the move to Scrum, but the transition turned out not to be so easy for everyone. Chunking the working into pieces was a new skill for some, but everyone on the team got through it. The team members also started using new tools, like Balsamiq for sketching designs. They were used to using Photoshop, but switching to Balsamiq made it easier to churn out design ideas quickly. Since the learning curve for Balsamiq is fairly low, especially relative to Photoshop, this is an easy skill to acquire and can be almost as natural for sketching as working with pencil and paper. The team also started using Axure because it was having trouble really showing complex interactions, especially for controls like trees and tables. She found that it is a good tool. The members got great feedback, and their PM is impressed with the quality of the prototype they can produce quickly. They have also used it a few times to produce a prototype for usability testing. They do testing in their own lab and also go on site with customers or at conferences.

The UX team members have a solid idea of where they want to go and just need to get there. However, she feels that cultural issues still need improvement. She thinks that they need an organization more focused on user experience. While the company talks about user experience quite a bit, things have not yet evolved to the point where UX is such a priority that the company would be willing to hold the release because of a UX issue. In very few companies could a UX issue hold up a release. Many of us have heard leadership say that UX is important but not necessarily follow through with actions that show this commitment to be true. This can occur for so many reasons. Sometimes, the organization wants the customers to think it is concerned with improving their experience but is not entirely prepared to spend time and resources on figuring out how best to do this. What often can help resolve this issue is creating visibility around UX activities, their benefits, and how little investment is required to effect significant change in the products. In other situations, leadership is genuinely interested in making the UX of the product better, but it does not know what to do so or how to get there. When facing this dynamic, the UX team can gain traction by doing some education around UX methods and having a specific proposal to pitch to leadership. She also finds that both the company and the release cycle are still very feature driven. This means that if a trade-off needs to be made for any reason, it is likely that UX work will be dropped in deference to features.

Another issue that has arisen since the move to Agile is that the organization has become very big on metrics. Development is completely focused on their velocity, and that function often is very averse to changing the UI because it thinks that would make it look like their velocity was decreasing. As often happens when metrics become a primary driver, people work toward the metric rather than the spirit of the metric. Part of the problem here is that, if reworking the UI is having a negative impact on the metrics, the work is not being tracked properly. Refactoring work, which is supported by Agile, is still work and should show up positively in the metrics. Another frequent problem is that the project team would come to the end of the sprint and end up with stories not having being done. This in itself is a very big red flag, especially if it is a recurring issue. It means that the team is either overcommitting to the amount of work that it can do or churning too much over the work during the sprint cycle. The fact that it continues to happen is an indication that the team is not raising or resolving their issues during retrospectives.

In addition, she has seen a struggle between boundaries of product owner and the UX team. The views have a lot of natural overlap, but the product owner is a single person. This tension is not uncommon, especially if the product owner defined many of the UI elements in the past and is reluctant to give that over to the UX team. It can also simply be an issue of the product owner feeling as though, in defining the interfaces, the UX people are stepping too far into the territory of "owning" the product. She has seen a lot of arguments over who had the final say on a disagreement. This resulted in a rule that the product owner has the final say, but this has not always worked out well for the UX team. The UX team members feel they do not have as much of a voice as they would like. This can be very frustrating for a UX team working hard to adapt to a new process and work at a faster pace, only to see that if the members disagree with how something is being done, it is unlikely that their viewpoint will be supported.

Overall, it still feels really waterfall and not very Agile to her. She thinks if development could see the usability sessions and the users actually using the software, this might help. Since so much testing is done on site with the customer, only one or two developers can come with them. Involving the development organization more in feedback sessions might be quite effective, as it seems that much of the needed changes are at the team level. She finds hope in the fact that smaller projects that get big wins tend to influence change at their organization, and this represents an opportunity for her team. She also thinks that it is good to know where you are and where you want to go, so you can figure out how to get there. This means identifying a goal for the team and how it wants to support the organization then working toward it. She recommends this as a first step to moving to an Agile environment, the plan can be revisited, but it is important to at least start with a specific vision and end state to guide choices along the way. Another piece of advice she gives to UX teams is that they need to recognize that you cannot boil the ocean in a single day. Change is an ongoing process, and you need to be patient but proactive as your team switches gears. She definitely sees benefits to working in an Agile way. In the past, she had to justify everything and mo longer has to. She can see progress, even if they are far from where they want to be.

As with most organizations, there is certainly room for the organization to mature in its Agile application, but the UX team has been able to make the most out of the transition. Members can streamline their work process, and they discovered new tools like Balsamiq to support their efforts. They see many of the challenges as opportunities and approach these daunting changes with a positive attitude. The team is also able to be tremendously effective, despite their relatively small size and fairly extensive workload. This helps it build credibility and support for its efforts. The UX team has certainly not failed to integrate into the Agile process, it is simply in a situation where the organization needs to continue to evolve and find a way to increase collaboration.

Key points

- If your organization still has a lot of room to grow into a mature adoption of Agile, focus on the small wins and the places where the UX team is able to gain traction. Change does not always happen overnight and identifying the small successes can not only keep up morale but help affect change elsewhere. Be strategic, and target the projects where you anticipate you will be successful; leverage these to get more support, more resources, or whatever else is needed by the team.
- When people hide behind the Agile process, work around it. Agile is not about metrics and hiding incomplete user stories. That does not mean that Agile teams do not often get caught up in things like this because of organizational pressure from above. If you happen to be in a situation where this occurring, taking the issue head on may not be the path to success. (Although, if it seems like it is possible to resolve it, by all means go for it!) Instead, work with the development team to figure out a way to track the velocity in a way that supports reworking the UI while meeting the metrics.

AUSTIN GOVELLA, AVANANDE

Austin is an experience design manager at Avanande, a provider of business technology and managed services. He has practiced Agile for more than five years in his current role and at a previous employer. He has a very well-thought-out philosophy on Lean UX and has been very successful in adapting his approach to situation needs. While still executing on the deliverables for the release, he focuses much of his energy on strategy and gives priority to his time spent on strategic activities.

When discussing his experience with Agile, the first thing he points out is that no two Agile teams are ever the same. This statement comes from Austin's experience of having worked with different teams and at different companies, but it is generalizable to the broader Agile world and is worth calling out, because it does not got expressed often enough. Many of us will work on Agile projects at more than one company or with different teams within the same company. If you approach each project as if it is the same, you may not be as successful as if you adjust to fit the team at hand. This is not unique to Agile, it is something that UX practitioners often do to be effective. However, since Agile methods depend so much on the project team being as high functioning as possible and able to communicate well enough to promote teamwork, it is especially important.

Austin describes himself as practicing a form of modified Scrum. He has learned from experience that, if he is on more than one project, he cannot go to all the meetings for each project. It is really important to know your limits when working in Agile. As designers, we always want to be able to help produce as many good designs as possible. Unfortunately, trying to support multiple projects and attend all of the meetings compromises our bandwidth. Since the process works in cycles, measured in weeks and not months (or years), it becomes apparent very quickly when you are in over your head. He feels that the key to Agile is really committing to a sprint's worth of work, delivering on it, and maintaining constant communication. He thinks that, compared to waterfall, it is a big commitment. Instead of agreeing to a set of work that may, or may not, take place over a long period of time, the team is agrees to do very specific things in a short amount of time. Working this way means so much more accountability. There is also an implicit agreement that the team will work together, which is never a factor addressed in a waterfall cycle.

He has a three-month release cycle and lots of meetings, although maybe not daily ones. He finds that the urgency of everything increases in an Agile environment. This is certainly true since the most time you have to turn around a single task might be three weeks. On the project he was working on at the time of our interview, his team built up a backlog and was doing preplanning activities. Austin was able to write some of the stories, which is very helpful, as he can make sure that they are written with the appropriate customer focus. The planning meeting that they is more high level; they do not hash out the tasks during this event but rather do that outside the meeting. This serves to keep the planning meetings somewhat focused and able to finish in a reasonable amount of time.

The development team for the project he is working on is in Buenos Aires, and he estimates that at least 50 percent of the work that he did the last few years has been done remotely. He uses Campfire, a persistent chat room, where he can post files. He and his visual designer are on that site all day, working together virtually. (The visual designer is in the remote location.) They spend time commenting and critiquing each other's work, and the site is a place for him and the designer to work collaboratively. It is a space where the UX team can talk openly about the design issues. It works better than any kind of instant messaging, which is too immediate to use across time zones, and is better than email because it has a dedicated and focused purpose. Austin is the architect and constructs wireframes, the visual designer is focused on the front end, and together they produce the overall design.

Prior to the kickoff of his most recent project, he put together a strategy for the architecture and how the pieces fit together. He likes doing this, because having that kind of document and presenting it to the team provides a common language and framework from which everyone can work. This up-front work saves time and reduces the number of course corrections needed later. Business needs and user needs are embedded in the document, and it is a compact way to communicate all these things. He describes the strategy document as "just a description of the Lego pieces," in essence saying, "these are the things we'll have." He posted the document and did all of this work ahead of staffing the development team, so the document really drove the definition of the project. Essentially, he took advantage of the downtime before the project really ramped up to produce the document and get buy-in for it. Not only did this lay the groundwork for the project, but it is much easier to do before the work is underway.

He developed two personas for his current project. He presented it generally and casually, and since there was no pushback, they are now they are part of the process. Every story in the backlog is built around these personas. Having a high-level artifact, such as personas, and making sure that it feeds into the more detailed user stories are excellent tactics for creating a coherent deliverable that fits together in a consistent way. He also uses the story as a basis for the wireframes and references it. Each wireframe has a description that contains a mini-story, which includes for whom it is targeted and how it will be used. This fleshes out the wireframe and gives it enough context that the other functional area can have a solid understanding of not only the design intent but its rationale. He was able to do a bunch of user interviews for competitive research. He also reread *Designing Social Interfaces* (Crumlish and Malone, 2009) to prepare for working on the designs. He did workshops with business and technical stakeholders to get insight into their expectations and customer needs. Business stakeholders said that they wanted him to produce a list or a backlog, but they got a strategy presentation and document instead, which was more useful in setting a clear direction for the project work. He notes that UX practitioners sometimes have to provide what is needed and not necessarily what is asked for.

There are no explicit "stories" for the wireframes and visual designs. Since he wrote the stories, he feels that there is an inherent relationship between them and the design work, so it is not necessary to create separate items. He and the designer do have tasks for the design work, but Austin manages those independent of the rest of the team. His velocity is not tracked because he straddles different projects and tracking his work would provide no insight into how the team is progressing. For deliverables, the UX person is actually producing the front end .html and handing that off to the development team. Austin also uses wireframes to illustrate workflows and creates site maps. He finds that the site maps are usually a great communication tool because everyone can understand them. Those always get bang for the buck relative to other efforts.

When it comes to user testing and validation, he finds that he can just schedule testing, and it happens. He was also planning to get the original interviewees' reactions to the wireframes. After the first release, he will run through basic tasks and get feedback. In a typical sprint, the team spends a half day planning, three and a half to four days of coding, three to four days quality testing, then the team has a retrospective. The first release happens after three sprints, and that pattern going continues two or three cycles. For tools, the team is considering using TeamForge, but it had not deployed it at the time of our interview. He is still using his original Excel document to manage the backlog.

Austin acknowledges that Agile heightens all the communication issues any team might have. In a waterfall environment, communication occurs at a slow rate and problems may go unnoticed or get lost in the noise. However, a problem, such as a team member who prefers to work in isolation and is uncomfortable working cooperatively, will reveal itself very quickly. The same is true for other dysfunctions that might exist. He also recognizes that "it is easy for someone to hop on the backlog train and drive it wherever they want to." He emphasizes that Agile itself is neither good nor bad, but it works best if everyone has a shared vision.

He also likes to track the improvement in UX across releases. He incorporates this into the process by including, in every story comparison criterion, that this has to be as good as, better than, not as good but useable than before or than a competitive feature. He finds that the developers are not very interested in these comparisons. They do not tend to participate in this activity, but it is very effective to use when communicating with the product owners. Executives love it, and charts and graphs can illustrate the progress or the lack of it. Sometimes, there is no real world comparison; then he uses the wireframe or prototype as the baseline. Austin notes that you can also use something like a "UX health check," which is inspired by Jon Innes's (2011) UXI matrix (see www.slideshare.net/balancedteam/uxi-matrix-jon-innes for more information on this matrix and its application). Both techniques are ways to analyze the overall robustness of the design and can identify areas for improvement.

One thing Austin learned along the way is that it is not designers or developers who create products, it is the organization as a whole. He points out that every project problem is a team problem. If someone does not want to do testing it is not because the person is lazy, but because the value of doing it is not clear to them; and it is the responsibility of the UX team to show its value. It is important to realize that, if you want to change the way things work, you have to influence the organization. (See his presentation on this topic on Slideshare; Govella, n.d.: www.slideshare.net/austingovella.) This is really an important consideration when deciding what strategy to use with the team on a given project. The role of the UX person is not to simply churn out sketches but contribute to a good customer experience in every way possible. This means helping to define the strategy, the personas, and the user stories as much as possible. It also means considering how to contribute to a high-functioning team and promote an understanding on the team of the users and how to meet their needs through design.

He also advises to make your process visible. This can be the most effective way to create understanding of and support for your work. If you do a project well, then people will copy your process and you will influence the culture. He suggests putting your work on walls and engaging in collaborative design. In a meeting he had once, everyone sketched ideas for a page. With nine people in the room, they wound up with eight pictures (one person abstained). This kind of activity can produce an appreciation for and awareness of the design process, as well as generate multiple design solutions very quickly. It is also an effective way to propagate UX techniques, since part of the goal should be to help give developers the skills to make the best design decisions they can. Austin also advises that focusing on strategy is more important than the production of wireframes. He feels that, if you can put an idea in to the team's head, it will infect everything the team does. The wireframes can be implemented in ways over which you have no control, so it is more important to focus on influencing the mindset. This is a better investment of UX effort and will contribute to a better outcome. He also recommends that UX practitioners engaging in Agile read the Balance Team (n.d.) blog (www.balancedteam.org/) and Jeff Gothelf's (n.d.) blog www.jeffgothelf.com/blog) to learn more about Lean UX. These blogs tend to focus on strategic efforts and how the UX team can work as efficiently as possible, all very important when working in an Agile environment.

When starting with Agile, it can be very easy to get hung up on or caught up in all the details of the process and lose sight of the big picture. It can certainly be easy to get fixated on the progress of burn-down charts, obsess over the details of the process, and keep your eyes focused exclusively on your next piece of work. However, if you wait until it is time to generate deliverables to try to guide or influence the process, your efforts will be much less impactful. Austin's story serves as a good reminder that defining the way people speak about the work by using personas and driving the overall strategy of the effort is the most effective way to affect the culture and the design. This is an especially valuable message for those of us with limited UX resources.

Key points
- Fancy tools are not required. The fact that Austin is managing his backlog with an Excel spreadsheet shows that the tools are much less important than the intention. You cannot judge the maturity of an Agile implementation by the tools the team uses. And, if the tool of choice is getting in the way of the team's work, consider keeping things simple. Plenty of fancy tools are available to Agile teams, and many of them provide great benefit, but in the end, they are just tools. If the team has problems, they need to be solved in a way other than by purchasing new software.

- While it is easy to get caught up in the deliverables, the wireframes, and the sketches, the most influential work is done on the front end. Being a part of the story definition process has the most bang for the buck, especially since the design tasks will fall out of that. Austin makes a very good point that you cannot control the implementation of the wireframes. However, if you can help drive (or win) the user story definitions, you may be able to worry less about some of the smaller details.

JOSH O'CONNOR, NATIONAL COUNCIL FOR THE BLIND, IRELAND

Josh is a senior accessibility consultant at National Council for the Blind Ireland's Center for Inclusive Technology and often works as a consultant to evaluate the accessibility of a client's website. He does usability testing with visually impaired people on websites and public domain sites. From the vantage point of a consultant, he has the opportunity to view many organizations and the way they approach Agile.

Josh is a big fan of Agile, although he acknowledges that, on paper, it can look like more work than traditional methods and it needs a champion within the development organization for it to be successfully adopted. Plenty of executives are excited by the idea that it just makes things happen faster, but those who are closer to the production of software worry about the additional overhead and process changes required to go Agile. He thinks the products produced via Agile methods tend to be better because of the iteration and customer involvement. However, he has seen quite a few environments that claim to be Agile, but once you scratch the surface, it is clear that this is just lip service. This is a fairly common phenomenon, since there are places that want to be Agile but have not yet figured out what that really means or how to get there. They may co-opt a given method in a superficial way and leave it at that. Suffice it to say, these organizations are likely to bear a stronger resemblance to waterfall processes than to Agile. Organizations that have taken on Agile in such a shallow way are likely to have the same approach to accessibility.

Since he is brought in as a consultant and companies are not obligated to implement his advice, he is often in the position of having to negotiate with cultures that are closed to complaints about accessibility. In his experience, the degree to which a team is proactive about accessibility issues has to do with the corporate culture's awareness and its history with supporting people with disabilities. While Josh is speaking specifically to accessibility, this is can be applied to broader user experience issues. If the company recognizes the value in improving these things, either from a revenue standpoint or simply because it is the right thing to do, there are fewer battles in which to engage. Since this is not always the case, he has found that the best way to get support and buy-in for accessibility design ideas is to show the developers cool solutions. Everyone likes cool things and being shown a better way to do things. He advises being really aware of what is new and how the technologies work. This goes hand in hand with the idea that UX people should not just point out all the flaws in the work. He recommends reinforcing what is good and doing it in a really, really supportive way. When you say what is wrong, have a solution, a way to fix it. This advice can be applied not only to design issues but also Agile adoption. Acknowledge that the team has done good work, but that it could be better if x, y, or z is done. Make the team your partners in producing a great product. Stay aware of the current technologies and be able to show the development team the cool things hey could be doing and help them make the change possible.

Josh has an interesting perspective as a consultant, because he comes into a culture that is already defined and he is not in a position to directly influence the organization. However, because he is brought in as an expert in accessibility and as an outsider who does not carry the same baggage as a team member, he is remarkably positioned to influence the people with whom he comes in contact. Focusing on solutions and showing developers a cool way to do things is a technique that any UX person could benefit from using.

Key point
- Just because an organization says itis Agile does not mean it really is. If an organization is only giving lip service to the method rather than genuinely engaged, you end up with the worst kind of process. When working in this situation, it is best to try to get what you can implemented, model good Agile behavior as much as possible, and focus on the small wins.

ADRIAN HOWARD, QUIETSTARS

Adrian is a consultant with Quietstars, in the United Kingdom, and specializes in Agile. His thoughts on Agile show up in many forums, at many conferences, and a quick overview of some of his answers on "how to be Agile" can be found online (Howard, n.d.; to see what Adrian has to say, go to www.quora.com/Adrian-Howard/answers/Agile-UX).

He recalls first reading about Extreme Programming and thinking that it would never work. He came from an architecture background and had been taught that you design your system first. The idea of designing as you go along ran opposite to everything he had learned. He decided to give it a try despite this and thinks that the appeal of working this way is that the process is iterative, feedback driven, and teamwork oriented. Once he started working in an Agile fashion, he felt the process just worked better.

He feels that there is often a divide between the coders and the "artists"/designers, which is harmful to the product. Having a pretty skin and an ugly inside does not work to, they have to connect. After all, the gorgeous graphical treatment looks much less appealing to a user who is completely frustrated by the quality or performance of the application. Agile can help bridge this divide by increasing communication and encouraging more conversations. Rather than engage in a more classic "us vs. them" dynamic, the team needs to work as a team and collaborate.

He feels Agile makes more explicit the need to do the design work throughout the project. There may have been a latent need for this in waterfall, but it may have only occasionally actually occurred. However, with Agile, the need for iterative design is the basis of making the process work and is, in fact, required by Agile methods. He points out that the design problems do not occur only before you build and Agile supports that reality Too often in traditional processes, the issues are identified after the code is written, and it is almost always too late in the cycle to change anything but the most catastrophic of issues.. He acknowledges that Agile can be more overwhelming, but sometimes, you end up doing less work, because you can get feedback more quickly and spare yourself from heading in the wrong direction or spending time on designs that will never see the light of day. In more traditional environments, you might never get feedback that the design is flawed until late-cycle usability, when only minor design refinements are feasible. If you get significant feedback in one sprint, you can completely rework the design and validate it in the next round. As chaotic as the pace may feel, efficiencies are to be gained by working this way.

He likes Agile, because what he likes best about design is not the creation of wireframes but seeing the design in the user's hands and seeing it going well.(Although he acknowledges that, sometimes, you watch them curse the application out of frustration, but that provides important feedback as well.) He thinks that getting customers involved with the design early on happens more often in Agile environments. The process is more feedback oriented and customer focused and, done right, can be better positioned to achieve a good user experience. Certainly, Agile has built-in support for involving the customer, so if you previously found resistance on this front, it is likely that you will no longer have that problem. He also finds less resistance to Agile than there used to be and wonders if the people who are anti-Agile are really criticizing Agile itself or are reacting to someone's bad implementation of Agile. It can be hard to divorce a single bad experience from the process itself. And, since many people have only the experience of a single company or team, it can be easy to write the whole thing off as a disaster if that is all a person known. It would also seem that more and more people are having positive experiences with the process, if the resistance to it is going away. Even for those working with imperfect adaptions, it is clear to see that there are benefits. Few UX people will be sad to say goodbye to the large specifications they were responsible for writing.

When talking with Adrian about Agile and UX, it seems like such an obvious fit that it is almost surprising that anyone struggles to make the two work well together. Obviously, many of us do struggle to be Agile, but Adrian's words are a good reminder that the values of Agile and UX are a natural pairing. If there are tensions or resistance, it has to do with people and the dynamics of the team. The processes themselves are a naturally good fit.

Key points

- Agile is very immediate and can seem like more work than traditional waterfall. In reality, because of the speed, the whole process tends to have less waste; and if feedback is a big part of the cycle, it might be possible to get to the best design quicker.
- Up-front design has been the norm because of the prevalence of waterfall, but it is not the natural state of things. While it may seem exhausting to commit to constant iteration formally, it tends to be what happens anyway. But, because Agile recognizes this, it is more likely that the iterations occur under the guidance of a designer rather that in isolation in a developer's cube.

ELISA MILLER, SENIOR USER EXPERIENCE ENGINEER GE HEALTHCARE

Elisa is a senior user experience engineer; in her role she supports multiple teams and serves as the sole researcher in an Agile environment. When I first heard about her situation, I fully expected to hear a story of frustration and difficulty. After all, working research into a tight sprint cycle can be a challenge for usability people who support only one project; I could not imagine how difficult it would be for someone juggling multiple teams. What I actually heard was a story of someone who embraced the challenges and the pace of Agile and made it work for her, managing to conduct frequent usability tests.

Her teams are composed mostly of systems engineers, who are a blend of user interface designers and business analysts. They create the requirements, define the user interface, and identify what graphic elements they will need for the project. The UX team is made up of 17n people who work on multiple products. Three are managers and the rest are designers who also do design research.

She is the only one doing usability testing on her product. The other UX staff members work very closely with the systems engineers on a project and with Elisa.

She supports two main product areas, each with multiple projects. One product represents the features associated with electronic medical records (EMR) and the other is practice management software. A third product area that she supports addresses scheduling and registration, which allows users to manage the use of rooms and equipment as well as streamline the patient registration process. Those modules are currently stable, so most of her focus has been on the EMR and practice management modules. She alternates one sprint on EMR efforts and the next on practice management software.

When we had our discussion, Elisa and her teams were about a year into their Agile journey, far enough along to have established a good rhythm in some places but early enough that they were still trying new things. They were about to embark on an eight-week project with Elisa supporting multiple teams and having a one-week Sprint 0. The previous rounds of sprints were two weeks long, and Elisa had sorted out a way to divide her time. The sprint reviews for each team occurred every second Thursday. The company's sprint reviews do not serve as a means of communicating to stakeholders but rather function as an integration meeting for all the teams working on the product.

On Friday, she would meet with the systems engineers and the product managers of a team that she would be supporting in the following sprint to discuss their needs and concerns and identify the areas for testing. On Monday, she would create a test plan. She would spend the rest of the week recruiting and walking through the tasks on her own, then with other people to make sure that the test plan was solid. She would also make sure that she had access to a virtual machine with the right product build, including the set of features, needed in the test environment. On Monday and Tuesday of the following week, she would run the usability sessions with customers. Her time on Wednesday and Thursday would be spent writing up the results, and she would deliver the findings on Friday.

In the Friday meetings with the product owner and the systems engineer, she will present a set of slides to summarize the usability testing results. The presentation will give an overview, the top issues, some screenshots, and recommendations. She sometimes gives demographic information about the participants to provide context and always includes user quotes, so that the audience can hear the voice of the customer. While she invites the team to attend the session and makes the notes from and recordings of them easily available via OneNote, it is not always possible for the team to attend sessions, so hearing the actual voice of the customer during the presentation is very valuable. All in all, she will present 10 or 12 slides and make the presentation short and sweet. The feedback is handled in different ways, depending on the team and the type of issue. If the problem is minor, needs time to be designed, or is unlikely to be addressed in the next sprint, then most teams put issue in the backlog to be worked on later. If the issue is serious and its resolution is clear, then most teams fold it into their next sprint.

She has tested on everything including paper prototypes, Axure prototypes, and development environments. Her favorite is to use html or Axure prototypes, because they allows her to test the interactions before they are coded. She might put together a prototype for the test session, but she does not always have the time to do that. Her UX colleagues or the systems engineers may also produce a prototype using Axure, Expression, or even PowerPoint, depending on the time they have and which tool is the most comfortable to use. Her tests are done remotely, using WebEx and a virtual machine. In two days, she generally can test with 8–10 customers and tries to achieve a mix of people from small and large practices. Elisa does not find remote testing to be the most informative, but it produces great data. Testing remotely also allows her access to a broader pool of users and a mix of representation. Her customers are very interested in providing feedback. Some of them have been using the product for 10 or 15 years and are very invested in the products. Recruiting is not that difficult for her, especially since she can leverage the working group for referrals and the user group meetings.

In addition to her efforts within the sprint cycles, she has touch points with the customers. In April and October, they have user group meetings that last for three days and are attended by as many as 600 customers. She is able to get customers in a conference room and test features and functions with 10 customers a day through 30 or 40 minutes that are quite focused in their scope. She has been able to use these opportunities to test out design ideas on areas that contain known issues and try out potential design solutions. She had a feature set that they were trying to refine and was able to have the customers perform four tasks on the existing UI then do the same four tasks on a prototype and received great feedback. The product also has working groups that meet every two weeks to review prototypes. Since this audience is reviewing prototypes early and often, she does not have them participate in the usability sessions.

Since she is juggling in-sprint testing and other activities and may not be doing work for a specific project team during the course of a sprint, Elisa adopted office hours. Every day, for a few set hours, her door is open for everyone, regardless of what project they are on or what kind of question they have. This allows her to be constantly available to all the teams she supports, but in a manageable way. Having the office hours not only helps to control when and how to support multiple teams, it sends a really clear message to those teams that she is committed to ongoing and continual communication.

As all of these sprint-based activities are going on, the UX team is looking at ways in which it can be more efficient and streamline the process. Because some of the products were acquired from different companies, there are natural differences in how certain things are done in the UI. Between the EMR and practice management applications, there are four or five different calendar controls, which is not an unusual situation for many legacy software systems. Since they are moving the code over to WPF (Windows Presentation Format), the team had to build a new calendar control. Elisa took this opportunity to make sure that the new control had all the functionality of the previous controls, so that when the old code is updated, the team can move to the new widget without a loss of functionality. Similar opportunities have arisen for standardizing column controls, tab controls, and other widgets. In addition to guiding the design of new components, the team is working on putting things into a pattern library, with snippets of code, so that the developers can access the detailed information about the design and get the code all in one place.

Her advice to UX practitioners who are starting out with Agile is to be flexible. If the team that she is scheduled to support during a sprint has nothing that needs her attention, she finds something else to do. When she first found out that she was going to work on an Agile projects, she simply pulled out a calendar, took a look at what the sprint schedules were, and figured out how to fit into that. Once she had an initial strategy, she pitched it to the product managers and product owners to see if they were comfortable with it and thought it was feasible. She also sat down with the systems engineers and asked them if they thought it would work. Elisa has been superflexible throughout her career and feels that this skill has served her well. When she looks at how to fit her work into Agile, she takes the perspective that it is all about risk and managing that risk. If something in the product needs attention, she flags it for testing and gets it in front of the users. As for being textbook Agile, there is some flexibility around that as well. The reality is that her company is fundamentally a manufacturing firm not a software firm, and certain processes arc in place because of that. The Agile methods that the team uses must fit into this larger framework, although if there are places where it must see a change to work more effectively, there is some room to request changes.

Elisa's other piece of advice is to make friends and bring cookies. She finds it critical to the process that everyone knows who she is and that she is there to help. It is important to communicate that the UX person and the process are not about being punitive but really about working together and making the product better. It is important to make everything feel inclusive. The team needs to be invited to the usability sessions, even if their schedules are unlikely to allow them to attend. It is important to convey the attitude that "you did not do it wrong" and focus on what the requirements are and that they can be satisfied in many ways. Sometimes, it might be best to make sure that the UX team is involved, since their job is to represent the user. She really tries to let her team members know that she wants to make them look good. She feels that her role allows her to see how things are built across products, which keeps her aware of what everyone is doing. This helps her guide and advise her team members more effectively. Now that she spent a certain amount of time working in Agile, she loves the chaos of it. Since she has a very low tolerance for boredom, working in a highly adaptive, fast-paced environment suits her very well. The fact that Agile UX is in its experimental stages in so many companies makes the process more exciting for her.

She wishes she had been able to have had her formal Agile training earlier. Most of the team was able to take its training in December, but she was unable to attend. She did not take her training until April. She had worked on an Agile project at a previous company, but that team was very small and cohesive. The team had official sprints, and their daily standups were often as short as five minutes. The team members were working on a tabbed interface, and she would design the bulk of the tab ahead of time, then refine it based on the requirements. She describes it as a fabulous experience working with a really smart group of people who worked well together. The outcome was a very good product. However, this did not necessarily give her the more formal training that she needed to support her current products, and she felt as if she could have had the answers to a lot of process questions sooner if she had been able to train with the rest of the team. When she did take her training, she also opted to attend the product owner training, just to have a broader perspective. She will not be a product owner but appreciates having insight into what their role is and what that means to the project. She found it tremendously helpful that the company doing the training had extensive experience with her company and was able to tailor its instruction to provide guidance on how to be Agile in that environment.

A lot of effort in general centers around communication and creating a better understanding of how to provide a better user experience for the customer and how to work with the UX staff. She recalls working with one developer who had more of a system focus and was trying to work with her to identify tasks for usability testing. In the end, she was not really able to get the information she needed, so she was inspired to write some guidelines for the systems engineers about how they can help support the usability testing. The team is building itsw pattern library, which allows everyone to contribute to a better design. They are also looking into doing a quarterly newsletter about the UX team and what it does to help create a better understanding of how the team works. This is still in the early stages, but it is an important tool for communicating internally. The team is also taking advantage of the interest in and growth of the UX team to do activities like creating personas. It has not always been able to do this, and this has not necessarily been a problem, because the company has a good understanding of its customers. However, Elisa sees the existence of the personas as a way to personalize the process for the systems engineer and developers. Instead of them just knowing that some users work this way, they can hear her referring to "Joe" and think of a specific person instead of an anonymous set of customers.

So much inspiration can be taken from Elisa's example. She may not be in an ideal Agile situation—she supports multiple projects as the sole researcher and works in an environment that cannot be completely Agile. But, she clearly embraces the values of Agile and is working on creating a process that works for her and her team. And, she has been successful. Her example should serve as inspiration that it is possible to do research in an Agile environment, as part of the cycle. Focusing on how to make it work and moving past any apprehension or preconceived notions about what it will be like frees you up to be a more effective participant in the process. At the time of our discussion, Elisa also served as the directory of professional development for the User Experience Professionals' Association (UXPA), so I hope to hear more about her Agile evolution at future conferences and in presentations.

Key points
- Focusing on how to solve the problem will lead you to a solution. It would have been very easy for people in Elisa's role to wring their hands and complain about how impossible their task was, they certainly would have found many sympathetic ears. That would have done absolutely nothing to change the circumstances, however. Taking a candid assessment of the situation, figuring out what could work, and getting buy-in for a strategy is a path to success, and it is exactly what Elisa did.
- Never forget that you are a part of a team and make sure that everyone knows that this is your philosophy. It would be very easy for Elisa's client teams to feel ignored or that she was not fully invested in their efforts. But, by establishing a collaborative tone, having a specific schedule of support that was vetted with her teams, and supporting office hours, she has made it clear that she is there for her teams no matter what she is focusing on in a given sprint. This is important in any environment, but critical in Agile environments where there may be less time to work through trust and relationship issues.

SUMMARY

The most successful Agile UX teams do not start out that way, but they put effort into identifying what they are doing well and work to correct the things that are going wrong; this self-reflection leads to success. In hearing the stories of how other teams practice Agile UX, it is clear that a wide variety of tools, techniques, and methods can be used. There is no one-size-fits-all solution for Agile UX teams, and the trick is to find the right fit for your project. Some UX teams find the transition easier than others because the pre-existing corporate values fit well with Agile, being more comfortable working with short time frames, or simply because the team has a natural affinity for working the Agile way.

Often, UX teams first engaging in Agile projects do so with a lot of trepidation. Some of that fear is healthy; after all, it might require some fairly drastic changes in how you do your work on a day-to-day basis. However, the skill to make it work is one of the core competencies that most UX people share. We are highly adaptive, out of necessity, and are always trying to fit our work into the culture around us and figure out how we can do more usability testing or increase customer involvement in the design. These are the same issues faced when moving to Agile. Sure, the pace and the rhythm and the events of the process might be different. Overall, moving a UX team to Agile is a design problem—gather your research, understand your user, propose your best solution, and iterate until you get it right.

References

10-Week Residency, n.d. LUXr: The Lean UX Company. Retrieved April 7, 2012, from http://luxr. co/programs/lean-ux-residency/.

Adrian Howard's Answers on Agile UX, n.d. Retrieved April 7, 2012, from www.quora.com/Adrian-Howard/answers/Agile-UX.

Balanced Team, n.d. Retrieved April 7, 2012, from www.balancedteam.org/.

Block, K., 2012, April 5. Geographically distributed teams in Agile software development Retrieved April 12, 2012, from http://kaylablock.com/agile-geographically-distributed/?goback=%2Egmp_3315113%2Egde_3315113_member_105723713.

Crumlish, C., Malone, E., 2009. Designing Social Interfaces Principles, Patterns, and Practices for Improving the User Experience. O'Reilly Media, Beijing.

Ethnio: Recruiting for User Research, n.d. Retrieved April 11, 2012, from http://ethn.io/.

Gothelf, J., an.d Beyond Staggered Sprints: How TheLadders.com Integrated UX into Agile. Retrieved April 2, 2012, from http://johnnyholland.org/2010/10/beyond-staggered-sprints-how-theladders-com-integrated-ux-into-agile/.

Gothelf, J., n.d. Jeff Gothelf—Lean UX Advocate, UX Designer, Information Architect, Usability Specialist, Agile, Interface Designer, Interaction Designer, Design Team Leader in New York City, New Jersey, Connecticut, tri-State Metro Area. Retrieved April 7, 2012, from www. jeffgothelf.com/.

Govella, A., n.d. Abandon all [Agile] ye who enter here Retrieved April 7, 2012, from www. slideshare.net/austingovella.

Innes, J., 2011, September 26. UXI Matrix (Jon Innes). Retrieved April 7, 2012, from www.slideshare.net/balancedteam/uxi-matrix-jon-innes.

Life at Snagajob—About Snagajob, n.d. Retrieved April 7, 2012, from www.snagajob.com/about-us/life-at-saj/.

O'Kelley, S., (n.d.). Autotagger: A Case Study for Lean UX | AppNexus Tech Blog. AppNexus Tech Blog. Retrieved April 2, 2012, from http://techblog.appnexus.com/2011/autotagger-a-case-study-for-lean-ux/.

Portigal, S., 2010, June 3. Culture: You're soaking in it. Retrieved April 7, 2012, from www.slideshare.net/steveportigal/culture-youre-soaking-in-it.

Smith, C., 2010, August 12. Getting started with user research, Presented at Agile2010. Retrieved April 7, 2012, from www.slideshare.net/carologic/getting-started-with-user-research-presented-at-agile2010.

Smith, C., 2011, August 11. Faster usability testing in an Agile world. Presented at Agile2011. Retrieved April 7, 2012, from www.slideshare.net/carologic/faster-usability-testing-in-an-agile-world.

Tedesco, D., Chadwick-Dias, A., Tullis, T., n.d. Freehand Interactive Design Offline (F.I.D.O.): A new methodology for participatory design. Retrieved April 7, 2012, from http://legacy.bentley.edu/events/agingbydesign2004/presentations/tedesco_chadwickdias_tullis_fido.pdf.

CHAPTER 4

Common Success Factors

CONTENTS

Introduction 121
Project Over Process 124
Team Dynamics 127
Communication 129
Define the Big Picture 133
Training 134
Resources for learning about agile 135
Adapt and Evolve 139
Summary 146
References 146

INTRODUCTION

In analyzing the different stories of how each organization implements Agile methods, it is clear that Agile UX teams tend to fall along a spectrum of success. On one end are the teams that have only "the scent of Agile" on them. These are the people who use the term *Agile* to describe what they do and claim to follow the process, although a close look at their day-to-day efforts might paint a different picture. In examining how these teams operate, it is clear that they do not really engage in the core values of the methodology and often skip many of the recommended steps prescribed by their chosen method. Because these teams are not actually applying Agile methods in concert with adopting the values and principles, it would be hard to see them as successful adopters of Agile. Since they are not necessarily following any particular development process, despite what they might think, they often embody the worst of all the styles that influence their work. It is typical to see on these teams a lack of

Agile User Experience Design. http://dx.doi.org/10.1016/B978-0-12-415953-2.00004-2

training to educate individuals about their Agile method and therefore a lack of real understanding of what it means to follow a particular process. It is also common for these teams to have many problems that are symptomatic of poor communication. The teams tend to struggle; and not only are they not effectively using Agile, they have trouble hitting their release dates with a good level of quality and containing the features that they committed to delivering. They are failing not just because they are not practicing Agile but because they are not following any defined process.

At the opposite end are the teams that achieved a kind of organic rhythm with Agile to the point where the process just disappears and they are no longer even aware of the process—they just do it. These teams have not only realized an expertise in practicing Agile, they are also putting out great products quickly. Being able to do this is the purpose of becoming Agile, so it is no surprise when an expert realization of the process results in robust and timely releases. The process has become so transparent to them that, when talking to members of teams that have been able to achieve such a seamless Agile process, it can be hard to pin down the details of the day-to-day efforts that the rest of us are so focused on navigating properly.

When I asked Christina York if her team used a Sprint 0 for planning, she told me that it did so at first but was evolving out of the process, because it did not really allow time for much research. That does not mean that the team is not doing research or planning but that it is *always* doing research and planning and is in a constant state of preparing for the next sprint or release cycle. It does not need a dedicated period of time to do this activity, because it found a way to plan constantly. I like to describe this of state as being effortless, but that is just how it looks to an outsider, as it probably takes a considerable amount of time and effort to get to that place. Since supporting ongoing research efforts is one of the questions that Agile UX teams have the most difficulty figuring out, the fact that her team could do this and make it a natural part of its rhythm is an indication of a very mature practice.

This kind of proficiency is a really great sign that a teams has been tending to the process: identifying what works and what does not and evolving its functioning at an optimal level. Jeff Gothelf describes this maturation process as progressing to the point where there is no process. He often compares it to the big fight in the *Karate Kid*, where our hero is no longer waxing, he is just doing karate without thought or effort. Once the values of Agile and the techniques have become ingrained in the way that the team works, it requires no conscious effort or hours of discussion to know how best to follow the process. It just becomes the way that the team works. Even the process of reflection becomes less of a ceremony and more of a natural conversation that occurs as a matter of course during the sprint cycle. This is an embodiment of the Agile Manifesto's values of giving priority to "individuals and interactions over process and tools." It can be easy to get caught up in all the trappings of Agile methods and lose sight of the real core values. There are so many events to execute: daily scrums, planning poker, retrospectives, and demonstrations. Checking off these activities can provide a sense of accomplishment, not to mention their ability to keep a whole team of people very busy and occupied. The real value of Agile is not in the ability to attend as many meetings as possible or aggressively keep them limited to the recommended time. The intention of these events is to provide the team a way to become highly efficient and collaborative, if it is not in that state already. A team can evolve beyond these methods or at least mature to the point where the process can be done without much conscious thought. When this happens, it is possible to give a seasoned team the ability to operate at the speed appropriate for the members and allow them the freedom to focus on completing the work and not on hitting prescribed deadlines.

A team just beginning its Agile journey should realize that the teams that have achieved this kind of seamlessness did not get there overnight, nor did they get there without some pain and suffering. The ability to transcend process comes from trial and error and, in some cases, years of effort. Achieving a seemingly effortless workflow first needs an exertion of effort to build the team's skills. No one starts out achieving a perfect adoption of Agile in the first sprint, and certainly no one immediately realizes an ideal integration of UX into the release cycle on Day 1. The ability to overcome obstacles and redirect the team's efforts is what ultimately determines the ability to move toward the more successful end of the Agile spectrum. The team's skill in navigating rough patches is almost more important than the success or failure of a single sprint. Learning from failure helps prevent additional issues down the road, if the team sorts out what went wrong; one bad sprint will not compromise the release but repeating the same mistakes will.

Also, many teams do not fit these extremes and fall somewhere along the middle of the spectrum between struggle and enlightenment and land solidly on competency. While I consider the teams that achieved a picture perfect process to be living at the optimal end of the spectrum, it is certainly possible to be a successful team without achieving this advanced expertise. Many teams live happily and indefinitely in the broad space in the middle, where things go well, the work gets done, and there is lots of process, hours of discussion, and plenty of negotiation around that effort. At the end of the day, these teams still release great high-quality software in a reasonably short period of time and with a wonderful user experience. It just might take them a little more thought and effort to get there. You need not feel less successful because your team has not achieved a totally organic practice of Agile. It might not be realistic for your situation, and it may not even be necessary to get to that state. However, there is comfort in knowing that it is possible and informative to see how it is done.

We can learn from all the use cases on both ends of the spectrum to identify what contributes to the success, or lack thereof, for any given team.

PROJECT OVER PROCESS

Not to be confused with the oft quoted "People over Process" from the Agile Manifesto, this speaks to the balance that successful teams strike between process activities, which keep them on track and moving forward, and the production of the software. The process is helpful only as long as it supports the release; and when it is not, a process refinement needs to occur. Agile methodologies provide a framework for a team to function as empowered, self-organizing individuals in support of a common goal. Before you can move beyond the process itself, you have to experience it and learn what things helpi the team be productive and efficient and what things inhibit the delivery of a high-quality product. When you first start looking at Scrum, it might be easy to think that a daily scrum meeting is a waste of time, only to learn, once you have gone through the process, that is actually a great team-building tool and very effective at increasing the communication and transparency of the team. The different methodologies should be seen as a starting point in the effort to create a more highly functioning work environment.

Unfortunately, a myopic focus on details can distract from the real issues and sometimes interfere with the team's ability to work as efficiently as possible. When I asked Archie Miller how long his team's sprint cycles are, he said they

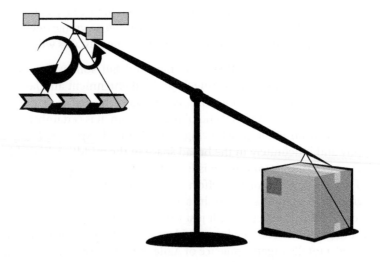

FIGURE 4.1
Project over process.

tend to be a week at minimum once they are out of the discovery phase. He did not have a definite number to give, because the team uses Kanban and choose to allow the work to move at its own natural pace. Because he is a part of a highly functioning Agile environment, he views the timing of the cycle a little bit differently from people who are still working within prescribed sprint cycles, saying, "Releases are like breathing for the team and nobody likes to hold their breath." If his team were working in an environment where it was on a strict sprint schedule, that could easily interfere with the cadence and become a disruption or even a source of frustration. This is a company that took to Agile like a duck to water, and the corporate culture is such a good fit for Agile values that the people do not require as much scaffolding to support them in their efforts to focus on the project.

It might make more sense to see the more well-defined, prescriptive Agile methods as training wheels, providing a more solid structure and guidance around how to work, as everyone learns to think differently about the business of creating software. If a team has never worked with any type of Agile method before and is not certain of where the challenges will be, it is probably more helpful to use an Agile method like Scrum, which provides a very specific approach with which to work. However, there is no need to force a perceived evolution to a less-defined process, just because there is a certain amount of expertise with Agile. The process is just there to help to produce the work, if it is not getting in the way, then there is no need to "fix" it. If the team looks at a different technique, like Kanban and Lean UX, and sees the potential to help it work more efficiently, then it could be worth making the change. But if the process is not broken, fixing it may not be the right answer. The purpose of the process is to support the production of the software; if that is going well, then what problem would be solved by imposing a change to the process? In the end, the process is not the most important thing; the degree to which the team can function at an efficient and productive manner is.

The different elements of the techniques should be seen as tools and used as such. Since the tools might be new and different, they have to be tried out before they are refined or discarded altogether. If playing planning poker does not yield dividends over the course of several sprints, then the team should assess whether to continue investing its time in doing that. Most teams utilize the standup in some way, but if someone who is straddling multiple projects is already well integrated into the team, it is not uncommon for that person to attend standups only when his presence is necessary and skip the rest. And if the team agrees to this and it works, then this is an appropriate adaption of the methodology. The methods are not sacred, they are just guidelines known to be effective, and the team should not be afraid to question them once it has seen how they work for a given project. If, however, if the infrequent attendance erodes trust or inhibits communication, then the team must find another way.

Perhaps, the split resource needs to take on less work each sprint to allow enough time to attend the meetings and build relationships. It might be worth mentioning that it would be very unusual to completely eliminate the daily standup altogether. Even for teams across multiple time zones, some form of daily communication summarizing progress and identifying problems happens in one form or another. Having a meeting that occurs every day serves the purpose of good hygiene for keeping the team in the habit of interacting with each other and providing transparency into their actions. Many elements of Scrum get tweaked by different teams, but some version of this event should remain a part of the routine.

To look at what it means to value the project over process, we take the example of two imaginary teams at the same company. One team is committed to its daily standups, planning meetings, retrospectives, and daily review of burndown charts. However, the standups routinely run 30 to 45 minutes rather than the recommended 15 minutes. Planning meetings similarly run long, and the team is overcommitted for each sprint. Some team members are often scheduled at 200 percent of their capacity; and while the team reviews these numbers, adjustment to the workload are not made. Retrospectives are awkward and do not contain candid communication or resolution of issues. Not surprisingly, the team routinely fails to complete the scope of work it took on for the sprint.

At the same imaginary company is a second team, which does not conduct planning meetings but allows the individuals to estimate its tasks at a high level only to the degree they need to in order to identify how much work they can fit into the sprint. The team does not track velocity, but it does deliver everything on time and within sprint. Planning and commitment meetings require little time, as the team has a very clear understanding of the work. Daily standups are quick and do not serve as the single point of communication. The team has a sense of where it is in the cycle and what work remains.

The first team feels that it is Agile: It can check the box next to all the steps it has been told are necessary. And, since team members do not feel they are empowered to change, resigned acceptance seems the only answer. But they are not delivering working code within the time to which they commit, and many tasks go uncompleted during each sprint. The fact that so many meetings are running long is an indication of insufficient communication among team members and that they are not seeking out each other outside the scheduled events. A quiet retrospective indicates a level of discomfort among the team members that is inhibiting problem solving. The second team agreed to skip or minimize many of the steps prescribed by Scrum but the level of communication is very high and the members are executing successfully everything to which they commit and deliver the product on time, with high quality, containing the features they originally scoped, and with a great user experience.

If process is the success metric, then it might be tempting to describe the first team as successful. However, it is pretty unlikely that the team members feel that way, even if they cannot actually put into words what exactly is going wrong. If we instead look at the project work, it becomes very clear that the team is struggling. The second team may be skipping a few meetings and techniques, but the work is getting done quickly and with a healthy level of iteration and collaboration. The steps described by any Agile methodology are helpful only if they help the team make progress on the project and supports it to do the work more efficiently. If that is not happening, then the team needs to take stock and decide if its application of a given technique needs to be refined, if the particular tool needs to re-evaluated as to whether it should be in the repertoire, or if the team simply needs to try harder to make it work.

While it is important to make sure that the process is working and the team is not engaging in time-wasting activities or simply failing to accomplish its purpose, equally important is to go through the prescribed process before making modifications. Whether a team has chosen Scrum, Kanban, or something else, follow it as prescribed before discarding elements of it. This is not to say that the team should have a fear of modifying the process, but skipping over pieces of the methodology without actually trying them then having the team discuss its efficacy might mean missing out on applying techniques that may have sounded odd or time consuming but could be very helpful or easy to do. Teams often grumble about the daily standups and the planning meetings, but in the end, both events add tremendous value and they rarely get discarded. The other reason to go through the process before tweaking it is so that the changes can be precise and impactful. It may be that you do not need to eliminate the daily standup, but streamlining them so that some functional areas can have a single representative at the meetings to make it more efficient for teams that straddle multiple projects. To fix a problem, you have to actually know what it is and why you are fixing it, if you want to get to the right solution.

TEAM DYNAMICS

Ideally, the values of the larger organization would be such that moving to Agile would be a process that dovetails seamlessly with Agile principles. Archie Miller describes a carefully curated culture at Snagajob.com that, by design, works to balance the individual with the higher-level goals. Having such an environment makes the transition much less painful, because the core values expressed in the Agile Manifesto are already embedded in the corporate culture and the everyday behavior of the staff. It is even better if the company has made such a commitment to Agile that they invest in facilities to support a cooperative and collaborative environment. Christina York describes the kind of facilities support that many of us can only dream of; where the UX team members actually have two seats. One seat is with their project team, so that they can spend some of their time being colocated, and the other seat is with their fellow UX teammates, so that they can share product knowledge across the UX team as well as function as a cohesive group. This setup also balances the need for privacy by providing phone booths but still recognizes the need for collaboration with its flexible seating assignments for "chickens."

There is no question that being in such a nurturing environment makes it easier to make the move to Agile methods. But, many of us are not as lucky as Archie and Christina, and this does not mean that we cannot achieve a certain amount success with these development processes, despite our organizational cultures. Multiple office spaces are great, a really neat idea, but they are not required. Many teams have managed to engender a solid team environment across continents, so sitting on a different floor than your team is not the end of the world. An Agile friendly organization smooths the way for an Agile adoption, but it is not an absolute necessity, since most of the activities occur at the local project level. The only culture that is critical to the success of a given project is that of the project team. A dysfunctional team in an amazing company can still fail. But, if the team's dynamic is healthy and communicative, it can survive and thrive in the most hostile of corporate atmospheres. And, if the team's dynamic is not where it needs to be, then the team and not the organization can correct this.

Just as it is important to value the outcome of the project over the details of the process, it is crucial to make the healthy functioning of the team a priority. This means breaking down silos and not writing off issues because a problem affects another functional area. If the QE team is floundering because it has a hard time keeping track of the progress of the features and which items are done, this is a sign of a larger communication problem. As a UX person, when you hear an issue like that raised, it might be tempting to write it off as something that the development team and quality team will sort out, as it has no impact on your work. However, the only way that an Agile team can be effective is if it operates at a high level of efficiency, and that requires a cohesive team. If something is not working for one member of the team, then it is not working for the entire team.

This is something about which UX teams need to be especially conscious. Since we are so used to shrinking to fit the time allowed or just making it work, there is a tendency to try to get the work done and suffer in silence if the schedule is too tight or not enough time is planned to incorporate customer feedback into the design process. However, as an Agile team member, it is everyone's responsibility to flag obstacles and work with the scrum master to remove them. If the UX person cannot complete tasks on time, perhaps he or she is overcommitted to the sprint and needs to adjust, take a sprint to do some high-level design, or discuss the requirements more thoroughly with other team members or stakeholders. The problem belongs to the team and can be solved by the team.

This goes beyond just being a good team member, a typical Agile schedule contains little slack; and if one team member is having a challenge, the downstream effects are immediate and often snowball quickly to turn into bigger problems. An issue does not affect just the UX person but the developer who needs to implement the design, the QE person who needs to write a test case, and the documentation person who needs to write the help for it. It is important to recognize any symptoms that might indicate an underlying problem, identify the root cause, and come up with a targeted solution. Delaying the work of one, or all, of these team members can have implications for the overall timeline of the project. Making life better for one team member increases the quality of life for the entire team.

Another challenge that some UX teams struggle with is that this process does not lend itself to what Christina York refers to as "design divas." For the manager of a UX team making this transition, that is an area where team members might require some coaching and support. Some people are used to working on a design and handing off the resulting work of art to the development team for implementation, which may or may not match the design intention. For some UX professionals, this is the most comfortable way to work. It allows them some quiet time to really think through the design problem and work at their own pace to hash out a solution. Also, a certain amount of glory accrues to the person who solves a tough problem with a fabulously elegant solution that is presented in highly polished, pixel-perfect screenshots. You can spend time looking for around for inspiration and craft some gorgeous images that impress everyone. It can be tough to let go of being the hero who saves the day and always comes up with the coolest solution. When a UX team engages in an Agile process, these contributors need to get comfortable with the idea of working collaboratively and not necessarily owning the design. Some rock stars can learn to be part of a band, while others will be more comfortable remaining solo acts; for them, Agile will not be a very good fit.

COMMUNICATION

How do you improve the health of the project and the team? Communication is the grease that makes those wheels turn. The process provides a support for communication, creating opportunities and reasons to communicate and identifying the places where interaction is most important. However, the teams

FIGURE 4.2
Communication.

must engage in these activities with a genuine interest in sharing information and learning about what other teammates are doing. Otherwise, the structure only highlights existing dysfunctions. The process provides only the framework; the team needs to bring the right attitude to bear on the work. The good news is that good communication skills can be taught and nurtured if they do not exist already.

Events around grooming the backlog afford the chance to contribute to and discuss the user stories, which is where the team can exert the most influence over the process. Since these items are constructed to communicate the user viewpoint, any team discussion around them furthers a customer-centric perspective. The team can define acceptance criteria, specify the definition of *done*, and break the user story into specific, actionable tasks. Not only are the user stories structured in such a way that the team becomes habituated to speaking from the perspective of the user, but all the discussion around the user stories create a shared understanding of the customer needs. The work done around stories to turn them into tasks also serves to create a sense of ownership over the work. That is quite an accomplishment for something essentially the equivalent of functional requirements.

Sprint planning activities allow each person to commit to only what he or she can execute and control his or her workload. Not only does it give the team members the authority to choose what they can realistically achieve, but since they made the commitment explicitly, they are responsible for honoring it. Often, accountability can be diffused in traditional processes, and when no one has clear responsibility for something, there is also no real ownership and things tend to falter. The planning sessions also provide an opportunity to discuss a given task with other team members, if clarity is required.

Daily standups are designed to flag obstacles that need to be addressed and let the rest of the team know what each person is working on. Not only does this help catch and resolve problems as they occur, it creates the habit of frequent communication and teaches the team that talking and sharing information does not need to be a time-intensive activity. With its specific format and short time limit, it models the example that a meeting should be productive and efficient and not be held just for the sake of having a meeting. This meeting ensures that everyone knows what each other is doing, and it accomplishes that goal every time. This is a definite improvement over the more traditional meeting, where everyone's eyes glaze over as they listen to endless status reports or repeatedly glance at clock as someone rambles on in an attempt to fill the time. Even though people new to Agile often chafe over this meeting, as they consider it disruptive to the rhythm of their day, most teams end up keeping it in some form or another. It is a cheap investment and serves as good communication hygiene for the team, not unlike brushing your teeth in the morning.

The retrospectives at the end of the sprint are meant be a forum to discuss what went well, identify the opportunities for improvement, and suggest potential solutions. This meeting requires a degree of candor that is not quite as necessary in other discussions; this is the designated time to talk openly about problems that need resolution and work together to solve them. The Agile values and the intention of the meeting give everyone the permission and freedom to raise concerns without being branded as a complainer, and it channels the discussion in a productive direction. To avoid having a gripe session, there should be a habit of presenting a concern and immediately moving the conversation to identifying the root cause and possible actions to correct it. The ability to have a candid retrospective may not happen during the first sprint, but as the team builds trust and confidence in the process, the dialog will become easier to engage in.

These checkpoints should not be the only moments where mindless conversation occurs, they really are meant to set the tone and create habits, so that the team members get accustomed to working with each other. Even for teams experienced in Agile, if the team itself is made up of people who have not worked together previously, then this might still require effort until the team gels. Even when the individuals are used to the practice of Agile, they may not be used to working with each other, and the meetings give them the chance to orient to one another. If team members do not interact with each other outside these meetings, that will show up pretty quickly, as the scheduled meetings will routinely run long and not be very productive. The team members need to be in constant communication and comfortable reaching out to each other when they need something. In-person chats, emails, instant messages (IM), and the occasional formal meeting are great mechanisms for between-meeting inter-actions. The key is frequency and effectiveness. If you have a teammate who is more comfortable chatting over IM than face to face, then accommodate that and make it the preferred way to work with the person, if it results in more conversation and a better working relationship. Face to face is ideal, preferred, and should be encouraged, but individual styles should be respected.

Also take a look at what team building activities might be helpful. Collabo-rative design sessions can be a fun activity that brings the team closer together, especially if food is involved. While the team has many chances to connect and bond over work-based events, do not overlook the value of simply having lunch together. Spending a little time to get to know each other outside the context of meetings and talking about what you did over the weekend can go a long way to helping new team members feel like part of the group.

If the team is not entirely colocated, then there is a greater reliance on electronic methods. Austin Govella talks about having a virtual workroom that is a safe place for the UX people to interact and that allows him to bridge the gap with his colleague in another country. It is like having a virtual conference room, where he can put sketches up on the wall and have meetings. Having a persis-tent and dedicated place where design ideas and dialog can be shared, in privacy, can be the electronic equivalent of a recurring design meeting. Wiki pages can also help facilitate the communication between remote reams, but as they tend to be more public, they may not necessarily be a tool for engendering candid discussion. In addition to the day-to-day communication and dialog, some amount of design documentation may be helpful to facilitate a common understanding of the design, when teams are working at a distance. While Agile emphasizes not producing documentation for the sake of recordkeeping, nothing prohibits the production of an artifact if it benefits the team. Of course, it is best if that document is one of the items already naturally produced as a part of the design process—sketches, wireframes, html mockups.

Share these electronically, adding comments where they are needed. It is fairly important to share these items when they are created along the way, as they can help to provide insight into what the UX team is doing. Put your work up on the walls for on-site team members to see, post it virtually for remote colleagues. The purpose of doing this is not just to share information, some of the items on the wall might have no annotationsl, but to build a strong design culture. Designs that are tangible and somewhat omnipresent help immerse the whole team in the work of creating a great user experience. The UI stops being something on which the UX team works and specifies and becomes a living thing they look at every time they head to the kitchen. This may spark conversation and ideas that might not otherwise occur and builds a much greater awareness of design.

Regardless of where people sit, it is important that the ideas in one team member's head somehow make their way to the rest of the team. It is equally important that the information does not just go out but is processed by the others and that a healthy dialog ensues. Just like the events and ceremonies, the goal is not to have conversation for the sake of having a conversation but to engage in a real exchange of thoughts and ideas. Otherwise, everyone will drive each other crazy with nonstop chatter without actually adding any real value to the process or the product. Creating a genuine discourse is what allows the team to produce the best work possible.

DEFINE THE BIG PICTURE

Most of the people I interviewed for the case studies mentioned the need for an overall vision to help guide the work done during the course of a release. Agile teams can be especially susceptible to getting lost in the details of the work and lose track of how their tasks are meant to fit together. While many UX people mention the need for providing a framework for the design work, everyone seems to have a favorite way of providing that.

Personas can be a very effective technique to give the context to the design efforts. They are easy to produce and work into everything that the UX person touches. Because they are so easy to remember, it is easy for the entire team to use them as a touchstone to inform the decisions made throughout the process. Some UX people mention having a high-level design in place at the beginning to serve as a roadmap for the rest of the detailed design, which is developed during the release. This may not always be possible, but something visual that people can keep in the back of their minds as they move through the release can be a powerful tool to contribute to a coherent-looking release. This high-level design can be as simple as a workflow diagram or a quick sketch of one or two main screens. It cannot be too detailed, since it is created at the beginning of the cycle, when so much has yet to be defined. And it needs to be sufficiently vague so as not to stifle creative solutions that might be uncovered during the detailed design. Having such a design document in place from the beginning can serve as a veritable roadmap for the UI and a reference point for the entire team. Another tool often mentioned is a reference library. This tool is best used to increase consistency across the product rather than to indicate a specific design direction. However, these can be very useful when pulling several products together, extending the reach of a scarce UX resource, or minimizing the amount of unnecessary variation within a product.

TRAINING

Every successful team engaged in some form of Agile training, with many of them receiving training and coaching from Jeff Patton himself. Since many of the teams that are struggling had little or no training and are working a bit blind, there seems to be a pretty clear connection between training and a better implementation of Agile. On the extreme end, Suzanne O'Kelley and her teammates were able to participate in the LUXr residency program ("10-Week Residency," n.d.), a 10=week program where they were able to work on their real project problems in an environment where they received coaching. This level of training can be a factor in success, not just because it means the team receives a good, consistent education, but also because it indicates an organizational commitment to the process and a supportive management team. Other organizations routinely bring in coaches, so that the training is not a single event when they first begin to engage in Agile activities, but is a continuous effort that allows the teams to refine their process and get the guidance that they need to evolve. This also benefits employees who are new to the organization and were not onboard for earlier rounds of training. Not only have they the chance to be trained, they do so in the context of the environment in which they will work. This achieves consistency in the application of the process and a reinforcement of the best way to work at that company.

Unfortunately, not all of us can have Jeff Patton to provide coaching or attend a residency program. This does not mean that no other options can provide similar, although certainly not equal, value. Christina York started out with one user interface engineering session Jeff Patton presented. While no replacement for in-person coaching, it can be a very inexpensive way to get a lot of high-quality information into the hands of the team. It is even better if the entire team attends the training and then debriefs afterward over what the members learned. With one fairly inexpensive event, you can achieve some of the same education and team building results that come from a more formal training. You miss out on the tailored content and discussion, but it is a great replacement when the other options are not on the table. Another thing to bear in mind is that, after Christina's team achieved some success and the process was more ingrained at the company, there was more support for having team members attend conferences to stay current on Agile techniques. The organization saw that the process was working, and as time went on, it chose to invest in honing the skills that contributed to that productivity. Her tactics shows how to get your foot in the door and prove that investing in training for the team can contribute to good results and encourage continued investment.

However, even if you are in a situation with virtually no budget or organizational support for training, you should still engage in some kind of learning to equip yourself and get a good understanding of the road ahead of you. Many resources are available that require little or no money. When Jeff Gothelf started out, he simply reached out to practitioners who had experience and arranged to talk about their stories. It is amazing how generous perfect strangers are willing to be with their time, and a 45-minute conversation with someone can yield tremendous benefit and inspiration. Books, newsgroups, blogs, and local professional groups provide many opportunities to learn what your colleagues are doing in your neighborhood or around the world. Some of these resources might be broadly focused on Agile in general, while others are more specific to Agile UX. Explore the options available in both categories.

As much as possible, these resources should be leveraged for team-building events. Either the UX team should engage in training activities together or the entire project team can participate in the activities. Read the blog articles together and discuss them, have a book club, and share links to cool websites. Do not be afraid to share articles on Agile UX with other functional areas, after all they need to feel comfortable with how the UX team supports the project. Given how much training can contribute to the establishment of a high-functioning team, do as much of it as you can, and continue to do it even after you feel comfortable with Agile. It is an evolving methodology, and new information and ideas are coming out all the time that can inspire and help you solve problems. Your process and your team is evolving all the time as well, so a technique that held no interest for you a year ago might be incredibly relevant to you now.

Resources for learning about agile

When first starting out, it can often be difficult to even know where to look to learn more about Agile and Agile UX. I compiled a list of resources that I found to be helpful, but new forums are always cropping up, so do not be afraid to put your favorite search engine to use to find more.

Book

There are many books about Agile as a development process and quite a few of them get good reviews. There are fewer books about Agile UX, but this is likely to change. One book is a good starting point, no matter what your area of interest is or what you are looking to learn about, *Agile Software Development* by Alistair Cockburn (2002). This is the primer and the definitive book about Agile software development. The focus is on development, this is not a book that is going to speak about user experience or product design. Since this is *the* book about Agile and Alistair Cockburn is one of the original authors of the Agile Manifesto, reading this book provides a great insight into the values that started it all.

Online resources

Many resources are available online—blogs, discussion forums, and training. I like online options because they have so much immediacy, you can find what you need when you need it. This allows you to stay current with the newest ideas and techniques. You can access these items from anywhere in the world and supplement your locally available offerings. The list contains the sites I found most helpful and informative, presented in no particular order. Bear in mind that this is just the tip of the iceberg of what it out there.

- **LinkedIn, Agile Experience Design group.** For those of you who have LinkedIn accounts, joining this group, moderated by Anders Ramsay, is a great way to participate in or listen to conversations about Agile with a specific focus on design. It also lets you see who is interested in the same issues ast you and puts a face to the broader community. Much diversity is found in the type of questions that arise in this forum. It is an easy way to hear what people are talking about and learn from the ensuing discussion.

- **www.agileproductdesign.com.** This is Jeff Patton's website, and it is a goldmine of information about Agile, with a focus on incorporating user-centered design into the process. On this site is his blog, an archive of some of his presentations, links to articles he wrote, descriptions of the training he provides, and a calendar of the events in which he is participating. It is incredibly comprehensive and one of the single best resources for designers and researchers interested in learning more about Agile. It is not too strong a statement to say that, if you only go to one site to learn about Agile, you should go to this site.

- **Jeffgothelf.com.** Jeff Gothelf and his experience at TheLadders.com constitute one of the case studies in this book. Jeff is also a thought leader in the Lean UX movement and has quite a bit of insight to share on the topic. In fact, he wrote a book, *Lean UX: Applying Lean Principles to Improve User Experience* (2013), on the topic. His blog, links to published articles, and many of his presentations can be found on this site. There are articles and presentations about his experience of bringing Agile to TheLadders.com and you can also find his presentation "Lean UX: Getting out of the Deliverables Business." So much valuable content and up-to-the-moment discussion on the most current issues are on the site that this should be required reading for UX person finding his or her way with Agile.

- **www.balancedteam.org**. The organization's description says, "Balanced Team is a group of people who are interested in furthering processes and methodologies to create great things." The site has a cross-discipline focus, but many of the discussion center around UX. The blog on this site is a great read, slides from the Balanced Team Conference are also posted, complete with audio. If you cannot attend conferences or training events, spend some time with these materials.

- **www.agilemanifesto.org.** This is where the Agile Manifesto, and its principles, live. There are no blogs or discussion groups, and a little history. This is the source of it all. You might see the Agile Manifesto reprinted or referenced, including in this book, but it is worth a visit just to know that you have gone to the original source and seen the original text as it was first written.

- **www.scrumalliance.org**. This site is focused on Scrum, specifically from a development viewpoint. Some interesting articles are to be found under the Resource Center, as well as some information about training. For a nondeveloper, the most valuable part of the site might be its "Scrum 101" page, under "Scrum Basics." In a few paragraphs, it tells you everything you need to know, at a high level, about Scrum.

- **www.extremeprogramming.org**. The first thing you see when you get to this site are the words "Extreme Programming: A Gentle Introduction" and that it exactly what you get on the homepage. The rest of the site is more geared toward developers, providing links to white papers, articles, and books. If you are looking for some quick information about Extreme Programming, the first page of the site is the right place to go.

- **Andersramsay.com.** This site is broadly focused on user experience, but Anders is also an Agile coach and has many postings that speak to Agile and UX. On this site, you can find his presentation "Learning to Play UX Rugby," which is not only entertaining but describes some interesting techniques for UX practitioners. "The UX of User Stories," Parts 1 and 2, are great blog posts about what user stories mean to the UX practitioners. It contains some practical advice, and these posts are very helpful for a UX person looking to influence his or her Agile environment.

- **UIE.com.** This is the site for Jared Spool's User Interface Engineering consultancy; it provides a variety of content on Agile, including training and events that the company offers on the topic. There are also several blog posts and articles on Agile. In Jared's article "Essential UX Layers for Agile and Lean Design Teams," he describes a mental model for thinking about UX and how to fit it into Agile that is quite interesting and can help a UX team define, or possibly redefine, its approach to integrating with Agile methods.

- **Mountaingoatsoftware.com.** I admit that part of why I like this site as much as I do is because the company makes the coolest set of planning poker cards, with goats on them. The site, which is done by Agile coach, consultant, and author Mike Cohn, has a wealth of information about Agile and Scrum. It is development focused and aimed toward educating people about the practice of Scrum specifically and Agile in general. Many training offerings are available, including some very reasonably priced "eLearning" sessions, which would be a very helpful resource for organizations where training is needed but there is not much budget to provide any.

- **Agile-UX.com.** This site belongs to Jean Claude Grosjean, an Agile coach and UX consultant. He has some great presentations and blog posts, but my favorite by far is "Collaborative Workshop and the Letter to Santa Claus" series of blog posts. This series is probably one of the most entertaining, adorable, and accessible examples of collaborative design.

- **UXMatters.com.** If you have not been to this site before, it is essentially an online magazine of really good articles about UX. As a whole, it is not Agile specific, but the subject comes up in a handful of articles, authored by experts. "Clash of the Titans: Agile and UCD" by Richard Cecil definitely wins the award for best title but is also a very thoughtful look at what Agile means for user-centered design. "Developing UX Agility: Letting Go of Perfection" is an interesting case study from the UX team at ProQuest about their adoption of Agile. I also found that the panel Q&A in "Integrating UX into an Agile Environment" to provide a nice summary of common concerns with great perspectives from a variety of contributors.

- **Johnnyholland.com,** As the site says, "Johnny Holland is an open collective exploring interaction design. Oh. and Johnny loves you." How can you not love a site that loves you back? That aside, it is a really cool site with a broad focus on interaction design and frequent contributors who bring the discussion around to Agile and Lean UX. Greg Laugero's article, "Lean UX Is Dead. Long Live Lean UX," is a thought provoking take on Lean UX as a strategic, rather than tactical, tool. A lot of content on this site will make you think differently about Agile specifically and design in general, so explore it at your leisure.

- **Nomad8.com,** Sandy Mamoli, whose title is "director of all things Agile" at Nomad8, has an Agile blog on this site that contains some of the most practical advice on Agile I have seen. Sometimes, the common discourse about Agile can get a little abstract or too philosophical for everyday use, but her posts on things, like "Should We Choose Agile or Iterative Development?" are accessible without being simplistic and her checklists for seemingly everything are a great resource for teams in the early stages of Agile adoption. Her "10 Ways to Fail with Agile" presentation is well worth viewing, and not just because it is a presentation that does not use PowerPoint.

- **leansoftwareengineering.com.** This site is full of essays from Corey Ladas and Bernie Thompson and their thoughts on a variety of Agile topics, including Scrumban, on which Corey actually wrote the book. While the content is a few years old, it is still relevant and interesting and worth a read for their practical take on Agile processes, especially if your team is interested in exploring the use of Kanban (or Scrumban).

- **Slideshare.com.** This slide deck repository has everything, if you are willing to do a little digging or have time to get lost in the related links. Not every deck stands on its own very well, but so many presentations are there that you can easily move along to one that does. It also turns up more specific content than your average search engine, so it can make a great jumping off point for your Agile research.

ADAPT AND EVOLVE

The most powerful moment in Jeff Gothelf's story is when he has a UX team-only retrospective, and the team shows the flowchart it created, where every path leads to the conclusion that Agile "creates a negative environment that fosters failure and generates low morale." This very compelling that this moment is not the end of the story, but just one of the turning points in the team's Agile evolution. The team examined the problems, sorted out a few key issues, and kept going, eventually realizing a very successful process. The key was to have the kind of environment where it was safe for the team to express its dissatisfaction and acknowledge that a problem needed to be addressed. But, it is not enough for issues to be brought up—that is the easy part—commitment is needed to work to find a solution and a rhythm that is a better fit for the team. Most if not all teams will find that their transition is a rocky road, and rarely does team get it right from Day 1. But, with an environment committed to making things work for the team, it is possible to get over the initial hurdles.

As a UX person, it is highly likely that you will work with more than one project team. This means that even though you have managed to achieve an organic rhythm with one team, you might find yourself starting all over again with a new team. And perhaps, this time, the team members are scattered all over the world; the team has less Agile experience than your previous team; the team already began the project without you; any number of less than ideal factors can affect your preferred approach to Agile. This is where you adapt. Every Agile project is different because it comprises unique individuals. Feeling skilled at the process is the first step, the next is to have mastery at working as efficiently as possible with every group you support. For less-experienced practitioners, adaptation can be challenging, since it is hard to know whether you are making a reasonable and appropriate change to the process or abandoning it. Training can go a long way in giving a higher level of confidence with this, and returning to the Agile core values and principles helps keep you on track. More-experienced practitioners need to keep an open mind and look

FIGURE 4.3
Adapt and evolve.

for opportunities to increase communication and enhance teamwork while accommodating whatever logistical challenges might be present. So much evolution occurs with Agile methods, especially with respect to UX, that it is almost impossible not to learn new tricks that help your own growth as an Agile UX practitioner.

CASE STUDY—SARAH KAHN, ADZERK

While there are many interesting stories, it is rare to find one that embodies so many of the success criteria. Sarah Kahn and Adzerk are that special situation. They are an example of what can happen when the team focuses on how the least amount of process can be used to support their work, working together and getting along well, healthy communication and interactions, and adaptation of the methods to fit the group's needs.

Sarah is a UX engineer at Adzerk, a small startup whose software helps content publishers optimize their advertising inventory. As the fourth employee, and currently the only UX person on the staff, she is in the unique position of helping

define the process as it evolved at the company. Adzerk has a small team and a very strong culture of collaboration and communication, which it consciously created. The decision to adopt an Agile process was born out of the need to have a more-defined process in place as the team grew, married with a strong dislike for doing anything that takes the team away from writing code or introduces bureaucracy into the members lives. Sarah's story tells of an organic process that works very well to support the needs of the team and its customers.

When Sarah joined the company, the entire team could sit around a table and talk, so there was no real need for any kind of a process. They were able to simply decide what needed to be done and do it. As the company grew, it recognized the need for a more structured framework to support the development efforts and keep things moving forward in an organized way. However, many of the developers had negative experiences with heavy-handed traditional processes and did not want to spend their time doing paperwork or estimation exercises. They wanted to use the barest method possible, which naturally led them to Agile and its most lightweight method, Kanban. Sarah describes the company's version of Kanban as being more "Kanban inspired" than a by-the-book implementation of the process. The company took what it needed from Kanban and adapted the process to make it their own. As a UX person, Sarah was accustomed to fitting her work in wherever she could and in a lightweight manner. Since formal tools are expensive, she is used to making do with what she had. She always relied on pencil and paper and whiteboard sketching to get her work done. This spirit of working quickly and lightly fits well into her small startup and makes her transition to working with Kanban a little more seamless.

Adzerk originally thought it would have three columns for its Kanban board—"UX," "Working," and "Acceptance." Once ity started examining the workflow, it realized that the UX work really fell into two phases. The first phase would be the time when Sarah is doing initial design work and testing with customers. In the second phase, she would be debugging the designs and refining them. The real difference in moving an item from the first phase to the second is that it indicates that the UI design is ready for the backend to be developed. The second phase still holds the potential for rework, but the design is solid and stable enough for some coding to begin. Sarah also does the UI front-end development, so this piece of work is being done by her within the UX phases. Having adjusted so that the UX work is in two phases, the resulting Kanban board has four columns "UX Working," "UX Acceptance," "Working," and "Acceptance.. One of the firm rules is that a card moves only forward, never backward, on the board. Customer testing can occur either before the UX working phase or during it, as needed. Sarah also talks to customers as a part of rolling out new features, to validate them before turning feature flags on for a broader audience. The only drawback in talking to customers so frequently is a certain amount of feedback burnout because of the high frequency of customer contact and feedback solicitation, so Sarah is always looking for new ways to recruit users and get information to help the designs. When she is looking to explore an issue like language or buttons, she uses social media to gather feedback.

A task can be created and added to the team's backlog in four ways. An item can be a bug fix from a previous version. Sarah also works with customer support to identify rough spots and feature requests that need to be included in the backlog. They also include competitive features that are identified internally, often by their CEO. The final category is contract-driven feature work. When an item is created and put into the backlog, generally, some initial discussion takes place around it, maybe even a quick whiteboard session to do some design thinking. When the backlog is populated, each item is given an initial T-shirt size representing a rough level of estimate. XS might represent a half day worth of work, and L might map to a week's effort. If it is larger than that, then it requires the team to break it down further. Each item has two sizes, a UX size and a development size. Sarah assigns the UX T-shirt size and the developer that pulls the task assigns the development size. The team does no formal planning, since it has no traditional release cycle. There are no branches in the code base, once you commit code it goes in to production. This does not mean that the team does no planning at all; it is just more loosely structured. For more information on how Adzerk uses Kanban, see their blog (http://team.adzerk.com/post/12289837931/agile-ux-and-kanban-at-adzerk?goback¼%2Egna_3315113.)

The company started using AgileZen to help it to manage its backlog. It has no formal roadmap as much as a big wish list of items. It found that constantly staring at huge list of items could be a bit overwhelming, so it is useful to have a tool to manage the list. Each week, team members pick a few items to focus on for the week or two duration of the sprint. Sprints themselves can be of flexible length, depending on the situation. If a customer has a specific need and date that needs to be met for contractual reasons, then the timing and duration of the sprints are geared toward supporting that effort. One of the benefits to using AgileZen is that it is very visual, which makes it easy to see what is happening to the tasks. If things are stuck, then the column turns red, and everyone can sees that there is a blockage and where it is. This allows the entire team to have clarity on where the issues are and when they need to drop what they are doing to pull together to resolve a problem and move things forward. Sarah also feels that it reminds everyone that all of them are working on the same thing. The fact that team members are able to work like this is a testament to their ability to work in a highly collaborative and communicative way. It is important to understand that the ability to work in such a natural rhythm is a result of this culture. It would not be possible for a larger company with big projects teams and a history of communication issues to work this way and be effective.

The team has a pretty cool way of managing the features. Since there are no branches and code submission is automatically part of the production code, they put in a simple "if" statement that allows them to control the visibility of and access to a feature. The team built in a simple UI to allow product management and customer support people to turn flags on and off, although the simplicity of the dialog started to decrease as more and more feature flags were created. They also found that, once the feature was released and the feature flag turned on for a customer, it might be forgotten about for broader distribution. This happened partly because the task would no longer be in AgileZen, since it had been completed and the features required a certain amount of time to solidify and have the bugs worked out. There also needed to be an opportunity to notify customers about new features, so that the ground was not constantly shifting beneath them. Given the potential for a lag between the task leaving AgileZen and being turned on for everyone, the company needed a way to track the items. The team gives the feature flags their own Kanban board. This board has three lanes: "UX," "Dev," and "Ready." A card is created at the same time as the feature flag. A date is associated with each item as it moves through the columns, so it is easy to see if an item is stalled in one section or another. Once a feature is robust, Sarah has a list of beta testers to exercise the feature. They agree to use the feature for a week, and if their feedback is positive, then she can turn the feature on for everyone. Once a feature is "on," information about it needs to be posted to the company's blog and the customer support team also does a write-up. See Adzerk's blog post on managing feature flags for more details on this technique (http://team.adzerk.com/post/20129347973/a-word-on-managing-feature-flags).

Since Sarah was one of the earliest employees, she has been able to be a very active participant in defining the process and how UX fits into things. She acknowledges that she has been quite lucky and management has been very supportive, essentially telling her to figure out what she needs and go ahead with it. She also admits that it always helps to be in a place where UX is valued. While she is currently the only UX person, she is fairly confident that the process currently in place could extend to accommodate more UX team members. When asked if she would practice Agile techniques if she ever found herself in an environment with a more traditional development process, Sarah thinks that she would. She feels that there is still room to fit in Lean UX, even in a waterfall environment. She thinks that, if she were in that situation, she would talk about it in terms of timeline to get it accepted into the process. Since waterfall methods move so slowly, she feels that there is plenty of room for doing smaller cycles and fitting iterations into that.

When I asked Sarah what advice she would give to UX folks trying to find their way with Agile, her first piece of advice is not to read a lot of Agile books or worry so much about your process. She feels that if you worry about your customers and how to meet their needs and figure out to support that, you will work out the process that enables it. She quotes the Agile Manifesto, "People over Process." The other advice she gives is for the UX team to be constantly communicating and chatting with the rest of their teammates. This means engaging each other in emails, virtual chatting, and face-to-face discussions to keep the flow of information going and support relationship building. She recommends instituting team lunches and getting outside of your department. Getting to know each other as people and connecting in ways outside the project work helps the team to gel and be better able to work together. Sarah acknowledges that Adzerk is really lucky about the blend of people that it has, although this has been a fairly conscious part of the hiring process. It has been able to hire for fit. The resulting team is a group of self-motivated individuals who are friendly and close knit. They have team lunches and spend time together in addition to executing work projects. Their CEO has been very clear about the culture he wants to create. He wants a company of friendly, easygoing people and has mandated that there be no more than one formal meeting a week. She also thinks that it helps that everyone on the team has worked in other places before Adzerk, and many of them had negative experiences with project management and want to avoid recreating those experiences.

Sarah likes that working in an Agile way virtually removes all the friction from her job. She feels empowered to do what she needs to do without having to justify it. She has laid out the process, everyone who works with her knows what it is, and she is able to just do it. Such a transparent process helps build the trust around how the team works. It is a very collaborative way to work. Nothing goes into the backlog without a little discussion. The company is so committed to this transparency that it extends that to its customers as much as possible. However, when you empower your users so much, it can be easy to get derailed by their requests. The way that they manage this is to just be honest with the customers. If customers have asked for something that is in the backlog but not likely to be released for a few months, the company just tells the customer that it is actively being worked on. It acknowledge that the request is a good idea but that the customer probably will not see it for a while. This works, because the company has credibility with the customers from the work done previously. Sarah is also able to leverage these customer requests to recruit for usability testing. The transparency that the company creates with its customers through the constant interactions, blog posts, and the collaborative spirit builds a high levels of trust, which makes this dynamic possible. The team blogs not just about product features but also about the process;d these blog posts can be found at team.adzerk.com.

The level of transparency that this team has about its process, both internally and externally, is a testament to its commitment to creating a circle of trust. The posts doe not just advertise their successes but include candid discussions that speak to the evolution of the process and acknowledge things that it realizes require refinement. This kind of self-awareness and sharing of information shows how deeply ingrained Agile values are in the culture. This is why it can take a very lightweight method like Kanban, use it, and modify it to fit its needs. By nature, thecompany is highly collaborative, Agile, and lean; it just needs a framework around what it does so that its natural process is extensible and can accommodate a growing team.

Key points

- Often, we focus on the mechanics and tactics of the process. We look to meetings and tools to help build a certain culture. However, Sarah's point that the team is cohesive because the members spend time together getting to know each other as humans is a something often overlooked. Sometimes, instead of having a retrospective or hashing out issues, we should invest time getting to know each other as people and talking about things other than work. Have lunch, maybe even off site, as a team and talk about what interests you. Team building occurs in many ways, and it always contributes to a better working environment.

- Do what feels right for your team, especially if your team members really know who they are. It might be a little unusual to have a separate Kanban board to track feature flags, but it works for the team and came out of identifying a gap in the process. They could been hung up on whether doing the second board was Lean enough or properly Kanban, but that would have been wasting energy instead of solving the problem.

CASE STUDY—ANONYMOUS 3, A COMPANY SPECIALIZING IN DIRECT MARKETING PRODUCTS

Success stories are educational, but it can be equally informative to look at teams having more difficulty to see what contributes to their difficulties. This case study tells the story of a team that is missing most of the success criteria, and the UX staff member finds herself in a situation that is confusing and chaotic.

Anonymous is a senior designer at a company that develops Web-based products for small customers to facilitate interactions with their own customer bases. On the surface, it might sound as if her company is employing the same Kanban techniques that Archie Miller describes in his story; however, the result is drastically different. This story stands in stark contrast to Snagajob.com and serves as a reminder that the process is not the biggest driver of success but the people and the culture.

When she started with the company a few years ago, the teams had already adopted Agile and some had moved to Kanban, or at least a loose interpretation of it. Despite internal experts in the methods, most people had no formal training and a lot of individual interpretations of how the process should work. While varying interpretations are fine, if they are done to improve the flow of work, the lack of training can be a problem. It increases the likelihood that some of the variations are not thoughtful adaptations but come from a lack of knowledge. The

UX team at this company is centralized and supports multiple teams; this is challenging for many reasons, but the variability among the approaches to implementing Kanban added an unnecessary level of complexity for staff members who were not able to generalize to one approach.

Each UX designer is responsible for his or her own time and is a project manager. (At the time we spoke, the team had no manager and had been in the process of looking for one for quite some time. This is a pretty unusual and extenuating circumstance that contributes to some of the chaos around the UX team.) The designers really just try to keep up and go with the flow, since they are dealing with a fairly large workload.

In describing the overall process, she says that a request would come in and the designer would get scope from the product manager. The product manager would break down the tasks and do this as an isolated activity, without the involvement of the development team or any other team members. The PMs also set task priorities based on their vision, and other functional areas are not involved in this activity either. The result of working this way is that the team has no opportunity to voice its opinion and share their insights. A development team could easily identify items that might be risky or difficult and help the PM to make decisions based on this information. Even more unfortunate is that, by keeping such close control over the process, the PM actually decreases the likelihood that the work will be implemented as he or she intended. With no conversation around these items when they are created or prioritized, the team loses out on understanding the rationale behind the requirements and the priorities and has less insight into what the PM is trying to achieve with that item. Additionally, the company has no analyst to help define and clarify scope and requirements based on real metrics. This makes her feel like she is working blind, in many ways, especially since there is no use of metrics to inform any decisions. She also worked on a single project that had 200 or 300 user stories with no epics to tie them together or establish any relationships among the stories. Trying to track that many user stories using a Kanban board is pushing the limits of the technique and makes things harder for the team to manage. To have so many stories with no overarching epic or clearly identified relationship reduces the amount of understanding that the team has of the work and makes it more challenging for it to have an overview of the project.

At the project kickoff, these user stories would be in place as created independently by the Product Manager. At

the meeting, the rest of the user stories would be defined by the development team and UX staff. A project-level sticky note would go on the Kanban board. This is great for visualization and a quick overview but does not really show the scale of the work needed for each item, and she found that a lot of complexity would be hidden by that simple sticky note. This makes it harder to use the boards to get a real sense of the progress of the project, since six sticky notes representing small efforts may have made their way through the process, but one sticky note stalling at the beginning represents a very large piece of work. Plenty of tools are in place to support the project. JIRA is used to manage and track tasks, but this is a development-centric activity, and the UX team's work is excluded from the system. Wiki (Confluence) pages are used for sharing information. Balsamiq is used for design sketches. Visio is used for wireframes, and Visio .pdfs are often attached to the Wiki page. The QE team uses these .pdfs as a reference.

The main form of communication for the UX people with their product teams is conference calls, since many developers are located throughout the United States and the United Kingdom in addition to the development staff colocated with the UX team. These calls are often used as wireframe review session. The wireframes are posted and communicated out as soon they are created, with review sessions scheduled afterward. The main deliverables for the team are wireframes and sketches, although there seems to be some confusion around those deliverables on some of the teams. The UX people are also responsible for research and usability testing. When they conduct usability testing, they document the results and post them. They also generate an email containing a short summary with links to the more detailed report.

She also struggles with the fact that there is no master Kanban board to provides an overview of all the projects. The closest thing to an overview is the UX team's Kanban board, as it documents the efforts of all the team members, but it is not granular enough to provide high-level insights in to the states of the projects or how they fit together. It might not be necessary to have a summary Kanban board, but there is a clear need in her organization for some overview of the work, showing where the efforts are at and how they relate to each other. This is especially valuable for her and her teammates, because they support multiple projects, need a better sense of the big picture, and are not able to get it.

In assessing how the process is working for the organization, she says that it is really difficult for her to work this way, as it feels like the worst of waterfall. Everyone is doing his or her work but without seeing the big picture, and the design team is just trying to stay current with all the work but is never able to get ahead. She is frustrated when she tries to plan for a release and finds that no one is thinking in terms of a phased approach and considering whether or not design just needs to happen in the end game, at the beginning, or all along. The teams interprets this process as relieving them of the burden of planning.

It is hard for her to put her finger on what is keeping the process from being successful, she thinks that part of the trouble for the design team is that the organization is not really sure what design is and thinks of the whole process from an exclusively development-centric perspective. There is no real integration among functional areas, which may be the root of the problems, so it is hard for her to say specifically what these teams should do differently to achieve a more positive outcome, because there is tremendous room for improvement.

The UX team that works on the company's website had a contrasting experience: That development team also practices Agile but is having more success. The projects are smaller, and that team relies on usage metrics to drive what features it work on. This makes the workload more manageable, because the number of overall user stories is smaller and easier to track. Having metrics to guide the work also allows the team insight into how the users actually use the site and the site's relative importance to the user community.

It can almost be more frustrating to see that the Agile process can work at the company, because it feel less like a broad organizational issue. In fact, in looking at her story, it does seem pretty clear that the trouble with the company's adoption of Agile relates to the product team organization, communication of high-level goals and priorities, and a broader scope of work than some of the projects might be able to accommodate. The first warning flag for me is the idea of the user stories being written with no involvement from other functional areas. This might give the PMs the illusion of tighter control over the release, but it really just obscures their general intent and leaves things open for interpretation by the development team. It also completely undermines the focus on communication and transparency at the core of Agile values. From the start, the teams are disconnected from what it is that they are supposed to achieve.

There is also a lack of colocation among the development teams, but I do not necessarily see this as having significant impact on the overall success of the team. While not ideal, geographical diversity is a reality for most people and generally with much larger gaps in time zones than this team has to deal with. In this case, colocation may simply be exacerbate existing communication issues but is probably the least of the problems to address for the process to work more effectively.

These projects seem a questionable fit for the Kanban technique, or at least the way that technique is being applied is not quite right. It seems that the Kanban boards are cover such a broad scope of work that they are not effectively communicating effort and progress as they are intended to. It also would seem that the projects might bear some breaking down a bit, so that a single Kanban board does not represent such a large amount of work. More important, it seems that the culture at the company, or at least within her part of the organization, is not well suited to such a lightweight Agile method. There are clearly gaps in communication and silos between functional areas. It would seem that they might benefit with a form of Agile that has more framework to facilitate the resolution of such issues or at least more training and coaching to refine the existing process.

Key points
- A process is useless without a culture to support it. The success of an any Agile project depends highly on frequent discussion and teamwork. The product managers here are effectively undermining the process from the start by controlling the most critical artifacts, developing them in isolation, and throwing them over the wall to the product team. When the first step of the process is done in such a non-Agile way, it is very difficult for the team to successfully move forward and balance out the effect of that first misstep.
- Training matters and should be supplied to every functional area that supports Agile. While not every employee requires such training, there needs to be a critical mass of consistently trained "experts" who can speak up when the process starts to run off its course and no one has a great sense of how to fix it. People put their own spin on something they did not understand very well in the first place, which can be dangerous. It is okay to deviate, but you should have a solid understanding of what you are changing (and why) before you do so.

SUMMARY

Every Agile team, no matter how experienced, faces different challenges as it tries to work as efficiently as possible to produce a wonderful user experience. While the specific techniques and activities might vary from team to team, a few things clearly contribute to a group's ability to successfully engage in Agile and Agile UX efforts. Focusing the team's attention on the project and not the bells and whistles of the process, healthy team interactions and communication, ensuring there is a sufficient level of training, and continuing to refactor and improve the process lays the groundwork for a high-functioning team.

References

10-Week Residency, n.d. Retrieved April 2, 2012, from http://luxr.co/programs/lean-ux-residency/.

Cockburn, A., 2002. Agile software development. Boston, Addison-Wesley.

Gothelf, J., 2013. Lean UX: Applying Lean Principles to Improve User Experience. O'Reilly Media.

Kahn, S., 2011. November 3. Agile UX. and Kanban at Adzerk. Adzerk Team Blog. Retrieved April 28, 2012, from http://team.adzerk.com/post/12289837931/agile-ux-and-kanban-at-adzerk?goback=%2Egna_3315113.

Kahn, S., 2012, March 29. A word on managing feature flags. Adzerk Team Blog Retrieved April 15, 2012, from, http://team.adzerk.com/post/20129347973/a-word-on-managing-feature-flags.

CHAPTER 5

Frequently Asked Questions

CONTENTS

Introduction 147

Should we Even be Agile? 148

How Long Should Sprints Be? 150

What Deliverables Should UX Produce? 151

How Should the Ux Team Fit in With the Development Sprints? 153

How do you Get Developers to Talk About the Design of One
Thing While They are Busy Implementing Another? 155

What if Ux Team Members Have to Support More Than One
Project? 155

How do we Fit User Research Into the Sprint Cycle? 156

What if the Team Claims to be Agile, but Agile Values are
Nowhere to be Seen? 157

What if the Team is not Colocated? 158

What do i do When Someone Uses "That's not Agile"
As a Reason not to do Something? 158

How Does the UX Team Plan and Research for the Next Release? ... 159

How do you Manage Internal Stakeholders? 160

Summary 160

Reference 161

INTRODUCTION

At the beginning, it can be very exciting to move into an Agile process. You did your homework, memorized the Agile Manifesto, gone to a few training sessions, and read everything ever written by Jeff Patton and Jeff Gothelf; you are pumped up and ready to go. As you start to do the real work of putting all that theory into practice, you realize that you still have many, many questions. It is always a challenge to try to figure out how to fit your UX teams' efforts into what Agile looks like at your company. You may have come to realize that something about your team is less than ideal for a textbook application of the chosen Agile method, and you are not sure if you are making the right trade-offs or just compromising the method. As it turns out, every UX person faces this same struggle when beginning the Agile journey and trying to customize the philosophy to a specific situation. Here are some of the common questions that people have, and some solutions that might work for you.

SHOULD WE EVEN BE AGILE?

This is a valid, interesting question to ask, but the answer almost never belongs to the UX team. Realistically, most of us learn about the decision to switch to Agile once it has already been made, although a lucky few may actually be part of that decision-making process. However, since the UX team will be left to define how it fits into the chosen Agile method, thinking about this issue is worthwhile, so you can understand what you might be up against and where your challenges lie. Most projects can benefit from some adoption of Agile methods. In my most optimistic moments, I like to think that any type of project could be Agile, if an Agile method is applied in the right way and the project work was scoped appropriately. However, in a few varieties of projects, the team should proceed with extreme caution and know that it may face more difficulties than the average team.

The first type of project that requires extra care in the application of Agile is those large-scope projects that cannot easily be broken into smaller pieces. Large infrastructure projects often require a sufficiently large project team to make the constant levels of communication required by Agile unwieldy and potentially distracting. The conventional wisdom is that the best size for a scrum team is between five and nine members. Kanban teams seem to work most effectively at similar sizes. That is not to say that these methods cannot be used with a larger team, but at a certain point, maintaining the high level of communication, transparency, and collaboration that is the intention of engaging in Agile will be a challenge. No matter how cohesive a team is, how much pair programming occurs, or how aggressively colocated the team is, a team larger than 12 people will struggle with the process. Not only will the kind of overhead that the ceremonies of a process like Scrum entails seem to be a burden and not necessarily helpful for a large scale project, a Scrum-style standup meeting with 20 team members is completely infeasible. Now, if you are a part of a large team and there is a genuine commitment to going Agile, there may be some ways to mitigate the size. Have representatives from the functional areas rather than the whole group attend daily standups and make sure that everyone takes a turn in that role. Also, engage not only in pair programming, but pair designing and pair testing. Partnering within and between functional areas makes sure that at least a few members in the team are engaged in the kind of communication that occurs on a small Agile team.

Working incrementally on large-scale infrastructure efforts is difficult, since they are generally made up of very large pieces of work that need to fit together, rather than many small pieces that make up the whole. Defining the smaller units of work, such that they can be completed within a sprint, may require sprint lengths so long that the release cycle resembles staged development more than anything Agile. If your sprints are eight weeks long and there are only six of them, is that still Agile? The answer is "It depends" or "Kind of," although I am sure many people would be happy to shout "No!" It would certainly be a step forward in the Agile direction if the previous cycle was just one long 12- to 18-month stretch. However, it might be hard to have demonstrations of completed work or show evidence of progress and do many of the things typical of Agile. Some infrastructure projects cannot even be broken down to this level; and if that is the case, the decision makers should think about what they are trying to achieve in using an Agile methodology on that work. It might make more sense to take inspiration from some Agile techniques around collaboration and the tracking of tasks to realize something that is more efficient than waterfall but less than Agile.

It is also typical for these large-scale efforts to require significant architectural changes, which may not easily be broken into small pieces and may make for very awkward user stories. In Scrum terms, an architectural epic that cannot be broken in to sprint-sized tasks can derail the process. An infrastructure or architectural change that is not being done for any performance or customer-facing reason ise difficult to express in a user story. Obviously, work that is to clean up a code base, modernize the architecture, or any of the other reasons for engaging in infrastructure work has value. However, these reasons cannot always be translated into customer needs; and while I have seen user stories such as "As a system, I want to…," those are really not good Agile practice. This is not to say that these types of projects cannot be made to work in Agile but that the project and the team need to be defined and chunked to fit well into the rhythm and needs of the Agile cycle. Also, some of the out-of-the-box methods may not be a good fit for the work and the team will have to be very conscientious in its application of Agile. If you find yourself working too hard to make the fit happen, it is worth taking a step back and considering whether or not Agile is that right answer.

At a minimum, this kind of project would definitely not be a good pilot for an organization with no experience in Agile projects and really should be tackled (if at all) only by an experienced team. A middle ground might be more reasonable for a novice team looking to leverage Agile principles. When you add up the potential for trouble with team size and the type of work, making these kinds of projects fit into Agile clearly is such an uphill battle that the value in doing so is very questionable. Working in a phased approach (with three phases instead of one), creating transparency around the project, increasing communication, and empowering the team can all be incredibly powerful for a large project. While it is true that a mini-waterfall is still a waterfall, it is also true that an expensive and abject failure using Agile could cause a company to write it off indefinitely. Taking baby steps on projects that are not an ideal fit for Agile methods and embracing the values rather than trying to fully engage in an Agile process (or remain completely committed to waterfall) could be a good first step.

Agile can also be complicated for projects with upstream or downstream dependencies. In these cases, it can take longer to be "done" with a piece of work if the project team completes its task but it cannot truly be completed until that work is integrated with the work of another team. Additional challenges are introduced depending on whether the team is upstream or downstream of the dependencies. If the team is downstream and not in control of ground that can change beneath them, the rework can be unpredictable and difficult to manage in an Agile manner. As with the large-scope projects, it is certainly possible to use Agile values and processes partially or entirely. However, it is probably best to have some organizational experience and expertise with Agile before taking on such an effort.

HOW LONG SHOULD SPRINTS BE?

There is no magical answer to this question, unfortunately, but there seems to be a bit of a sweet spot around three weeks. In true Goldilocks fashion, three weeks is somehow not too long and not too short, although it would be hard to say that it is just right for everyone. This length cycle seems to allow for a good balance between getting tasks done, working collaboratively, and engaging in all the meetings that might be required for the sprint. For sprints that are two weeks or less, the ratio of work to ceremonies can often be a weighted a little too much in the direction of the ceremonies, and some of the efficiencies that could be gained with a longer sprint are lost. In determining the right length for a project, consider the team size and location, the amount of scheduled meetings, and the smallest average unit of work. If the smallest unit of work is typically around three weeks, then your team will likely want to start with four week sprints to allow for the majority of the tasks to fit in, with some cushion for meetings and collaboration. One factor might constrain the solution space, but all these elements need to be considered together to properly identify if the team should work with a two-, three-, or four-week sprint.

If a team is very small, and nimble, then a two-week sprint could be a very good fit. If the communication levels are high, the scope of work is clear, and the overhead of meetings is streamlined, then working in two-week iterations could be ideal. Conversely, a team that is very large may be able to tackle and complete more tasks in a shorter amount of time and fit comfortably within two weeks. In both cases, it would probably work best if the teams were located in the same geographic location. Any diversity in the location can lead to a lag in communication, which can slow down the work effort. Having any kind of significant delays introduces a challenge in working within the shortest of sprint cycles but could be mitigated by adding additional time to the cycle. The most limiting factor in selecting a timeframe are the tasks themselves. If the smallest, or most typical, work unit is less than a week's worth of effort, then a short cycle is feasible. For something like a large architectural project in which the typical task takes a week and a half, it might make more sense to go with a three- or four-week cycle to achieve a more coherent piece of work within the cycle. Maybe the most important thing to bear in mind is that these numbers are not written in stone. If the team decides to work in two-week increments and, after a few cycles, finds that this is not working, then by all means adjust. Let the team decide what a better rhythm might look like and if adding a few days would make the difference.

The UX person also needs to consider, and have the team take into consideration, what the interaction with UX will look like as the team moves through the release cycle. Are you going to work a sprint ahead and need some dedicated time from the developers to support working collaboratively? If that is the case, the development team needs to accommodate that time. Or, are you going to work within the sprint and need a considerable amount of time from several team members? In this case, more time is needed to work together but overall the tasks may close out more quickly and result in a net gain in velocity for the team. All these things affect the velocity of the team and its ability to fit into a sprint cycle. This is not a problem, just something that the team needs to take into consideration, preferably before the cycle kicks off.

WHAT DELIVERABLES SHOULD UX PRODUCE?

This is a good place to invoke the classic usability practitioner answer for everything: "It depends." It would also to be fair to mention that this is another question that many Agile folks, especially those of the Lean UX persuasion, would quickly answer, "None!" Agile strongly encourages teams to move away from specifications to focus on more immediate and interactive forms of communication. Jeff Gothelf (n.d.), "Getting out of the Deliverables Business," is a very insightful article that does an eloquent job of expressing the rationale behind this idea. The proposal is to eliminate traditional deliverables and instead work off a rapid prototype that can be used both for testing and iterating with customers and becomes the artifact shared with the development team. It is the antithesis of the old-school specification document that is thrown over the wall and lands with a thud. Instead, this more interactive method of communicating design intent is many steps closer to resembling the actual implementation. And, if you are in a situation where you can do this, I wholeheartedly encourage you to do so. a certain amount of truth lies in the idea that creating a deliverable also creates unnecessary boundaries between the functional areas on Agile project. There are better and more efficient ways to share information about the design. If the level of communication and dynamics of the team allow for a seamless workflow that can survive and thrive without deliverables, then throw away the idea of specifications and do not look back.

However, in some environments, this ideal may not be entirely realizable. Sometimes, groups are spread across countries and time zones or encounter language differences that make nonverbal communication more effective than conference calls. In situations where some sort of deliverable needs to be created; the goal should be to produce the least possible amount of documentation. This cannot be emphasized enough. It really is okay to produce something if it supports the team's work, but there is a reason that Agile recommends eliminating it, so proceed with caution if you choose to ignore this advice. In generating any kind of document, the UX staff should also work with the team to determine the necessary amount of information and what it looks like. This not only sets expectations and goals but provides an opportunity to look for another solution to the problem that does not involve the creation of a document. The team should examine exactly why documentation of any kind is being produced and make sure that the needs are being met. It might help to think of these as communication-support items rather than deliverables, because that is really the purpose they serve. If a team is geographically diverse, smooth communication is not achievable through face-to-face discussion. Sometimes, posting a sketch or interactive prototype can facilitate communication immensely. The issue is more about sharing ideas effectively than handing off documentation. When large time zone gaps and language barriers are at play, such items can bring a common understanding more quickly than a meeting.

Long software releases, where the current version does not always represent the front-end design, can also lead to the need to create "speclettes." It is very easy for the Agile team to be aware of where they are "now" and the work going on in the current cycle. It tends to be a bit more challenging to remember where the team has been, how certain things have changed along the way, or where the team is headed. This information can be especially important for quality and documentation teams, as they try to stay on top of a moving target. To support these team, and generally remind everyone of the overall state of the design, it can be helpful to have some sort of document to which team members can refer when needed. I prefer to call them *speclettes*, because they are much more lightweight versions of their heavy duty cousin, the specification, and bear a much stronger relationship to a design brief. Usually, these documents contain a screenshot and a few words about an interaction for clarity. They may be grouped together by area or sprint for which they were designed or implemented. They can be attached to a design task, posted to a Wiki page, or printed out and displayed on the wall. Both the content and delivery mechanism are determined by the needs of the team, but minimal effort to deliver and consume should be the hallmark of these speclettes.

However, it is important to be very conscious of why any sort of documents are being produced. Sometimes, it will just be more comfortable for a UX person to produce something and publicly share it. We are so used to providing documentation, often to prove that what was designed is different than what was implemented and to have a point of reference for the subsequent bugs and change requests. It may feel as though, if we do not post such artifacts, then there is no way that resulting product will match the design intentions. In an Agile environment, this can end up being a self-fulfilling prophecy. Expecting a failure in communication will likely lead to such a failure because it means that there is no trust. If the request for documentation comes from outside the UX team, take a look at what is motivating the request. If the issue is that a functional area does not feel it has a sufficient understanding of what is going on in a given sprint or the overall release, simply posting a few annotated sketches may not address the root cause and may distract the team from solving the real problem. The design team is always creating sketches and it takes very little effort to share these on a Wiki page or attach them to a user story, but it important to make sure that doing so is not preventing or inhibiting a richer form of communication.

HOW SHOULD THE UX TEAM FIT IN WITH THE DEVELOPMENT SPRINTS?

A certain amount of debate centers around whether the UX team should work ahead of the development team or within the same sprint, on the same tasks. There are pros and cons to both approaches. The one thing we can all agree on enthusiastically is that the UX team should, at all costs, avoid working a sprint (or two or more) behind the development team. This can happen if the project was kicked off before there was a UX resource, often in companies where the few UX resources are distributed among many projects. Working behind the implementation leads to confusion among the entire team—no one can remember what the software is "really" supposed to look and act like, since some UI coding work will have been submitted prior to the design work then will need to be updated to reflect the design. The developers know that designs were discussed and reviewed and they remember seeing development tasks on that item occurring within the sprint, but it is a challenge to know whether the implementation included the design or not. This keeps the team from being able to trust that what they see is actually "done." It can also be much harder to affect change or appropriately influence the design.

While Agile environments are more open to rework or "refactoring" than traditional environments, there is a limit. The development team can cover the same ground only so many times before it is counterproductive to the schedule. And, as in waterfall, a design that requires an architectural change or a substantial rewrite of code will be a harder sell to get the development team to do it. Of course, that the UX team is behind the rest of the team is a red flag in and of itself; and while it may not be possible to change the behavior during a single sprint, the team needs to be aware that this is not a viable way to work. Bringing UX into the process late, regardless of the reason, might be a sign that other functional areas are not being completely integrated into the team, which is not a recipe for success.

Having the UX team work a sprint or two ahead of the development team, on its own velocity, is a conservative approach and can be great strategy for UX teams that are just finding their way with Agile. It creates the space for the UX team to really work on a design and iterate it, without affecting the time needed for implementation. This can also allow the UX team to dedicate a sprint to high-level design, usability testing, or another type of user research. Having a separate stream of work also creates a certain amount of visibility in to what the UX team is doing, which can be quite beneficial in an organization where the value of the UX team is not always clear. It is also an ideal approach for organizations where members of the UX team support multiple projects and need to build time into their schedule for that. One potential pitfall to this approach is that it can easily turn into a mini-waterfall. UX creates a design in Sprint 1, documents and hands it off to the development team to code in Sprint 2. If you take away the word *sprint*, you have a good, old-fashioned waterfall method on your hands. The best way to avoid this is communication. The UX team needs to make sure that it is working iteratively with customers, stakeholders, and the development team. In the fast-paced world of Agile, make sure that there is time for formal and informal communication among team members, even if it means assigning "support the UX team" tasks to critical team members to ensure their availability for and engagement in the UX sprint.

Working within a sprint on the same task as the development team, so that a given item is designed and implemented in a single sprint cycle, can be a challenge for a UX person new to Agile. However, it isa delightfully collaborative way of working, if a bit intense, and many teams are quite successful working this way. It is probably best taken on by teams that already have a healthy communication style, good working relationship, and are located in the same office. It may also be best if the UX resource supports only this project and does not try to balance several projects, as this type of approach is very fast paced and may not allow for load balancing on multiple projects. At a minimum, the UX person should take on only one major project when working in this style.

HOW DO YOU GET DEVELOPERS TO TALK ABOUT THE DESIGN OF ONE THING WHILE THEY ARE BUSY IMPLEMENTING ANOTHER?

Even in more traditional environments, this can often happen; it is just less explicit. However, it is a legitimate concern given that the pace of the Agile work might make it harder for the developers to be able to spend time on any activity that takes them away from accomplishing their work for the sprint. While bribing the team with candy and pizza is always an option, and one that I highly recommend, it gets you only so far, and a more sustainable solution needs to be found. Start by taking a look at what the issue is. Consider whether the developers are strapped for time or are just having a tough time switching focus, since either or both could be at play. If it is just an issue of time, try building in "UX-collaboration" time into the schedule. Have a task with a set amount of time assigned to the necessary resources and try to keep your collaboration work within those time boundaries to show respect for the developers' schedules. If the problem is more along the lines that you are asking them to multiprocess and it just is not working, then maybe the problem is that the UX team is working too separately. Consider an approach that has the UX team and the developer working together on the same problem, at the same time. This can take the form of in-sprint UX work or be as extreme as pair designing. The reality is this: If it is not working to ask a team member to help you out with one thing while his or her head is somewhere else, you should probably find another way to work together.

WHAT IF UX TEAM MEMBERS HAVE TO SUPPORT MORE THAN ONE PROJECT?

This is obviously a less-than-ideal situation but fairly common. Most UX teams have to face this reality and have found ways to deal with it. One approach is to have a UX person support one larger effort and one (or more, if it is feasible) smaller effort, so that the workload is balanced. This allows the UX person to spend time operating as a team member on the project that requires most of their effort and supports the ability to engage in as many of the team's event as possible. Giving the UX person the space to establish and foster a strong relationship with his or her product team is as important as having sufficient time to generate designs. Another way to tackle the work is to have the UX staff members work as consultants and integrate themselves with the teams only to the degree necessary. This approach can be tricky if the UX team or staff member does not already have a strong trust relationship with the team. Choosing to not attend certain meetings in order to spend more time working on the design may not go over very well with an Agile team unless they already feel comfortable with the designer. Additional care should be taken to make sure that the UX person engages in and encourages as much communication with the other functional areas as possible, informally or formally. Maintaining transparency is critical to building trust and keeping the collaborative spirit healthy.

HOW DO WE FIT USER RESEARCH INTO THE SPRINT CYCLE?

It is a common Agile UX practice to schedule regularly recurring usability sessions and get feedback on whatever is available at that moment. Sessions can be scheduled to occur on the same day every week or every month. Feedback can be solicited on design concepts, sketches, wireframes, prototypes, or working software. The user comments can be incorporated into new user stories and given priority by the team, no formal report necessary. When done routinely like this, customer reactions can be incorporated as seamlessly as observations made by team members and can function as a natural extension of the team. This is usability in the most Agile form.

If this is not possible in your situation, it is still possible to work standard research practices into an Agile framework. User research can be a part of the planning cycle and can include surveys, persona definition, usability testing, card sorting activities, or any other research technique used at this stage to help with the definition and clarification of requirements for the release. These activities can also be done within the cycle, as tasks assigned to the UX team in support of a specific user story or stories. As with any process, incorporating some user research is better than none, so create as many opportunities to do so as bandwidth allows.

Practically speaking, larger research efforts have to occur outside the sprint cycle, either using different resources internally or leveraging outside consultants. To a degree, Agile methods assume a good understanding of the customers and that in-cycle feedback will be sufficient to drive the product in the right direction. While this may often be true, it is not always enough. If your organization is entering a new market space, using of a new platform or other transformative technology, or expanding the product line in a direction that is more unknown, then up-front user research needs to occur. Ideally, this research occurs well ahead of the product cycle kickoff. Since we are often in fairly nonideal situations, this may not be an option. If the product cycle has kicked off and there is a need for research, coordinate with the team and conduct the research in as streamlined a way as possible while the developers work on architecture issues or other efforts that do not require design decisions to already be in place.

WHAT IF THE TEAM CLAIMS TO BE AGILE, BUT AGILE VALUES ARE NOWHERE TO BE SEEN?

I describe this as having the scent of Agile on it. Those involved call themselves *Agile* and give lip service to a method, but they does not practice Agile methods in any real way. Unfortunately, this is a fairly common phenomenon and can be one of the hardest challenges to overcome. It can happen for many reasons and sorting out the root cause is the best way to know whether or not the issue is intractable and, if it is not, identify potential solutions. It is entirely possible that it might just be the result of an overly enthusiastic scrum master, fresh off of Scrum training, who is dazzled by all the new things to do and fixates on them at the expense of Agile values. In this case, a candid team discussion might be warranted. If enough team members recognize and speak about the problem, they may be able to effect change and influence the culture of the team.

It is also very common, oddly enough, that no one on the team has any kind of training in any Agile beyond reading the Agile Manifesto (and maybe some teammates have not even done that) but are nonetheless speeding down the highway toward delivering the product using an Agile process. Conquering this dynamic requires members of the team who care about having a better understanding of the process. If there is an interest in genuinely applying the method, a champion who educates him- or herself and shares this knowledge can inform the team and create an Agile value-driven environment. Plenty of online training classes, articles, and blogs can be leveraged in place of more formal training or coaching. Doing some of these activities as a team not only increases the team's knowledge of Agile and allows it to be more effective, it can also serve as a team building activity that brings everyone closer together. However, if the team is happy enough to continue as it is, perhaps, doing so to simply avoid a more rigid process by calling themselves *Agile*, then the options for influencing cultural change are a bit more limited. In that situation, modeling good behavior as a team member and encouraging similar behavior might be the most effective option to shift the attitude of the team.

Then, there are the times when the problem is at a higher level of the organization. Executives or stakeholders who do not know or understand some of the basic details of Agile may simply view it is an interesting trend that should allow them to move faster. They want to do some of "that," but do not necessarily know what that means from a day-to-day perspective or realize that a certain amount of training and organizational support is needed for it to really succeed. When this is the case, these people may not understand the benefits in moving to an Agile process and may have unrealistic expectations of what to expect as a result of moving to an Agile process. In this environment, a successful project is the best way to get attention and support. Success would mean not just an effective adoption of Agile, but also an enthusiastic customer response and great revenue numbers. Showing that a team can not only deliver with Agile but t deliver products even better, more effectively, quicker, or more fully featured if the organization with support, training, coaching, or whatever is needed can be a very powerful message that gets the attention of people who are more removed from the process.

WHAT IF THE TEAM IS NOT COLOCATED?

Rarely is an ideal Agile team described in a way that includes teams in multiple time zones, but for most of us, this is becoming a common reality. Many of the teams interviewed for the case studies where in this situation, and more than a few of them were quite successfully Agile. Distance certainly represents communication challenges but nothing that cannot be overcome with a little bit of technology and creativity. The key is to identify which elements of the process need to be modified to accommodate the situation and where the communication gaps are. Wiki pages are a great way to post daily happenings and key bits of information. These can serve as a repository for different things that need to be shared and accessed asynchronously. Easily editable and informal types of communication like this can help fill the gap of daily standups when there is no convenient, common time zone in which to have a daily conversation with the entire team. The greater the distance between time zones, the more helpful an online communication tool can be. For remote meetings, tools that allow for both conversation and screen sharing can help replicate the dynamics of in-person demonstrations and discussions. If people are simply in different offices, without drastic geographical differences, IM chat tools can support the immediacy of communication that is more common when everyone sits together in a common area.

WHAT DO I DO WHEN SOMEONE USES "THAT'S NOT AGILE" AS A REASON NOT TO DO SOMETHING?

The first thing is to do is to consider if the statement is actually true. It is entirely possible that someone may be suggesting a course of action that completely undermines Agile values and violates it principles. However, do not be too surprised if this is not the case, and definitely do not take the comment at face value and assume that it is true. While individuals and teams do many things to undermine the Agile process, if someone is tossing around this particular phrase, it should raise a red flag. Agile methods are not particularly dogmatic in their approach, and it is entirely possible and very common to alter the method a bit to fit a particular situation while still achieving an Agile environment. If something is not working for the team, it should be discussed by the team and resolved in a way the team is comfortable with. Unfortunately, a person who responds to any kind of idea with that phrase is effectively shutting down the conversation and failing to address whatever it is to be resolved. Even if the solution would absolutely not work in an Agile environment, a problem lies underneath that should be investigated to see if there is a more-Agile solution. A more-Agile response would be to ask, "Why?" or "What are we trying to achieve with that?" and sort out what is actually going on and identify the best solution.

If a team member proposes to do away with all the daily scrum meetings, which goes against what the method recommends, the right answer is never to simply dismiss the proposal by saying, "That's not Agile." The more appropriate response would be to find out why the person made the suggestion in the first place and see if there is an issue that needs resolving. Maybe this is a knee jerk reaction representing a deep-seated mistrust of daily meetings of any kind, which might not require any more corrective action than to have a discussion about why the team has that activity. Or, that person could feel completely overwhelmed by the workload, and a daily event, even if it is only 15 minutes long, feels like one stress too many. This situation would obviously merit a different kind of discussion and potential solution. Really, the "Agile" thing to do is make sure that the team is communicating and feeling empowered.

HOW DOES THE UX TEAM PLAN AND RESEARCH FOR THE NEXT RELEASE?

This can be a difficult question to answer from an Agile perspective, since Agile methods really are focused on the "now" of the current release and the immediacy of the development work. The UX team can do a few things to facilitate this. If there is a central UX resource, it can be used to support the research efforts and coordinate with the product team to deliver the information in a timely way. It will also be important for the resource to think about making its findings fit easily into an Agile process, so he or she might want to look at how to write good user stories as a method of communicating research results.

If there is no central resource and the same person that supports the product and its design also needs to work on the research, then a little more finesse must be applied to the timing of these efforts. Consider whether or not the team uses a Sprint 0 for planning and if the sprint provides enough time to complete the necessary research. Depending on the length of the release and the sprints, maybe just using a sprint during the cycle for the research could provide enough time. This most likely will work best at the beginning or end of the release cycle, where there is often fewer design activities, but it is certainly possible for the UX person to pick a sprint at any point and dedicate time during that cycle for research. Depending on your team's schedule, the lengths of the sprints may or may not lend themselves to being used a period of dedicated focus. Perhaps, the timeframes are too short to do all the necessary research activities and analyze the results. If this is the case, the UX person could have a set of tasks dedicated to research activities that occur throughout the sprint. If the efforts are forward looking, it may be a little awkward to make these tasks fit in as part of the Agile method t being used. If this is the case, then simply do not make it part of the Agile method. Ideally, everyone on an Agile team is a dedicated resource, but this often is the case only for the development team, and many of the other functional areas support other projects. It could make sense to treat the research work as another project, which it is. The UX person simply adjusts the available time for the project team and carves out the time the need to work on the research. The time spent on research can vary throughout the release, and the UX person simply takes on more or less project work to accommodate it.

HOW DO YOU MANAGE INTERNAL STAKEHOLDERS?

Some touch points with internal stakeholders are built into the process as a part of the planning activities and in the demonstration of the work done during the sprint. This is mostly intended to communicate with immediate stakeholders that are somewhat involved in the project and have a good sense of the work that is occurring. However, there might also be a need to work with stakeholders who have less contact with the team, especially if it is a pilot project to explore the methodology. This may require an occasional meeting with these people to let them know what the project is tackling and the kind of progress it is making. It is probably worth doing these meetings as dedicated events, separate from the day-to-day work and involving only necessary team members. There is a natural tendency to want to invite these interested parties to attend the demonstrations at the end of the sprint, but try to resist that temptation. Meeting as a team to discuss what was achieved during a specific sprint is a different conversation than talking to management about the project, and trying to do both at once will likely prevent the right level of communication on either front.

SUMMARY

There are many questions about how to get started with Agile UX, and the answer to most of them is "It depends." As design professionals we need to be comfortable with a certain amount of ambiguity, and it might help to think of fitting into Agile as a design problem. Consider the project team to be the users, identify their needs, and create an elegant solution. There are many best practices but few definitive answers on to how to practice Agile UX.

Reference

Gothelf, J., n.d. Lean UX: Getting out of the Deliverables Business, Retrieved April 2, 2012, from http://uxdesign.smashingmagazine.com/2011/03/07/lean-ux-getting-out-of-the-deliverables-business/.

CHAPTER 6

Using Agile Concepts for UX Teams

CONTENTS

Introduction 163

Creating a User Experience Backlog 164

Recurring User Testing 165

Breaking the Work in to Smaller Pieces 165

Constant Feedback and Iteration 166

Recurring Events and Rituals 166

No Design Divas or Heroes 167

Focusing on Communication Over Documentation 168

Thinking and Communicating in Terms
of User Stories 169

Defining Acceptance Criteria 169

Using Less Up-Front Design 170

Summary 170

INTRODUCTION

User Experience teams can borrow Agile practices, even if they support projects and development teams that do not use Agile methods. A process focused on iteration, integrating user feedback and customer needs has something to offer any UX team. Most UX teams do not even consider how Agile could be integrated into the user-centered design process until they learn their organization or team adopting an Agile process. If your team is part of a more-traditional process, you might think that there is no point in figuring how to practice Agile UX, because it cannot be possible to do so if the development team is not doing the same. However, the core values and principles of Agile are very well suited to any team practicing user-centered design. If you are looking to evolve the practice of your

Agile User Experience Design. http://dx.doi.org/10.1016/B978-0-12-415953-2.00006-6

team or just your own practice, plenty of inspiration is to be found in Agile practices and you need not wait for your development teams to lead the way.

CREATING A USER EXPERIENCE BACKLOG

In most Agile environments, the backlog of user stories and tasks is local to the project team. However, after hearing Catherine Robson's description of having a centralized UX backlog, clearly, this idea could be helpful for many UX teams regardless of the development methodology. One issue UX teams face time and again is the return on investment for the design effort, and it is often necessary to prove to management that the design team adds value to the production process. Even if the UX team is in an organization where these requests are not explicitly made, this does not mean the issue will not come up in the future. After all, with changes in leadership, the new executives have no prior experience with UX or your team, so it can be very helpful to be able to illustrate the contributions of the UX team and mitigate the need for conversations around the value of UX. While some groups can come up with benchmarks and usability testing metrics that show the effect of their efforts, most are unable to show such concrete measurements and oftenare at a disadvantage when trying to justify head count or budget.

Having a process by which requests for UX support are created by the development team and submitted to some sort system adds an element of thoughtfulness to the act of seeking UX support. Instead of just wandering in to a UX person's cube and suggesting he or she look at something or viewing the UX person as an on-call resource whose tasks require no advance planning, having to formally request the UX person's times gives the sense that the UX work requires time and effort and needs to be planned for. That is not to say that teams that do not request UX support do not value the work, but when the client teams have to put the requests in to writing and think about what they need, it imparts a certain sense of worth to the work. Having the tasks come to UX in writing from the team also provides some clarity about what kind of help sought and an opportunity to discuss what activities are most appropriate or beneficial. Many times, a team thinks it needs one thing but could really benefit more from a different activity, which can turn the discussion around the request into a powerful teaching moment.

Having a backlog of requests can not only help a UX team balance its load balance more effectively, it can be a valuable artifact to illustrate both the supply and demand for the team. The UX group can also gain insights into where the members spend most of their time and determine if they need to adjust. The team need not be centralized for this to be effective. Even if designers are dedicated to specific projects or products, the backlog can be structured to support individual efforts but roll up into a summary that gives an overview of the entire group. When UX teams are not centralized, having such a reporting mechanism can also identify potential efficiencies that might be realized. Regardless of the UX team organization, having a backlog can increase visibility, awareness, and understanding of what the team does.

RECURRING USER TESTING

In a waterfall cycle, it is easy to schedule user testing to occur after a specific milestone. That milestone often slips out of the schedule, taking the usability testing with it and possibly pushing it to the point where customer feedback cannot be incorporated into the shipping release. It can be even easier to continually put off scheduling user testing because the product is not ready or there is so much design work to do and specifications to write that it seems like there is not enough time to run the sessions. The intentions are good—wanting to wait until the design is "done enough" before showing it to users, the desire for a sufficiently robust prototype, or resolving bandwidth issues. We know that the more "done" a product is, the less likely the user feedback is to be incorporated in to the product, but there is often internal pressure not to show customers a rough prototype that may give the wrong impression. Looking at Agile teams that embrace a "test what you have" mentality can inspire you to find some ways to get around this pressure. Instead of trying to show a prototype that is so rough the feedback may not be as meaningful as it could, show the customers sketches or wireframes or have a conversation about workflow. None of these concepts is unique to Agile, but seeing how user research is incorporated into such tight timeframes can certainly undermine any excuses not to do research in a release cycle that is a year or longer in duration. If someone with a three-week or three-month release cycle can make time for weekly feedback sessions, then surely someone with more time can do so as well.

Agile encourages frequent user feedback sessions and the ideal state is to have a predictable, recurring event happen weekly, biweekly, or monthly. There is no reason not to adopt this in a waterfall cycle. It might mean testing with rough digital or paper sketches, but the same holds true in Agile environments. It may even mean to have nothing to show the customer but simply use the opportunity to do collaborative design or engage in a conversation for feedback. The sprint cycle provides an incentive for testing, because there is an opportunity to get the customer issues into the backlog and influence the direction of the next sprint. There is no reason the outcome of a testing event in a non-Agile environment could not simply influence the next week of design or implementation.

BREAKING THE WORK IN TO SMALLER PIECES

A problem with more traditional methods is that they deal with very large pieces of work, such as "create a mobile application for product *x*" and ask only that you get it done by a given point in time. Not breaking the work down into smaller units makes it harder to track progress against the goal. For a designer, it can also make for an overwhelming task. Identifying the pieces that make up the whole and tackling those incrementally allows for a more focused effort. It also supports the designer's ability to seek feedback throughout the cycle. It is clear that the designer who focuses on the entire mobile app as one task and waits to have a design review until the whole thing is designed will take considerably longer than one who narrows the first review session to address the high-level architecture and a few key screens.

CONSTANT FEEDBACK AND ITERATION

The motivation to have so many user feedback sessions comes from the Agile intention to keep the customer needs at the forefront of the team's consciousness, but it is also encourages a more accepting approach to reworking and refining the product in a direction that will create the best user experience. Since refactoring is an accepted and even encouraged concept in Agile, the team is mentally prepared to refine the product and revisit different aspects of the design throughout the release cycle.

If you are in a more traditional environment, the values around keeping the customer in mind and refactoring along the way may not be as dominant. However, the earlier in the cycle design changes are proposed, the less expensive they are and the more likely the changes will make it into the product. Regardless of whether you are validating designs with usability testing or having design review sessions with the team, you should solicit feedback as often as possible. Waiting until you have handed of a huge design specifications makes you more reluctant or able to make corrections. This does not mean that you should consider assaulting your team with weekly change requests. Instead, use regularly occurring sessions with internal and external stakeholders to guide and refine your designs before you hand them off to the development team. Doing this creates a stronger design that requires less rework for everyone and can free you up to focus on more valuable design validation later in the cycle. as you have managed to resolve the most glaring issues.

RECURRING EVENTS AND RITUALS

Some of the value in the scrum events is that they are predictable and repeatable. It is more of a break in the rhythm of the team to meet occasionally than to meet briefly every day. Similarly, scheduling a weekly customer feedback session can make it more natural to interact with customers throughout the cycle, and working their comments into the design becomes second nature. Take inspiration from this tactic and consider scheduling routine design reviews with your product team. Keep the meetings short, efficient, and relevant, since attendance is not mandatory or part of the official process. If you can keep the discussion interesting and everyone knows that there will be a design session at lunchtime every other Wednesday, it might just become a habit for the team to attend to see what you have to share and work collaboratively with you to improve the design.

NO DESIGN DIVAS OR HEROES

It is always fun to be the genius designer who swoops in with a fantastic solution at the last minute that makes the design amazing. The reality is that depending on one star performer to always independently create the best design solution is not very healthy. It is not collaborative and it creates a bottleneck if one (or two) people are the only ones allowed or expected to generate designs. Many people have gotten used to being in this role and enjoy it, but it is a good idea to move away from encouraging this kind of culture. Someone who is very attached to that dynamic will not last long in Agile environment, but that person should not be allowed to engage in such behavior in any environment. Part of valuing the individual and his or her skills in Agile means recognizing each person's unique contributions and skills, regardless of title. While the UX person is responsible for the design, that is not the same as "owning" it. It means that the person is the shepherd who guides the design to completion and is on the hook to do so. It does not mean that the UX person is the only one who can, or should, contribute to the design. Not only will team members have better insight into feasible implementation solutions, they often have domain expertise that the designer may lack.

This does not mean that design should be a chaotic activity, where everyone's design suggestion needs to find its way into the design or the team must vote on design solutions. However, team members should be viewed as design partners and contributors to work as collaboratively as possible. Working collaboratively also allows the designers to come up with ideas they might never have identified on their own, while discarding truly infeasible ideas quickly before investing too much time and energy in them. Although Agile values support this, the principles are equally valid in more traditional environments. Just because they work in a waterfall environment does not mean that development resources cannot contribute to the design in a meaningful way. Divalike behaviors are based on the assumption that the solution could not be made better with additional input, and it is hard to believe that this is true, regardless of what development process is in place.

Additionally, a good designer teaches design skills, in a "teach a man to fish" strategy. Not only does this enable more people to recognize and implement a better user experience, it allows the designers to focus on areas that require their attention instead of trying to be everywhere at once. When everyone on the team has a working understanding of good design principles, the resulting user experience is improved. The UX person cannot define every widget and label, especially in an Agile environment; and many, many implementation decisions are made by the developers as a matter of course and necessity. This happens just as frequently in more traditional environments, but when the finest detail is written in a specification document, there is an illusion that the outcome will match the specification, which is very rarely the case. This is why empowering all the team members to wear the hat of "designer" while giving them the tools to do so effectively makes the UX staff infinitely more effective.

FOCUSING ON COMMUNICATION OVER DOCUMENTATION

If your software development life cycle requires epic novel-length specifications, you will not be able to get them off the team's plate, but you can consider how to support a more effective way to share its content. If there is no hard requirement for such deliverables, consider examining your UX deliverables to see if they are geared toward supporting communication or simply documenting your intentions. Relieving your team of the burden of producing something that does not serve its purpose might be worthwhile. If the designers focus on engaging in collaboration with other functional areas and achieving common understanding through conversations, there is less to communicate in writing. In many cases, a simple sketch that reminds the different team members of the general design and direction might be enough. For functional areas that are less involved in day-to-day design activities or tend to come into the process later in the cycle, having a meeting to review the design might prove more effective, and quicker, than posting a long document.

The reality is that, even when long documents are required by the process, not everyone who should read them does so. Just as often, team members read an earlier version as part of a review process and never take the time to sort through the changes made with the final draft. If your team is in the business of writing such documents and your process does not allow for a different way of communicating the design, take a cue from Agile and think about additional delivery methods, such as a walkthrough of the design or a review and discussion of the critical design elements. This provides the other functional areas with a much richer opportunity to understand what the design is trying to accomplish and gives them a chance to ask questions and learn more about what the design is doing. This significantly increases the chances of the key elements of the design being implemented correctly.

THINKING AND COMMUNICATING IN TERMS OF USER STORIES

UX practitioners are accustomed to thinking in terms of personas, either formally developed and robust personas based on user research or more informal constructs that live in a designer's head based on customer interactions. Personas are valuable when thinking about intended audience and segmenting different user types and provide excellent guidance when working through the high level design. However, even personas can get a little abstract for people from all functional areas when they start to work on the detailed design. For some people, it is a challenge to move from the description of the person and his or her needs and apply that to a single interaction or set of controls. Thinking in terms of "What would 'Kevin' want?" still leaves plenty of room for interpretation on what exactly "Kevin" would want from a given element of the design. User stories can make a wonderful complement to personas, if you are already using them, or can be a technique that can change the language of the discussion. User stories are framed in terms of customer use instead of product requirements, which can be helpful as well. Despite anyone's best efforts, if the work is constantly defined by and spoken about in terms of features, the conversation can be constrained. As UX professionals, we always try to stay focused on the user, but when the dialog is always centered on the presupposed solution and not the problem, this can be a challenge.

DEFINING ACCEPTANCE CRITERIA

Many organizations have implicit or explicit release criteria that serve as gatekeepers for releasing a product. This can be quality criteria, performance criteria, or simply sign-off criteria. Depending on how seriously these criteria are taken by the organization, they can be effective at preventing products from shipping with major flaws. More local quality criteria might be applied to features or code submissions, and those can be very helpful in improving the overall health and robustness of the product. Release criteria, and even local quality criteria, are necessarily generalized and intended to enforce a certain set of standards across products.

The Agile concept of "acceptance criteria" can be helpful in any environment. The idea behind the acceptance criteria is that the team agrees on what needs to be a part of that user story in order for it to ship. For example, if the user story is, "As a student traveler, I want to book a cheap flight to Amsterdam," then the accompanying acceptance criteria might be "Show available flights to Amsterdam," "Allow the arrival and departure dates to be changed," and "Highlight low fares." The agreement is established ahead of the stress and the heat of an impending deadline, where the natural tendency is to ship what you have done and there can be pressure to compromise to support that goal. These criteria are tailored to the specific user story, with the unique goal of making sure that the user story is implemented in a way that satisfies the user's needs. This specificity gives these conditions greater impact on a specific feature and can drive feature completeness and a broader clarity about what the user story means. Without the framework of an Agile process and its many tools to support the creation of these items, it can be a little more difficult to work these into a more traditional process. If you choose to employee use stories as a technique, then discussing and agreeing on the acceptance criteria can be a natural part of the story creation. If that seems like it might require too much effort or you did not choose to use user stories as a method of communication, there is a still an opportunity to apply this technique. It works best to capture the acceptance criteria in writing, to make it easier to refer to and remember what the actual agreement was. The criteria can be stored in something as simple a publicly available Excel spreadsheet or attached somehow to an existing artifact in your process.

USING LESS UP-FRONT DESIGN

Before you panic, even in an Agile environment, "less up-front design" is not the same as "*no* up-front design." It really means that the design should not, and really cannot, be fully designed before being turned over to development. There is no handoff period in Agile, and things move so quickly you cannot do a complete design ahead of the implementation work, even if you want to try. If you are in a more traditional environment, you might wonder why you should even think about using this technique. After all, you have a lot of design work to do and really big specifications to write. If you think back to the last time there was a review of those specifications, someone probably caught an error or a design change needed to be made. It probably took you hours or days to update the sketches, screenshots, and wireframes and bring the document up to date. If, instead of laboring over the document alone in your cube, you conducted periodic reviews with the team and collaborated on a variety of design solutions and proceeded to document those efforts, you might save yourself a lot of time and effort. You might also find that you have not only produced a better design, but the implementation more closely matches the specification.

SUMMARY

It is not necessary to move an entire organization to an Agile development process to get some of the benefits from its values and tactics. Since there is so much overlap with Agile and user-centered design values, it is fairly easy for UX teams to borrow from Agile methods. Inspiration is to be found in treating the design as a deliverable that can be produced through a series of smaller design efforts and incorporates continuous feedback. Specific elements can also be translated into UX activities by using the language of user stories to describe customer needs, having recurring events to increase communication, and creating a collaborative culture. These ideas can help create a more high-functioning team, even when still working with a traditional process, and the UX team should consider how it can take advantage of using these methods.

Index

Note: Page numbers with "b" denote boxes.

A

Acceptance criteria, 22, 34, 130—131
  defining, 169—170
Adaptation, 139—140
Adaptive Programming, 3—4
Agile, defined, 2
Agile Alliance Conference, 95
AgileFall, 35—36
Agile Manifesto, 3—6, 16, 20, 73, 122—123, 127—128, 157
  customer collaboration over contract negotiation, 8
  individuals and interactions, valuing, 5—6
  "People over Process", 97—99, 124, 140b—143b
  responding to change over following plan, 8—9
  working software over comprehensive documentation, 6—7
  www.agilemanifesto.org, 137
Agile UX, 148—150
  coding, 54
  collaboration, 54
  communication, 51
  conversation, 54
  design activities, 64—66
  planning, 51
  prototypes, 54
  resourcing, 48—51
  sketches, 54—55
  speclettes, 55
  specifications, 51—54
  staffing, 48—51
  usability testing reports, 61—63
  user research, 55—61
  wireframes, 54—55
  www.Agile-UX.com, 138,
  see also UX (user experience)
AgileZen, 140b—143b
Anonymous 1, 92—94
Anonymous 2, 99—104
Anonymous 3, 143b—145b
Architectural epic, 149
Axure prototype, 54, 66b, 81—82, 90—91, 101—102, 114,
  see also Prototypes

B

Balsamiq, 101—103
Block, Kayla, 87—91
Books, about agiles, 135—136
Brainstorming, 63, 65, 77
Burn-down charts, 34—35
  daily review of, 126
Business people
  coordination with project development, 12—13

C

Card sorting, 57, 65, 156
Cecil, Richard, 138
Change, 100, 103
  changing requirements, welcoming, 11
  responding to, over following plan, 8—9
Chickens, 28, 127—128
Cockburn, Alistair, 36b—38b
Codesigners

  customers as, 65—66
  teammates as, 65
Coding, 54
Cognitive walkthroughs, 65
Collaboration, 54
  customer, over contract negotiation, 8
  team size effect on, 88
Communication, 51, 74—75, 129—133, 168
  based on user stories, 169
  electronic, 132—133
Comprehensive documentation, working software over, 6—7
Contract negotiation, customer collaboration over, 8
Conversation, 54
  face-to-face, 14—15
Courage, Catherine, 36b—38b
Crystal, 20
Custom Agile, 23—25
Customer(s)
  as codesigners, 65—66
  collaboration, over contract negotiation, 8
  experience, 39,
  see also UX (user experience)
  satisfaction, 10—11
Customer Bill of Rights, 20—21

D

Daily scrums, 5—6, 22, 29, 46, 49—50, 59, 66b, 75, 77—78, 88, 116, 122—127, 131, 148—149, 158—159,
  see also Scrum(s)

173

Daily standups, *see* Daily scrums
Deliverables, 151–153
Delivery, of valuable software,
        10–11
Demonstrations, 122–123
Design activities, 64–66
Design divas, 64, 129, 167–168
Design documentation, 132
Developer Bill of Rights, 20–21
Developers
    coordination with project
        development, 12–13
    involved in other activity,
        interaction with, 155
Distribution of work, 165–166
Documentation, 168
    comprehensive documentation,
        working software over, 6–7
    design, 132

E
Electronic medical records (EMR),
        113
Epic, 32
Events, recurring, 166–167
Evolving, 139–140
Extreme Programming, 3–4,
        20–21
    www.extremeprogramming.org,
        137

F
Facebook, 4
Face-to-face conversation, 14–15
"F*ckups and Wins", 98
Feedback, 6, 9, 11, 17, 19–20, 22,
        27–28, 42–43, 45–46,
        55–62, 74–75, 78–79,
        81–82, 100, 103, 111,
        113–114, 156–157
    constant, 166
Formal training, 72–76
Forums, 78, 131

G
Good design, continuous attention
        to, 17–18
Gothelf, Jeff, 36b, 122–123, 135,
        151–152
    www.jeffgothelf.com, 136
GoToMeeting, 14–15

Govella, Austin, 104–109, 132
Greenhopper, 96
Grosjean, Jean Claude
    www.Agile-UX.com, 138

H
Heroes, 167–168
Howard, Adrian, 110–112
Hybrid Agile, 23–25

I
Individuals and interactions, valuing,
        5–6
Inform user stories, 63,
    see also User stories
Interactions and individuals, valuing,
        5–6
Internal stakeholders, managing, 160
Iteration, 20–21, 47–48, 166

J
JIRA, 96, 143b–145b

K
Kahn, Sarah, 140b–143b
Kanban, 25–26, 30, 81, 86, 92,
        124–125, 127, 138–139,
        140b–143b, 143b–145b,
        148–149

L
Ladas, Corey, 138–139
Lean UX, 27–28, 73–75,
        125
Learning
    about agile, resources
        for, 135–139
    books, 135–136
    online resources,
        136–139
    from failure, 123
Less up-front design, using, 170
LinkedIn, 136
LUXr residency program, 134

M
Mamoli, Sandy, 138
Meetings
    commitment, 126
    planning, 126

Mental models, for aligning design
        strategy, 57
Microsoft
    Facebook, 4
    UX principles, for Windows,
        4–5
    XP, 4
Miller, Archie, 79–83, 124–125,
        127–128
Miller, Elisa, 112–117
Motivated individuals, project
        development around, 13–14

O
O'connor, Josh, 109–110
O'Kelley, Suzanne, 72, 134
Online resources, for learning about
        agiles, 136–139

P
Pair programming, 64, 148–149
Patton, Jeff, 36, 36b–38b, 57–58,
        134–135
    www.agileproductdesign.com,
        136
"People over Process", 97–99,
        124, 140b–143b
Person, present findings in, 63
Personas, 8, 12–13, 106, 108,
        133–134, 169
    creation, 62–63, 85–86,
        116–117
    definition, 73, 156
Photoshop, 101–102
Pigs, 28
Plan(ning), 51, 60
    following, responding to change
        over, 8–9
    poker, 5–6, 32, 122–123,
        125–126
Practice management software,
        113
Process, 122–127
Product backlog, 21–22,
        30–31
Product owner, 21–22, 28–29,
        31–32, 34, 64, 96
    and UX team, boundary struggle
        between, 102–103
Project, 124–127

Project development
  around motivated individuals,
    13–14
  business people/developers
    coordination with, 12–13
Prototypes, 11–12, 21, 44, 54, 78,
    81–82, 152, 165
  Axure, 54, 66b–68b, 81–82,
    90–91, 101–102, 114
  paper, 101–102, 114

Q

Qualities of agile, 158–159

R

Ramsay, Anders, 136
  www.andersramsay.com,
    137
Rapid Iterative Testing and
  Evaluation (RITE), 8,
    57–58, 60, 65
Rauch, Thyra, 77–79
Refactoring work, 102
Reference library, 133–134
Resources, for learning about agiles,
    135–139
  books, 135–136
  online resources, 136–139
Resourcing, 48–51
Retrospectives, 16, 19–20, 22,
    29–30, 43, 50, 66b–68b, 82,
    98, 102, 122–123, 126–127,
    131
Rituals, 166–167
Robson, Catherine, 66b–68b, 164

S

Sandler, Andrew, 36b–38b
Scalability, 96
Scrum, 3–4, 21–23, 88–89, 92,
    100–102, 104–105,
    125–127, 137, 148–149
  daily, 5–6, 22, 29, 46, 49–50, 59,
    66b–68b, 75, 77–78, 88, 116,
    122–127, 131, 148–149,
    158–159
  master, 29
  police, 29
Scrumban, 26–27, 92, 138–139
Self-organizing teams

architectures, requirements, and
    designs emerge from, 19,
    see also Team(s)
Simplicity, 18
Sketches, 54–55
Smith, Carol, 83–87
Software, working, see Working
    software
Specifications, 51–54
Speclettes, 53, 55, 152–153
Spike, 35, 95
Spool, Jared
  www.UIE.com, 137
Sprint(s), 22, 30, 82, 149
  cycle, 22, 25, 32, 49–50, 55–60,
    62, 100–101, 122–125
    fitting user research into,
      156–157
  development sprints, UX team
    working with, 153–155
  duration of, 150–151
  planning, 131
  retrospective, 22
  Sprint 0, 58–60, 89–90, 92–93,
    113, 122, 159–160
  Sprint 1, 154
  Sprint 2, 154
Staffing, 48–51
Story-point estimation, 32–33
Surveys, 57, 60, 156
Sustainable development, 16

T

Target user stories, 60–61
Team(s)
  acceptance criteria, defining,
    169–170
  agile claim by, 157–158
  anti-colocation of, 158
  communication, 168
    based on user stories, 169
  constant feedback, 166
  design divas, 167–168
  distribution of work, 165–166
  documentation, 168
  dynamics, 127–129
  effective, 19–20
  events, recurring, 166–167
  heroes, 167–168
  iteration, 166
  less up-front design, using, 170

next release, plan and research for,
    159–160
  rituals, 166–167
  self-organizing, 19
  size, effect on collaborative work,
    88
  user experience backlog, creating,
    164–165
  user testing, recurring, 165
  working with development sprints,
    153–155
Team Foundation Server (TFS), 89
Teammates, as codesigners, 65
Technical excellence, continuous
    attention to, 17–18
Thompson, Bernie, 138–139
Toyota
  Lean production process, 25
Training, 134–139

U

Us vs. them, 6, 111
Usability testing, 156
  reports, 61–63
User experience backlog, creating,
    164–165,
    see also UX (user experience)
User Experience Professionals'
    Association (UXPA), 117
User Interface Engineering (UIE), 95
  www.UIE.com, 137
User research, 55–61
  into sprint cycle, fitting, 156–157
User stories, 31–32
  communication based on, 169
  inform, 63
  target, 60–61
User testing, recurring, 165
UX (user experience), 4–9
  defined, 39
  deliverables produced by,
    151–153
  health check, 107
  Lean UX, 27–28
  peg into agile-shaped hole, fitting,
    42–48
  team members, support to
    multiple projects, 155–156
  teams
    acceptance criteria, defining,
      169–170

UX (user experience) (*Continued*)
  communication, 168
  communication based on user
    stories, 169
  constant feedback, 166
  design divas, 167–168
  distribution of work, 165–166
  documentation, 168
  events, recurring, 166–167
  heroes, 167–168
  iteration, 166
  less up-front design, using, 170
  next release, plan and research
    for, 159–160
  rituals, 166–167
  user experience backlog, creating,
    164–165
  user testing, recurring, 165
  working with development
    sprints, 153–155
work, 48–66
  coding, 54
  collaboration, 54
  communication, 51
  conversation, 54
  design activities, 64–66
  planning, 51
  prototypes, 54

resourcing, 48–51
sketches, 54–55
speclettes, 55
specifications, 51–55
staffing, 48–51
usability testing reports, 61–63
user research, 55–61
wireframes, 54–55
see also Customer experience
UXI matrix, 107

V

Values of agile, 4–9

W

Waterfall method, 2–3
WebEx, 14–15, 114
Windows Presentation Format
  (WPF), 115
Wireframes, 54–55
Working in parallel, 22–23
Working software
  delivery of, 11–12
  over comprehensive
    documentation, 6–7
  as primary measure of progress, 15
www.agilemanifesto.org, 137

www.agileproductdesign.com, 136
www.Agile-UX.com, 138
www.andersramsay.com, 137
www.balancedteam.org, 137
www.extremeprogramming.org,
  137
www.jeffgothelf.com, 136
www.johnnyholland.com, 138
www.leansoftwareengineering.com,
  138–139
www.mountaingoatsoftware.com,
  137–138
www.Nomad8.com, 138
www.scrumalliance.org, 137
www.slideshare.com, 139
www.TheLadders.com, 136
www.UIE.com, 137
www.UXMatters.com, 138

X

XP, 4

Y

York, Christina, 94–99, 122,
  127–129, 134–135

Printed and bound by CPI Group (UK) Ltd, Croydon, CR0 4YY

03/10/2024

01040324-0017